THE MORAL SENSE

THE
MORAL
SENSE

JAMES Q. WILSON

THE FREE PRESS
A Division of Macmillan, Inc.
NEW YORK

Maxwell Macmillan Canada
TORONTO

Maxwell Macmillan International
NEW YORK   OXFORD   SINGAPORE   SYDNEY

The Free Press
A Division of Macmillan, Inc.
866 Third Avenue, New York, N.Y. 10022

Maxwell Macmillan Canada, Inc.
1200 Eglinton Avenue East
Suite 200
Don Mills, Ontario M3C 3N1

Macmillan, Inc. is part of the Maxwell Communication
Group of Companies.

Printed in the United States of America

printing number
1   2   3   4   5   6   7   8   9   10

Library of Congress Cataloging-in-Publication Data

Wilson, James Q.
    The moral sense / James Q. Wilson.
        p.   cm.
    Includes bibliographical references and index.
    ISBN 0-02-935405-6
    1. Ethics.   2. Moral development.   3. Social ethics.   4. Values—
Psychological aspects.   Title.
BJ1012W5375   1993
170—dc20   93-18520
                                                            CIP

To David and Elizabeth,
and moral sensors yet to come

Contents

Preface

Virtue has acquired a bad name. To young people it is the opposite of having fun, to older ones it is a symbol of lost virtue that politicians now exploit for partisan purposes, and to young and old alike it is a set of rules that well-meaning but intolerant bluenoses impose on other people.

Yet the daily discourse of ordinary people is filled with oblique references to morality. We talk constantly about being or not being decent, nice, or dependable; about having or not having a good character; about friendship, loyalty, and moderation or fickleness, insincerity, and addiction. When we overhear these conversations or read about these topics in magazines and novels, we sometimes say that people are preoccupied with personal relationships: the problems of mother and child, of wife and husband, of lovers, friends, and co-workers. This preoccupation is not simply about relationships, however; much of it is about what those relationships ought to be. This preoccupation, like the adjectives with which we express it— loyal, kind, or nice; disloyal, selfish, or rude—is with the language of morality, even though we often disguise it in the language of personality. It is the language of virtue and vice. It is the language that this book is about.

I wrote this book to help people recover the confidence with which they once spoke about virtue and morality. I did not write it in order to make a case for or against some currently disputed moral question, but rather to reestablish the possibility and the reasonableness of speaking frankly and convincingly about moral choices. In doing so I endeavor to show that mankind has a moral nature to which we commonly and inevitably appeal when trying to defend our moral arguments.

Why have people lost the confidence with which they once spoke publicly about morality? Why has moral discourse become unfashionable or merely partisan? I believe it is because we have learned, either firsthand from intellectuals or secondhand from the pronouncements of people influenced by intellectuals, that morality has no basis in science or logic. To defend morality is to defend the indefensible.

Our public discourse has been shaped, in ways we may be only dimly aware of, by the teachings, or the popular corruptions of the teachings, of the great thinkers of the modern age. Charles Darwin taught us, we suppose, that a person is the isolated product of a competition for survival among selfish genes coping with material circumstances; his or her morals are entirely utilitarian and self-centered.[1] Sigmund Freud taught us, we suppose, that guilt is an unhealthy expression of a repressed impulse; to live well we must overcome guilt. Karl Marx taught us, we suppose, that we are driven entirely by economic impulses; the societies we produce are based simply on the power relationships that result from class warfare. Scholars who have studied these thinkers know that their teachings were more complex and subtle than this and, at least in the case of Darwin, quite different. No matter; the spirit of the age will shape how any message is understood.

That spirit has been one of skepticism. Science has challenged common sense; one theory of science holds that we can never have knowledge, as opposed to mere opinions, about morality. Anthropologists have shown how various are the customs of mankind; the dominant tradition in modern anthropology has held that those customs are entirely the product of culture, and so we can conclude that man has no nature apart from his culture.* Philosophers have sought to find a rational basis for moral judgments; the dominant tradition in modern philosophy asserts that no rational foundation

---

* I have just used the words "man" and "his." Before going any further, let me be clear that in this book the masculine pronoun, unless otherwise indicated, refers to both males and females. As the dictionary makes clear, that pronoun has been used since time immemorial to represent any person whose sex is not specified. Though it is fashionable to find circumlocutions to avoid "gender-biased writing," it is also awkward and wooden. I do not think it necessary to write "he or she" every time I want to refer to one person of unspecified gender. If you believe it is necessary, please supply the phrase mentally as you read along.

can be given for any such judgment. Whatever Darwin, Freud, and Marx may have said, the skeptical spirit has determined what we have remembered.

My understanding of our moral confusion is a bit different from that of many others. To some, the central problem is that modern man has lost his moral bearings or religious commitments so that he is now governed only by immediate impulse or calculating self-interest. Though examples of such a mentality abound, I do not think it is an accurate characterization of the general problem. I will argue in this book that most of us have moral sense, but that some of us have tried to talk ourselves out of it. It is as if a person born to appreciate a golden sunset or a lovely song had persuaded himself and others that a greasy smear or a clanging gong ought to be enjoyed as much as true beauty.

Many people have persuaded themselves that no law has any foundation in a widely shared sense of justice; each is but the arbitrary enactment of the politically powerful. This is called "legal realism," but it strikes me as utterly unrealistic. Many people have persuaded themselves that children will be harmed if they are told right from wrong; instead they should be encouraged to discuss the merits of moral alternatives. This is called "values clarification," but I think it a recipe for confusion rather than clarity. Many people have persuaded themselves that it is wrong to judge the customs of another society since there are no standards apart from custom on which such judgments can rest; presumably they would oppose infanticide only if it involved their own child. This is sometimes called tolerance; I think a better name would be barbarism. Some people have persuaded themselves that a child is born wicked and can only be beaten into decency. This is called discipline; I prefer to call it brutality and cannot imagine anyone embracing it who has watched an infant's first smile.

It is difficult to say what effects have followed from this effort to talk ourselves out of having a moral sense. We may have abetted, by excusing, the few who have no moral sense; we may have harmed vulnerable children who ought to have received surer guidance from family and neighborhoods; we may have promoted self-indulgence when we thought we were only endorsing freedom. I am tempted to say that people who have persuaded themselves to embrace non-moral standards should not be surprised if young people who have heard these ideas grow up taking drugs, cheating on tests, and shooting their enemies. I am tempted to say this, but I cannot do so with complete confidence. It is no easy task to assess the influence of bad ideas on human conduct; in any event, it is not the task of this book to make that assessment. It *is* a task of this book, however, to make us ask whether the mirror that modern skepticism has held up to mankind's face reflects what we wish to see. Do we really *want* to have the utterly malleable, slightly cynical, superficially tolerant, wholly transparent human nature that we claim we have? Are we prepared for the possibility that by behaving as if no moral judgments were possible we may create a world that more and more resembles our diminished moral expectations? We must be careful of what we think we are, because we may become that.

Our intellectual culture has left ordinary men and women alone to cope with this possibility. They wish to make moral judgments, but their culture does not help them do it. They often feel like refugees living in a land captured by hostile forces. When they speak of virtue, they must do so privately, in whispers, lest they be charged with the grievous crime of being "unsophisticated" or, if they press the matter, "fanatics." If we are to live as fugitives in so alien a world, it is necessary to find a way of speaking that will not offend anyone. We need a code word for virtue or morality. That word is "values."

When we discuss the prevalence of divorce and illegitimacy, some take it as evidence that the values of our society have collapsed, others as a sign that people now attach value to alternative life-styles. When we try to explain the high rate of crime, some argue that it is the result of young people's no longer having the right values and others claim that it is caused by social barriers that have prevented young people from attaining their values by legitimate means. Any discussion of drug abuse precipitates a lively debate between those who take such abuse as confirmation of the absence of decent values and those who interpret it as testimony to the problems that result when society tries to impose its values on people. Hardly anyone can discuss the problems of public schools without claiming or denying that these failures are the result of the schools' teaching the wrong values, or no values. No one can mention television or the motion pictures without either asserting that these media, by their portrayal of sex and violence, are corrupting our values or declaring that these entertainments are at worst a reflection of the values of our society or at best a much-needed attack on the last vestiges of stuffy, puritanical values.

Preface

We are engaged in a cultural war, a war about values. It is not a new war; it has been going on for centuries as part of a continuing struggle at national self-definition. Once the issues were slavery, temperance, religion, and prostitution; today they are divorce, illegitimacy, crime, and entertainment.

What is new, distinctive, and odd about the contemporary version of this age-old debate is the language in which it is conducted. It is about "values." But what do we mean by a "value"? A taste? A preference? A belief? A moral principle? A binding obligation? Most people flinch from answering that question, at least in public. Their instinctive and commendable tolerance makes them shun any appearance of imposing their philosophical orientation or religious convictions upon others. But beneath that tolerance there lurks among many of us a worrisome uncertainty—some of us doubt that we have a defensible philosophy or credible conviction that we would want to impose.

The word "values" finesses all of the tough questions. It implies a taste or preference and recalls to mind the adage that there is no disputing tastes. But of course we don't really mean that our beliefs are no more than tastes, because when we defend them—to the extent we can—our muscles tighten and our knuckles grow white. Arguments about values often turn into fights over values, with pointed fingers, shaken fists, and thrown punches. That is not the way we discuss our taste for vanilla ice cream. We are aware, then, that some values are more important than others, but we are not certain we can say why, or at least say why with enough conviction to persuade anyone else.

Our reluctance to speak of morality and our suspicion, nurtured by our best minds, that we cannot "prove" our moral principles has amputated our public discourse at the knees. We have cut off the legs on which any serious discussion of marriage, schools, or mass entertainment must stand. We suspect that "values clarification" is not the best way to teach the young but lack the confidence to assert a value that ought to be defended. We debate "family values" but are not quite sure what they are, and so we beat a hasty retreat when someone accuses us of wanting in the name of that phrase to reassert paternal authority or deny female rights.

But we need not retreat. There are standards to which we can repair that are very different from the slogans fluttering on the banners of our occupying army. They emerge from serious reflection about why we insist upon judging, morally, events and people around us. Students of child development have observed the emergence of the moral sense and given respectful and thoughtful accounts of it. However much the scientific method is thought to be the enemy of morality, scientific findings provide substantial support for its existence and power.

Rebuilding the basis of moral judgments requires us to take the perspective of the citizen, but the citizen has gone to great lengths to deny that he has a perspective to take. On the one hand, he is nervous or on guard when hearing someone speak of virtue or character; on the other hand, he regularly evaluates his friends and acquaintances in terms that clearly imply a standard of virtue and character. Moreover, while he may not tell another person to his face that he lacks character or virtue, he is often ready to say that it is the absence of those qualities that accounts for much of the crime, disorder, and self-indulgence he sees in the world about him.

The book that follows begins with an introductory chapter that tries to make clear that people necessarily make moral judgments, that many of those judgments are not arbitrary or unique to some time, place, or culture, and that we will get a lot further in understanding how we live as a species if we recognize that we are bound together both by mutual interdependence and a common moral sense. By a moral sense I mean an intuitive or directly felt belief about how one ought to act when one is free to act voluntarily (that is, not under duress). By "ought" I mean an obligation binding on all people similarly situated. I cannot clarify the word any more than this; as the great English philosopher Henry Sidgwick put it after struggling with the word through six editions of his magnificent treatise on ethics, "ought" is a word that "is too elementary to admit of any formal definition."[2] Aristotle would have agreed; you cannot discuss morality with someone who is devoid of any moral sense.[3] The fact that you *can* discuss morality with practically anyone suggests to me that the word "ought" has an intuitively obvious meaning and that people are, in the great majority of instances, equipped with some moral sense.

Toward the end of my opening chapter I confront the argument of cultural relativism, the argument that even our deepest moral sentiments, to say nothing of our more transient or ephemeral ones, are entirely the products of the culture in which we are raised and thus have no enduring significance outside that culture. The view

Preface

has become so pervasive that many people, otherwise quite secure in their moral convictions, feel timid about expressing them for fear others will think them unsophisticated or ethnocentric.

In Part One I take up four examples of such a moral sense: sympathy, fairness, self-control, and duty. I do not pretend that these four sensibilities exhaust what one might mean by a moral impulse or standard or that one might not define some of them a bit differently. Integrity, for example, does not appear here, in part because it is, I think, a combination of other, more elementary senses (duty, fairness, and self-control). Courage is missing; though it is akin to duty, it implies other qualities as well. Modesty is, to me, the most conspicuous and discomforting omission, but I confess that I have not thought the matter through to my own satisfaction. I have chosen to write about these four because I have something to say about them.

Let me also stress that these are four aspects of the moral *sense*, not four moral rules or laws. This book is not an effort to state or justify moral rules; that is, it is not a book of philosophy. Rather, it is an effort to clarify what ordinary people mean when they speak of their moral feelings and to explain, insofar as one can, the origins of those feelings. This effort is a continuation of work begun by certain eighteenth-century English and Scottish thinkers, notably Joseph Butler, Francis Hutcheson, David Hume, and Adam Smith. What I seek to add to this tradition is a knowledge of what the biological and social sciences have since learned about what they were the first to call the moral sense.

The standard supplied by one's moral sense is often, indeed usually, rather general and imprecise, and so my saying that people have a moral sense is not the same thing as saying that they have direct, intuitive knowledge of certain moral rules. People can feel strongly that they have a duty to tell the truth but still doubt that they should tell it so unsparingly as to wound the feelings of a beloved friend or reveal to a homicidal maniac the location of an innocent child. To some readers, this conflict condemns any discussion of a moral sense to irrelevancy; if a standard is too uncertain to settle a concrete case, then it is hardly a standard worth talking about.

To the contrary, our moral sense is worth discussing because it explains a great deal of our behavior. To the extent that what we do is affected by our moral senses, it can be affected by different senses under different circumstances. Consider altruism. Occasionally we make charitable donations, help people who are lost or in need, or volunteer to perform dangerous tasks. Such acts may have a wide variety of motives, ranging from pure self-interest (a desire to win a prize or impress another person in order to get a better job) to various other-regarding motives (a sense of fairness, a sense of duty, or a sense of sympathy). If this were a book about moral behavior, I would have to sort out in each case the many motives that can lead to the same action. I am interested in why people act as they do, but I am more interested in why people *judge* actions as they do. The moral senses are the basis for much of that judging, and it is these that I want to dissect.

Proceeding this way creates a problem for me and for the reader that ought to be faced immediately, though I confess to having found no solution for it. The problem is revealed by the following question: what is the evidence for the existence of a moral sense? You can only with great difficulty examine directly a person's beliefs, sentiments, or predispositions, though one can try by using psychological tests and personal interviews. Much of what we know about the moral senses has to be inferred from how people behave. For example: We observe somebody helping somebody else. Is the explanation a desire for a reward, hope for a reciprocal favor, or genuine compassion for the other fellow? The best one can do is to try to make a plausible inference from the facts as we know them. But of course that puts one in an awkward position. It can be tantamount to saying that our actions are sometimes influenced by our moral sentiments, but the evidence for the existence of those sentiments comes from having observed the actions. The reader will have to judge how well I have coped with this problem.

Part Two is an account of the sources of the moral sentiments—human nature, family experiences, gender, and culture. The reader is no doubt quite prepared to encounter chapters on family and culture, but may be surprised to find ones on biology and gender. He shouldn't be. We already know that criminality is importantly influenced by biological factors, including sex;[4] it stands to reason that noncriminality should be influenced by such factors as well. To believe otherwise is to believe that law-abidingness is wholly learned, while criminality is a quasi-biological interruption of that acquired disposition. That is, to say the least, rather implausible.

The chapter on culture is a bit different from what the reader might expect. Instead of summarizing the abundant evidence of the many ways in which culture shapes the way in which we express our moral nature and adds to that nature a host of conventional (that is to say, wholly learned) moral beliefs, it endeavors to answer what to me is the fundamental cultural and historical question: how did it happen that in the West people were induced to believe that our moral sentiments should extend to many, perhaps all, people, and not just to family, close relatives, and ethnic kin? My answer involves a bold leap of inference from scattered and incomplete facts, and so I will not be surprised if it is viewed as an inadequate solution to so great a puzzle.

In the concluding chapter I bring together the arguments I have been advancing and draw out some of their larger implications. They are not, by and large, public policy implications. Some readers will be relieved to discover this; others will be frustrated. But this book is not, for the most part, about laws, institutions, or policies, it is about human nature. To anticipate and oversimplify the conclusion, it is that an older view of human nature than is now current in the human sciences and moral philosophy is the correct view; thinking seriously about the kinds of animals we are will help us understand our persistent but fragile disposition to make moral judgments and the aspects of human relations that must be cultivated if that disposition is to be protected and nurtured. We are human, with all the frailties and inconsistencies that this implies; but we also wish, when we observe ourselves with any sort of detachment, to avoid becoming less than human.

Beneath our wars, crimes, envies, fanaticisms, persecutions, snobberies, and adulteries; beneath, that is to say, all of those human traits that might be said to constitute our original sin, there is a desire not only for praise but for praiseworthiness, for fair dealings as well as for good deals, for honor as well as for advantage. But to magnify the better side of our nature, we must understand its sources and the forces that threaten it.

Acknowledgments

F or many years the Alfred Sloan Foundation has supported my research and writing, even when what I was doing bore little relationship to the intellectual goals of that organization. Arthur Singer, vice-president of Sloan, has been the person who has kept Sloan and me in a productive partnership. As I have said in several previous books, without his support none of this would have been possible. Thank you again, Art.

A number of scholars have read and commented on the book as a whole: Edward C. Banfield, Robert Boyd, Peter B. Clark, Jean Bethke Elshtain, Grace Goodell, Richard J. Herrnstein, Jerome Kagan, Elisabeth Langby, and Heather Richardson. William Bouwsma and Steven Ozment read selected chapters. I am deeply grateful for all of their comments, even those I was unwilling or unable to accept. Were I smarter and more industrious, I would have benefitted from everything they said.

My wife, Roberta Wilson, read the manuscript and made, as usual, many sensible comments. But her contribution to this book long preceded her reading it or even my writing it. Though the number of references at the end may lead the reader to think that my views were principally formed by what I have read, they were not; they were shaped by living with a remarkable human being for over forty years. She has taught me by example what the moral sense is.

Four research assistants helped me find my way through the literature of several academic disciplines. I am indebted to Mariella Bacigalupo, Heather Elms, Robin O'Brian, and Geoff Waring. Finally, I am deeply appreciative of the support and enthusiasm of my publisher, Erwin Glikes; my editor, Adam Bellow; and my agents, Glen Hartley and Lynn Chu.

J.Q.W.

The Moral Sense

Since daily newspapers were first published, they have been filled with accounts of murder and mayhem, of political terror and human atrocities. Differences in religious belief so minor as to be invisible to all but a trained theologian have been the pretext, if not the cause, of unspeakable savageries. Differences in color and even small differences in lineage among people of the same color have precipitated riots, repression, and genocide. The Nazi regime set about to exterminate an entire people and succeeded in murdering six million of them before an invading army put a stop to the methodical horror. Hardly any boundary can be drawn on the earth without it becoming a cause for war. In parts of Africa, warlords fight for power and booty while children starve. When riots occur in an American city, many bystanders rush to take advantage of the opportunity for looting. If people have a common moral sense, there is scarcely any evidence of it in the matters to which journalists—and their readers—pay the greatest attention.

A person who contemplates this endless litany of tragedy and misery would be pardoned for concluding that man is at best a selfish and aggressive animal whose predatory instincts are only partially and occasionally controlled by some combination of powerful institutions and happy accidents. He would agree with the famous observation of Thomas Hobbes that in their natural state men engage in a war of all against all. In this respect they are worse than beasts; whereas the animals of the forest desire only sufficient food and sex, humans seek not merely sufficient but abundant resources. Men strive to outdo one another in every as-

1

pect of life, pursuing power and wealth, pride and fame, beyond any reasonable measure.

But before drawing so bleak a conclusion from his daily newspaper, the reader should ask himself why bloodletting and savagery are news. There are two answers. The first is that they are unusual. If daily life were simply a war of all against all, what would be newsworthy would be the occasional outbreak of compassion and decency, self-restraint and fair dealing. Our newspapers would mainly report on parents who sacrificed for their children and people who aided neighbors in distress. Amazed that such things occurred, we would explain them as either rare expressions of a personality quirk or disguised examples of clever self-dealing. The second reason that misery is news is because it is shocking. We recoil in horror at pictures of starving children, death camp victims, and greedy looters. Though in the heat of battle or the embrace of ideology many of us will become indifferent to suffering or inured to bloodshed, in our calm and disinterested moments we discover in ourselves an intuitive and powerful aversion to inhumanity.

This intuition is not simply a cultural artifact or a studied hypocrisy. The argument of this book is that people have a natural moral sense, a sense that is formed out of the interaction of their innate dispositions with their earliest familial experiences. To different degrees among different people, but to some important degree in almost all people, that moral sense shapes human behavior and the judgments people make of the behavior of others.

Morality versus Philosophy

At one time, the view that our sense of morality shaped our behavior and judgments was widely held among philosophers. Aristotle said that man was naturally a social being who seeks happiness. Thomas Aquinas, the great medieval theologian who sought to reconcile Catholic and Aristotelian teachings, argued that man has a natural inclination to be a rational and familial being; the moral law is, in the first instance, an expression of a natural—that is, an innate—tendency. Adam Smith wrote that man is motivated by sympathy as well as by self-interest, and he developed a moral philosophy squarely based on this capacity for sympathy. No one can say what effect these doctrines had on the way people actually lived, but one can say

The Moral Sense

that for much of Western history philosophy sought to support and explicate the more social side of human nature without denying its selfish and wilder side.

Modern philosophy, with some exceptions, represents a fundamental break with that tradition. For the last century or so, few of the great philosophical theories of human behavior have accorded much weight to the possibility that men and women are naturally endowed with anything remotely resembling a moral sense. Marxism as generally received (and, with some exceptions, as Marx himself wrote it) is a relentlessly materialistic doctrine in which morality, religion, and philosophy have no independent meaning; they are, in Marx's words, "phantoms formed in the human brain," "ideological reflexes," "sublimates of their material life-process."[1] To be sure, in certain places Marx wrote movingly of man's alienation in a way that implied that in their natural state people value self-realization and uncoerced communal living,* but he never explored in a serious way man's moral inclinations. Marx's followers, especially those that used his doctrine to justify their power (Lenin comes especially to mind), were alike in thinking that any means were justified to achieve the communist utopia. And Marx's own life is testimony to how little he was disposed to let moral considerations affect his political determinations or personal conduct.

If Marx hinted at morality without examining it, much of modern philosophy abandoned morality without even a hint. Analytical philosophers took seriously the argument that "values" could not be derived from "facts," and tended to relegate moral judgments to the realm of personal preferences not much different from a taste for vanilla ice cream. In 1936 A. J. Ayer asserted that since moral arguments (unlike the theory of gravity) cannot be scientifically verified, they are nothing more than "ejaculations or commands," "pure expressions of feeling" that have "no objective validity whatsoever."[2] Existentialists such as Jean-Paul Sartre argued that man must choose his values, but provided little guidance for making that choice.[3] Of course there are many other, quite different tendencies in modern

---

* To be alienated means, roughly, to lose one's essential humanity (in Marx's case, as a result of wage labor and private property). But for the concept of alienation to have any moral significance, you must first state what constitutes man's essential humanity; you must, in short, have a theory of human nature. Marx did not supply such a theory.

philosophy, but anyone who has spent much time in a classroom is keenly aware that the skeptical, relativistic themes have been most influential. Richard Rorty, perhaps the most important philosophical writer in present-day America, denies that there is anything like a "core self" or an inherently human quality, and so there is no way for us to say that some actions are inherently inhuman, even when confronted with the horrors of Auschwitz (which, of course, Rorty condemns, but only because history and circumstance have supplied him with certain "beliefs").[4]

What Marxism and positivism have meant for philosophy, Freudianism has meant for psychology. It is difficult to disentangle what Freud actually said from what he is widely believed to have said, or one stage in his thinking from another. But it seems clear that Freudianism was popularly understood as meaning that people have instincts, especially sexual and aggressive ones, and not moral senses; morality, to the extent people acquire any, is chiefly the result of learning to repress those instincts. Among the objects of the sexual drive are one's own parents. Repressing those instincts is necessary for civilization to exist, but that repression can lead to mental illness. People do acquire a conscience—Freud called it the superego—but not out of any natural inclination to be good; rather, their conscience is an internalized fear of losing the love of their parents.[5] Freud, at least, argued that conscience existed; some behavioral psychologists, such as B. F. Skinner, denied even that.

People who have never been affected by Marxism or Freudianism and who are indifferent to philosophical disputes may nonetheless have learned, at least secondhand, the teachings of many cultural anthropologists. All of us are aware of the great variety of social customs, religious beliefs, and ritual practices to be found around the world, especially among primitive peoples, a variety so great as to suggest that all morality is relative to time and place. And if we wish to confirm what our imagination suggests, we can find explicit arguments to that effect in some of the leading texts. In 1906 the great sociologist William Graham Sumner wrote that "the mores can make anything right."[6] Thirty years later Ruth Benedict's best-selling book *Patterns of Culture* was read to mean that all ways of life were equally valid. Published in 1934, just after the Nazis had come to power, it was probably intended to be a plea for tolerance and an argument for judging one's own culture only after becoming aware of an alternative to it. But by popularizing the phrase "cultural relativism" and discussing cannibalism without explicitly condemning it, she was read as saying something like what Sumner had said: culture and the mores of society can make anything right and anything wrong.[7]

Is Everything Permitted?

If modern man had taken seriously the main intellectual currents of the last century or so, he would have found himself confronted by the need to make moral choices when the very possibility of making such choices had been denied. God is dead or silent, reason suspect or defective, nature meaningless or hostile. As a result, man is adrift on an uncharted sea, left to find his moral bearings with no compass and no pole star, and so able to do little more than utter personal preferences, bow to historical necessity, or accept social conventions.

Countless writers have assumed that man is in precisely this predicament. Recall the phrases with which writers and poets have characterized our times. We have been described as "hollow men" living in a "wasteland" or "the age of anxiety," from which there is "no exit," part of a "lonely crowd" that seeks refuge in either "possessive individualism" or "therapeutic individualism." To escape from the emptiness of being we either retreat inward to mystical or drug-induced self-contemplation or outward to various fanatical ideologies.*

If this were true, then my argument that there is in human nature the elements of a natural moral sense would be untrue. There can scarcely be anything worth calling a moral sense if people can be talked out of it by modern philosophy, secular humanism, Marxist dialectics, or pseudo-Freudian psychoanalysis. But I doubt that most people most of the time are affected by these intellectual fashions. The intellectuals who consume them may be affected. If they think life is without moral meaning, they may live accordingly, creating an avant-garde in which "meaning" is to be found in self-expressive art, a bohemian counterculture, or anarchistic politics. But the lives of most people are centered around the enduring facts of human existence—coping with a family, establishing relationships, and raising children. Everywhere we look, we see ordinary men and women going about their daily affairs, happily or unhappily as their circumstances

---

* The authors of these phrases are, of course, T. S. Eliot, W. H. Auden, Jean-Paul Sartre, David Riesman, C. B. MacPherson, and Robert Bellah.

allow, making and acting on moral judgments without pausing to wonder what Marx or Freud or Rorty would say about those judgments. In the intimate realms of life, there will be stress, deprivation, and frustration, but ordinarily these will not be experienced as a pervasive spiritual crisis.

Two errors arise in attempting to understand the human condition. One is to assume that culture is everything, the other to assume that it is nothing. In the first case there would be no natural moral sense—if culture is everything, then nature is nothing. In the second, the moral sense would speak to us far more clearly than it does. A more reasonable assumption is that culture will make some difference some of the time in the lives of most of us and a large difference much of the time in the lives of a few of us.

An example of how modern intellectual currents have a modest effect on the lives of people who are exposed to them can be found in some of our educational fashions. Most pupils are well behaved; a few are not. Controlling the few who are not can only become more difficult if teachers embrace the view that their task is to address questions of right and wrong by helping children "choose" and "clarify" their "values." The "values clarification" approach to moral education that began in the late 1960s warned teachers to avoid "moralizing, criticizing, giving values, or evaluating." They were especially to avoid "all hints of 'good' or 'right' or 'acceptable.' "[8] One wonders what students thought of teachers who studiously avoided suggesting that any course of action was better than any other. There is no evidence that this bit of pedagogical idiocy had any direct effect on the beliefs of children,[9] but it may have had an indirect effect on their actions. If a child cheated on an exam, did the teacher respond by helping the student "clarify" the "value" he attached to honesty and dishonesty? And if the pupil valued a good grade even if dishonestly obtained, how was the teacher supposed to respond? This approach was so at odds with common sense and the requirements of everyday life that, not surprisingly, it fell into disrepute in many quarters.[10]

But values clarification—or more accurately, the philosophical premises on which it was based—left its traces. Ask college students to make and defend a moral judgment about people or places with which they are personally unfamiliar. Many will act as if they really believed that all cultural practices were equally valid, all moral claims were equally suspect, and human nature was infinitely malleable or utterly self-regarding. In my classes, college students asked to judge a distant people, practice, or event will warn one another and me not to be "judgmental" or to "impose your values on other people." These remarks are most often heard when they are discussing individual "life-styles," the modern, "nonjudgmental" word for what used to be called character. If students know anything at all about these folk, it is usually what they have learned from books written by anthropologists who believe that no other culture but their own can or should be judged. If asked to defend their admonitions against "being judgmental," the students sometimes respond by arguing that moral judgments are arbitrary, but more often they stress the importance of tolerance and fair play, which, in turn, require understanding and even compassion. Do not condemn some practice— say, drug use or unconventional sexuality—that ought to be a matter of personal choice; do not criticize some group—say, ghetto rioters—whom you do not know and whose beliefs and experiences you do not understand.

But tolerance and fair play are moral dispositions; a commitment to personal liberty is a moral conviction; a belief that one ought to enter imaginatively and sympathetically into the minds of others is a moral urging. When asked why people should be tolerant, act fairly, or respect liberty, many students will look at me as if I were merely engaging in professorial cleverness, while a few will attempt to construct intellectual defenses of these notions, defenses typically based on utility: for example, society is better off if everybody behaves that way.

Most people, however, do not act fairly or sympathetically because they have decided that "society" (whatever that is) will be better off as a consequence. It is not hard to think of cases in which "society" might be better off if at least some people were treated unfairly or unsympathetically.* In fact, when people act fairly or sympathetically it is rarely because they have engaged in much systematic reasoning. Much of the time our inclination toward fair play or our sympathy for the plight of others are immediate and instinc-

---

* Readers who have taken a course in philosophy will recall the standard objections to utilitarian justifications of morality. If imprisoning an innocent man or carrying out an especially gruesome execution will deter others from committing crimes, then the greatest good of the greatest number will be enhanced by imposing these sentences even though imposing such penalties seems to violate common notions of fairness and compassion.

tive, a reflex of our emotions more than an act of our intellect, and in those cases in which we do deliberate (for example, by struggling to decide what fair play entails or duty requires in a particular case), our deliberation begins, not with philosophical premises (much less with the justification for them), but with feelings—in short, with a moral sense. The feelings on which people act are often superior to the arguments that they employ.

These students are decent people. In most respects, their lives are exemplary. Thus it was all the more shocking when, during a class in which we were discussing people who at great risk to themselves had helped European Jews during the Holocaust, I found that there was no general agreement that those guilty of the Holocaust itself were guilty of a moral horror. "It all depends on your perspective," one said. "I'd first have to see those events through the eyes of people affected by them," another remarked. No doubt some per-petrators were caught up in that barbaric episode for reasons that we might understand and even excuse. What worried me was not that the students were prepared to accept some excuses, but that they began their moral reasoning on the subject by searching for excuses. They seemed to assume that one approaches a moral question by taking a relativist position and asking, "How, given the interests and values of another person, might we explain what happened?" Hear-ing them speak this way, I could better understand the popularity of Rorty, a philosopher who has embraced the failure of modern phi-losophy to find any rational (that is, scientific) basis for moral judg-ments. To him, and to many of my students, there is no human nature that renders some actions entirely inhuman: "What counts as a decent human being is relative to historical circumstance, a matter of transient consensus about what attitudes are normal and what practices are just or unjust."[11]

College students, like Professor Rorty, rarely have to cope with an atrocity or give a reason for condemning those they learn of. To them, the perils of accepting cultural relativism are purely hypothet-ical. One can get along most of the time with unanchored beliefs. Rorty argues that even "contingent historical circumstance" can pro-vide beliefs that "can still be thought worth dying for,"[12] and many of my students would probably agree. They are living decent lives in a society that, most of the time, values decency.

But for others the perils can be very great. If the moral sense is the result of nothing more significant than a cultural or historical throw of the dice, then it will occur to some people who by reason of temperament or circumstances are weakly attached to their own moral senses that they are free to do whatever they can get away with by practicing indulgent self-absorption or embracing an angry ideology. How common this may be is hard to say, and one must resist the temptation to ascribe all the ills of our society to a moral failure. There are many reasons for the high rates of divorce, illegitimacy, and drug abuse of which everyone is aware; for the rudeness and indecency of so many human encounters; and for the lewdness, cruelty, and senseless violence with which we have become so familiar.

These unpleasant actions are chiefly the behavior of young people who in all cultures and in every epoch test the limits of acceptable behavior. Testing limits is a way of asserting selfhood. Maintaining limits is a way of asserting community. If the limits are asserted weakly, uncertainly, or apologetically, their effects must surely be weaker than if they are asserted boldly, confidently, and persuasively. How vigorously and persuasively we—mostly but not entirely older people—assert those limits will surely depend to some important degree on how confidently we believe in the sentiments that underlie them. Some of us have lost that confidence. The avant-garde in music, art, and literature mocks that confidence.

Fortunately, most of us give unreflective allegiance to those sentiments. But some of us are disposed to examine them critically. If those of us so disposed believe that all principles are arbitrary or at best useful under certain circumstances, and if we frequently and eloquently proclaim their purely arbitrary or utilitarian character, we should not be surprised to discover that some people believe us and act on that belief.

Consider the problem of rising crime rates. Having thought about the matter for many years, I can find no complete explanation for the worldwide increase in crime rates that does not assign an important role to a profound cultural shift in the strength of either social constraints or internal conscience or both, and I can find no complete explanation of that cultural shift that does not implicate to some important degree our convictions about the sources and importance of the moral sentiments.[13] Rising crime rates worry Americans, but because they forget that the rise has affected virtually every industrial nation in the world, they sometimes suppose, incorrectly, that America has high crime rates simply because there is something wrong with America. No doubt crime rates might come down a bit if guns were taken from every American, extreme poverty eliminated, and the criminal justice system made more effective. But crime has increased over the last several decades in countries as diverse as England, Germany, and Italy, so much so that by 1987 the rates of burglary, auto theft, and heroin addiction were higher in England than in the United States.[14]

Industrialization and urbanization have played a part in this rise, but whereas in the late nineteenth century crime rates seem to have decreased during periods of economic growth, in the last few decades they have often increased during such periods. Over the course of the last hundred years the world has experienced a shift from an era in which crime chiefly responded to material circumstances to one in which it responds in large measure to cultural ones.[15] That shift had many causes, but one is the collapse in the legitimacy of what once was respectfully called middle-class morality but today is sneeringly referred to as "middle-class values."

The moral relativism of the modern age has probably contributed to the increase in crime rates, especially the increases that occur during prosperous times. It has done so by replacing the belief in personal responsibility with the notion of social causation and by supplying to those marginal persons at risk for crime a justification for doing what they might have done anyway. If you are tempted to take the criminal route to the easy life, you may go further along that route if everywhere you turn you hear educated people saying—indeed, "proving"—that life is meaningless and moral standards arbitrary.

Having said that the moral climate has probably affected the level of crime, let me now say that it probably has not affected it dramatically. To be sure, there is at least three times as much violent crime today as there was thirty years ago. But only a tiny fraction of all people commit crimes at a high rate, and that fraction seems, so far as we can tell, remarkably similar in different cultures and different eras. About a third of the young boys growing up in Philadelphia, London, and Copenhagen will get arrested at least once, but only about 5 or 6 percent will go on to get arrested many times. The criminal proportion of boys in the 1960s was about the same as it had been in the 1950s.[16] This small cohort of serious offenders has acquired, owing to prosperity and modern technology, the ability to commit crimes over a much wider territory, to reach more victims,

The Moral Sense

and to take more lethal actions than once was the case. But the cohort itself has not gotten much larger. To the extent that there is something in mankind that leads us to hold back from a life of crime, it must be something that, at least for most of us, is immune to the philosophical doubts, therapeutic nostrums, and ideological zealotry with which the modern age has been so thoroughly infected.

That immunity arises in part, I think, from our natural tendency to judge ourselves and others and to try, when not distracted by passion, preoccupied with greed, bound by organizations, or led by rascals, to live by the judgments we make. We do have a core self, not wholly the product of culture, that includes both a desire to advance our own interests and a capacity to judge disinterestedly how those interests ought to be advanced. Our selfish desires and moral capacities are at war with one another, and often the former triumphs over the latter. However great this war may be and no matter how often we submerge our better instincts in favor of our baser ones, we are almost always able, in our calm and disinterested moments, to feel the tug of our better nature. In those moments we know the difference between being human and being inhuman.

Even criminals believe in morality, at least as they grow older. David Farrington and Donald West have followed a group of working-class London males from early childhood well past the age of thirty. When asked, at the age of thirty-two, whether they would be "very angry" if their son or daughter committed a criminal offense, over three-fourths of those men who had themselves been convicted of a crime (and often of several crimes) answered yes. Even the most hardened criminals—those with at least eight convictions—agreed.[17] They may not be very good fathers, but they don't want their sons or daughters to be very bad children.

Now, criminal fathers do not ordinarily engage in much that we would call moral reasoning. Yet they have, at least with respect to their own children and during those moments when they are not yielding to some angry impulse, something that we might call a moral sentiment, however vague it may be. Most of us are not criminals, but most of the time we do not reflect any more deeply than do they on our ethical inclinations. This book is an effort to explore those inclinations, especially those that, insofar as the (very imperfect) evidence suggests, are common to almost all people. If we find such common inclinations, we will not have found a set of moral rules. Deciding that mankind has at some level a shared moral nature is not the same thing as deciding that men are everywhere in possession of a set of moral absolutes.

In sum, I am here giving the reader a cautious and guarded answer to the question, "What difference does it make if we believe or fail to believe that we have a moral sense?" If our passing intellectual and cultural fashions made a vast difference, it would follow that there could not be a natural moral sense of much consequence. If they made no difference, than the moral sense would be so strong that it would govern our actions regardless of the circumstances. The correct position, I think, is the middle one: we have a moral sense, most people instinctively rely on it even if intellectuals deny it, but it is not always and in every aspect of life strong enough to withstand a pervasive and sustained attack.

To say that people have a moral sense is not the same thing as saying that they are innately good. A moral sense must compete with other senses that are natural to humans—the desire to survive, acquire possessions, indulge in sex, or accumulate power—in short, with self-interest narrowly defined. How that struggle is resolved will differ depending on our character, our circumstances, and the cultural and political tendencies of the day. But saying that a moral sense exists *is* the same thing as saying that humans, by their nature, are potentially good.

Someone once remarked that the two great errors in moral philosophy are the belief that we know the truth and the belief that there is no truth to be known. Only people who have had the benefit of higher education seem inclined to fall into so false a choice. Ordinary people do not make that mistake. They believe they can judge human actions, albeit with great difficulty, and they believe that most disinterested people will make judgments that, if not identical, appeal to some shared sentiments. They are dismayed both by the claim that somebody is in possession of the absolute truth about all moral issues and by the thought that somebody thinks that there is no truth at all about them.

Modern science is often praised or condemned for supporting a relativistic conception of human morality. Certainly the scientific method, by insisting that factual statements differ fundamentally from value statements, seems to lead to this conclusion. But scientific findings, contrary to popular impression, do not unequivocally support it. I hope to show that there is a great deal in the literature of child psychology, evolutionary biology, and cultural anthropology

The Moral Sense

that is consistent with a quite different view of human nature, one that accords an important role to a moral sense. Science supplies more support for the "ancient" view of human nature than is commonly recognized.

The Moral Sense and Social Order

Most of us do not break the law most of the time, not simply because we worry about taking even a small chance of getting caught, but also because our conscience forbids our doing what is wrong. By the same token, most of us honor most promises, play games by the rules, respect the rights and claims of others, and work at our jobs even when the boss isn't looking. Most of us wait our turn in line and cooperate with others to achieve a common goal even when it would be more convenient to go to the head of the line or let others do the work. We usually are courteous to strangers, regularly leave tips for waitresses, occasionally help people in distress, and sometimes join campaigns that benefit others but not ourselves. We do so in part out of a fear of retribution but also out of a sense of duty, a desire to please, a belief in fairness, and sympathy for the plight of others.

We usually take for granted the predictability and peacefulness of most human interactions. Philosophers do not. They search for principles that can account for the existence of social order. As Jon Elster has observed, these tend to fall into one of two categories.[18] The first is rationalistic and individualistic: order exists because people, horrified by the anarchy of the natural world, find some rule or convention that can keep them from being part of an endless war of all against all. Thomas Hobbes argued that government is created because "every man is enemy to every man," driven by a desire for gain, for safety, and for glory to engage in constant quarrels. Only a sovereign power—a Leviathan—is capable of protecting every man from every other, and so to this sovereign each man surrenders his right to self-government in order to obtain that which each most desperately wants, which is to avoid a violent death.[19] Later writers—including most economists—dropped the emphasis on a powerful sovereign in favor of a self-regulating system of individuals linked together by market transactions, but they retained the Hobbesian view that society consists of people pursuing their self-interest. As Albert Hirschman has written, interests—that is, the calm and deliberate pursuit of personal advantage—were brought forward to tame the wild and unpredictable power of passions.[20] Adam Smith was only the best known of the many writers who sought to find a basis for social order by showing how interests could produce what could not be achieved by destructive passions or ineffectual reason.[21]

The second explanation is normative and communal: order exists because a system of beliefs and sentiments held by members of a society sets limits to what those members can do. Emile Durkheim believed that neither governments nor markets alone could produce order; instead, they presupposed it. He called our attention to social norms that induce people to live peaceably together. Those norms are part of a collective consciousness that produces, depending on social conditions, varying degrees of solidarity.[22] Society is the source of moral constraints; it is, indeed, the source of everything that makes man more than an animal. Societies will, of course, differ in their mores; each society has the moral system it needs.[23]

There is much truth in both views, but neither strikes me as entirely satisfactory. Durkheim's (and before him, Rousseau's) criticism of Hobbes (and by implication of many contemporary economists) are telling. For there to be a contract, whether to create a state or manage an exchange, there must first be a willingness to *obey* contracts; there must be, in Durkheim's phrase, some noncontractual elements of contract. No government can have authority by force alone, and few agreements will be observed if only fear of reprisal compels their observance. Thus, the citizen who obeys the law or observes a contract does so in part out of a sense of duty, a sense that cannot be created simply by a show of force.* The calm pursuit of personal interest can produce a more stable order and a more willing acceptance of mutually advantageous rules of conduct than can arbitrary power. But as Adam Smith was the first to recognize (and as many of his followers seem to have forgotten), what makes the pursuit of interest calm rather than unruly are the natural sentiments of people, and especially pity or compassion, "the emotion which we feel for the misery of others."[24] The existence of such a sentiment cannot be explained by the interests of those people whose behavior is shaped by it.

---

* Rousseau put it this way in *The Social Contract*: "The strongest is never strong enough to be always the master, unless he transforms strength into right, and obedience into duty.... Force is a physical power, and I fail to see what moral effect it can have" (1762:1.3).

The Moral Sense

While Durkheim was clearly right to call attention to the pre-existing social bonds that make governments and markets possible, the source of those bonds is far from clear. Whence the moral code that lies at the heart of the social bond? Does each society invent one? How does that invention occur?

Let us suppose that the social bond evolves gradually, growing in power and scope with the size of the human community and the complexity of group life. Clearly it is necessary for each generation to teach its young the rules of social life. But if parents teach moral lessons to their young, we would expect great variation in the lessons taught and learned, as well as many cases in which the parents decided to teach no lessons at all. Moreover, parents will differ in intelligence, temperament, and interests, as will their children. Over the thousands of years during which billions of people have walked their brief moments on this earth, surely we would find many examples of peoples with no social bond at all such that everybody lives only by the rule of personal advantage.* And we should find some societies whose members abandoned their children in wholesale numbers, having decided that nurturing and teaching them was a tiresome burden. But we find neither.

Kinship and the Moral Sense

The two most striking facts about human societies is that each is organized around kinship patterns and that children, no matter how burdensome, are not abandoned in large numbers. These facts are generally acknowledged (albeit with some amendments, to be dis-

---

* Readers familiar with anthropology will claim that such a group has been found. They are the Ik of northern Uganda, described by Colin Turnbull in 1972 as living amid a horrific war of all against all. Children were abandoned, familial affection was nonexistent, and the elderly were encouraged to starve. So dreadful was their behavior that Turnbull urged the government to disperse them forcibly so that their monstrous culture would be destroyed. The Ik family was "not a fundamental unit" (133); the people were "loveless" (234) and engaged in "mutual exploitation (290); coerced relocation was necessary (283). But other scholars have cast serious doubt on the accuracy of Turnbull's account. In 1985 Bernd Heine (who was much more fluent in the Ik language than Turnbull) found them to be a quite sociable people, much different from what Turnbull had described. But scholars seem to remember the Turnbull book and not the Heine refutation (Edgerton, 1992:6–8). A better, though less well known, example of a relatively unsociable people were the Sirioni Indians of eastern Bolivia as described by Allan Holmberg (1950: esp. 77–78). But even here, though the Sirioni often seemed indifferent to the fate of fellow members of the tribe, they loved their own children.

cussed below, involving infanticide), but they are often treated as mere facts. Yet they are more than facts; they are phenomena with profound moral implications. That is because kinship and child rearing cannot wholly be explained on grounds of personal self-interest; they involve an important element of obligation that cannot be enforced fully by threats of retaliation or promises of reciprocity.

Kin are loyal to one another in part because it is in their interest to do so. If I help my sister, she will help me. We are linked by a rule of reciprocity. That explanation, true so far as it goes, begs an important question. Are there not many circumstances under which the rule would be unenforceable? I live in California and my sister in Texas. We see each other no more than once every two years; meanwhile, we each are embedded in a network of friends who are much more helpful to us than we are to each other. My friends do not know her friends, and so if I neglect her when she asks for help, my reputation suffers only in the eyes of people whom I do not know and who can do nothing for me. Nonetheless, my sister and I acknowledge and act upon a strong sense of duty toward one another, a sense that ordinarily takes precedence over competing claims from friends. She and I are not unusual in this regard; almost everyone reading this has sisters and brothers, uncles and aunts, cousins and nephews who have claims upon them that, absent some intense quarrel or personality clash, require them to act in ways that are inconvenient or costly. We value the help that comes from acknowledging the norm of reciprocity. At one time, only kin could supply that help because only kin lived near us. But in modern times we usually live closer to nonkin, and so the norm confers greater mutual advantage among friends, neighbors, and business associates than it does among far-flung kin. Despite this change, kinship ties continue to exert a powerful pull on us.

Similarly with children. There may well be times and places when children are valuable assets. Caring for them through infancy may make sense to the parents if the children help gather food, raise crops, or hunt animals, and if as adults they support their enfeebled parents. These considerations may explain why parents expend effort on behalf of their children, but they cannot explain why the children should reciprocate those efforts. The youngsters are free riders who benefit from parental nurture whether or not they later support them. Yet grown children feel an obligation toward their parents and often act upon it, even though such actions are unprofitable. As the modern state assumes responsibility for the elderly we can expect the care supplied by children to decline sharply, but the sense of obligation to one's parents will not, I think, decline by nearly as much.

This book is in part an effort to explain the apparently irrational attachments of family members and to draw from those attachments the argument that they rest on a moral sense and a sketch of the way in which that sense develops.

This is not how many anthropologists interpret the central facts of human society. Most either look for universal standards of right and wrong or, believing that none can be found, content themselves with the task of documenting the exotic diversity of human communities and the infinite complexity of kinship patterns. Of late the latter group has far outnumbered the former, and so the study of culture has in general produced two conclusions: first, culture is everything, nature nothing; and second, no universal moral rules exist in all cultures.

The second is almost surely wrong. Take murder: in all societies there is a rule that unjustifiable homicide is wrong and deserving of punishment. To justify an exception requires making reasonable arguments.[25] My critics will rejoin that if only *unjustifiable* homicides are wrong, and if societies differ radically in what constitutes a justification, that is tantamount to saying that there is no rule against homicide. I grant the force of their argument, but I suggest in response that the need to make an argument—to offer a justification for the killing—is itself a sign that every society attaches some weight to human life. For murder not to be a universal wrong, one would have to imagine a society in which murder were subject to no general rule other than, perhaps, "only do it when you think you can get away with it."

There is also a rule against incest. Sexual intercourse between brothers and sisters or between mothers and sons is universally condemned. Where lawful exceptions occur, it is because of extraordinary circumstances that are carefully defined—for example, the need to preserve a royal dynasty when suitable mates cannot be found outside the first degree of kinship. For incest not to be a universal wrong, one would have to imagine a society in which sex between brothers and sisters was approved of, or at worst a matter of indifference. So far as anyone is aware, no such society has existed.[26]

But the existence of a natural moral sense does not require the existence of universal moral rules. (It would be odd if there were *no* universal rules, since their absence would imply that the moral sense is so weak as never to lead to a rule. Happily there are some such rules: that against incest, for example.) Most important human universals do not take the form of rules at all and hence are not likely to be discovered by scholars searching for rules. Even the incest taboo, though a universal rule, scarcely needs to be a rule because incest is so rare.[27] As Robin Fox has noted, what is cultural is the *rule* against incest; what is universal is the avoiding of incest.[28] Much of the dispute over the existence of human universals has taken the form of a search for laws and stated practices. But what is most likely to be universal are those impulses that, because they are so common, scarcely need to be stated in the form of a rule, and so escape the notice of anyone scanning indexes to ethnographic studies. The impulse to avoid incest is one such. Another—and to me the most important—is the impulse to care for one's children.

Were social norms entirely designed to suit the preferences of people, there would be far fewer children in the world today. Many people would have noticed the great risks, enormous burdens, and uncertain rewards of nurturing babies and decided not to do it. So widespread is the practice of child nurturance and so unreflective is the parental behavior on which it depends that this care must occur, not because a rule is being enforced, but because an impulse is being obeyed. Though a rule may be propounded to control the small fraction of people who prefer to let their offspring die, it is not the rule that explains the behavior of most people but their behavior that explains the rule. For this reason I doubt that the fundamental social bonds are entirely created by human artifice or preserved by human choice.

But this generalization, so plausible to the average person, has elicited strong scholarly objections. Many writers have asserted that until recently mankind—or at least its European and American variants—treated children with some combination of neglect, abuse, and abandonment.[29] John Locke was only the first of many to point out that infanticide is common in less advanced societies and not unknown in advanced ones.[30] If mothers still kill their own babies and if parents have only recently stopped sending them to foundling homes, the love of children must be a recently acquired and thus socially learned disposition.* Lloyd de Mause wrote that the history of childhood is a "nightmare from which we have only recently begun to awaken."[31] The further back in time we go, the more likely the child was to be killed, abandoned, beaten, terrorized, and sexually abused. Edward Shorter gathered data on the use of wet nurses and foundling homes in the eighteenth century that, to him, bespoke a "traditional lack of maternal love."[32] Childhood, and the love of children, is a modern invention, ascribed variously to religion, capitalism, or the Enlightenment.

It is odd that this view should have had so large an impact, since we already knew from studies of primitive societies, such as the San of the Kalahari Desert, that children are not only loved but indulged without benefit of modern science, enlightened teaching, or capitalist requirements.[33] In 1906 Edward Westermarck's magisterial two-volume account of the origins of moral ideas among primitive peoples concluded that "the maternal sentiment is universal in mankind" and that "parental affection is not a late product of civilisation, but a normal feature of the savage mind." He gave countless examples in support of this generalization, ranging from the peaceful Australian aborigines to the fierce residents of Tierra del Fuego, the Upper Congo, and the Fiji Islands.[34] Swaddling, supposedly evidence of parental indifference to infants, has been shown to arise out of a desire to protect the child when, during the necessary absence of the parents, it might be endangered by cold air or its own crawling.[35]

It is even odder that conclusions about how people felt toward children were inferred from data about how children were treated, since the treatment of children might well have been shaped by circumstances and not attitudes.[36] Wet nursing was used by women who, because of their employment in agriculture, could not breast feed their own infants and for whom no other safe source of food was

---

* I omit here a discussion of whether parenting is a distinctively female activity. Some writers have argued that mothering is a learned social role (Weitzman, 1975); others have argued that mothering is reproduced by the differential working out of oedipal relationships between mothers on the one hand and either daughters or sons on the other (Chodorow, 1978); still others that it is produced by the economic system (Lorber, 1981). And there are yet others too numerous to list. I am not satisfied with any of these explanations, but I postpone the reasons for my dissatisfaction to another occasion. In the meantime I commend to the reader the writings of Alice Rossi (1977, 1981).

available.[37] And in any event wet nursing was far less common than some experts would have us believe; perhaps 10 percent of all Parisian women, beyond the small percentage who were physiologically unable to nurse, put their children out to wet nurses.[38]

Such direct evidence as we have about the feelings of European parents and children toward one another is inconsistent with the view that a caring family is a recent invention. The painstaking research of Linda Pollock in over four hundred diaries and autobiographies, including many written by children, strongly suggests that from the sixteenth to the nineteenth centuries British and American parents and children felt toward each other much as we feel today: mutual attachment and great affection.*

But surely the existence of infanticide throughout history confirms the purely conventional nature of family attachments. How could a natural sentiment—affection for a child—ever coexist with the deliberate killing of that child?

This is a profoundly important question, and one that cannot be entirely resolved on the basis of the available historical and anthropological evidence. In 1974 William L. Langer published a brief but chilling history of infanticide, noting that it has existed everywhere since time immemorial as a means for disposing of deformed infants and limiting the size of the population during periods of extreme privation. Only with the advent of Christianity did there begin, in Europe at least, the widespread condemnation of the practice; only with the triumph of Christianity did the secular authorities make it a crime.[39] (The Jews had always condemned infanticide.)[40] In hopes of providing an incentive that would reinforce the sanctions of the criminal law, many states created foundling homes in which mothers could leave their unwanted infants. These hopes were realized beyond the capacity of the system to accommodate them. In 1833, 164,319 babies were left in French foundling homes. At about the

---

* Pollock's conclusion is worth quoting, resting, as it does, on the most systematic review of the evidence that we have: "Despite the individual differences in child-rearing techniques, there are limits of variation. These limits are the dependency of the child and the acceptance of responsibility for the protection and socialisation of that child by the parents. From the material gathered here, it is clear that the vast majority of parents from earlier centuries were operating within these constraints." (1983:271). A similar judgment about child care was reached by David Herlihy (1985) for medieval Europe, Steven Ozment (1984: ch. 4) for sixteenth-century Europe, and Keith Wrightson and Michael MacDonald (1982) for seventeenth-century England.

same time, one such home in Saint Petersburg had twenty-five thousand infants on its rolls, with five thousand being admitted yearly.[41] The crowding was so great and regulation so lax that conveying a baby to a foundling home was often tantamount to sentencing it to death from neglect.

While this grisly history confirms how often infants were killed or abandoned, it is not very clear about the sentiments and motives of the people who did it. Langer suggests that the motive for infanticide reflected extreme circumstances, typically a child who was either deformed or beyond the capacity of its poor parents to feed. To this motive must be added the threat of social stigma, moral obloquy, or penal sanction faced by unwed mothers. But these are only suggestions, not conclusions based on a close study of parental feelings. For the history of infanticide to shed light on the existence of a moral sense, it is essential to know how the parents, and especially the mothers, felt about what they did. What proportion disposed of the baby without remorse as a matter of convenience, and what proportion did so in anguish and out of necessity? Langer attributed the decline in infanticide in the late nineteenth and early twentieth centuries to the advent of modern contraception, coupled with more stringent state regulation. This is a troubling hypothesis, for it implies that convenience dictated whether or not the baby would be killed. It neglects entirely what may have been the more important causes of the decline: a rise in the standard of living sufficient to enable poor parents to support several children, a change in the attitude toward unwed mothers great enough to make it thinkable to keep an illegitimate child, and an improvement in medical care adequate to ensure the ultimate good health of sickly infants.

To the best of my knowledge, the only way to assess the moral significance of infanticide is either to examine the feelings of the parents directly or to consider what happens when the conditions giving rise to it change. As with child neglect more generally, it is a mistake to infer sentiments from actions. In the modern world infanticide still occurs, but there are no reliable data on how often.[42] The closest thing we have to systematic data is a survey of 112 preindustrial societies from which the authors concluded that infanticide was "common" in about a third of them.[43] The word "common" was not defined, nor does anyone have any idea how many times it actually occurs in any society.

Insofar as one can tell, infanticide occurs today under essentially the same conditions that it occurred (more frequently) in the past: there is so little food that the child cannot be fed (especially a problem when twins are born), or the child is so deformed or sickly that its chances of survival are slight.[44] Infanticide may also occur when the child's paternity is in dispute. Of the 112 instances in which a cultural justification for infanticide could be found in the anthropological literature, all but 15 involved three factors: food shortages, deformed infants, or uncertain paternity.[45] Less common were instances of female infanticide designed to minimize the number of girls for whom dowries must be provided.[46]

Suppose for a moment that mother-child attachments were purely a matter of convention such that infanticide was entirely governed by personal advantage or cultural practice. Under those circumstances one would expect to find some societies—perhaps many—in which babies would be killed even though food was plentiful, paternity certain, and the child healthy. After all, even healthy, easy-to-support children can be a great nuisance for many years. We would also expect to find some societies in which children were killed in the second or third year of life, rather than immediately after birth, especially since (as every parent knows) a two-year-old child is often a greater burden than a newborn infant.

But all of these predictions that follow from a purely relativistic view of human nature are, so far as one can tell, false. When economic stresses end, infanticide becomes far less common and, indeed, is almost always made a criminal act. Healthy babies of certain paternity are rarely destroyed. Infanticide almost never occurs after the first month of life; indeed, it rarely occurs except during the first few hours of life.[47] This suggests that infanticide must be committed before bonding can occur. If the baby does not die almost immediately, the mother's distress is very great, at least in those few instances in which scholars have been on the scene to record the events.* However natural, few sentiments are sovereign; each must

---

* Eibl-Eibesfeldt, 1989:193–94. There are two related issues that cannot be addressed here. Some see abortion as equivalent to infanticide, and so argue that prosperity and technology have merely shifted the form of infant killing from one means to a morally equivalent alternative. But from the viewpoint maintained here, they cannot be subjectively equivalent actions because the mother can only imagine a fetus but can see and touch a neonate. The difference between these subjective states is relevant to one's moral judgment, whether or not

compete with others. Maternal affection for one infant must compete with her affection for another and with her own desire to survive. In a poor area of Brazil, mothers cope with this competition by not naming the baby until its survival seems assured.[48] George Peter Murdock, an anthropologist who spoke out against his profession's bias toward cultural relativism, noted that every primitive people to whom colonial governments have offered improved technology, modern medicine, and communal peace enforced by disinterested constables has readily relinquished infanticide, cannibalism, and killing the aged.[49]

The Moral Sense and Natural Selection

This long excursion through murder, incest, child neglect, and infanticide was necessary to suggest that there are good reasons for supposing that the social bonds, which Durkheim rightly thought so important, are not entirely a matter of convention or accident or, if they ever were, that millennia of evolution have selected for those bonds that are most suited for the perpetuation of the species.

If Darwin and his followers are right, and I think they are, the moral sense must have had adaptive value; if it did not, natural selection would have worked against people who had such useless traits as sympathy, self-control, or a desire for fairness and in favor of those with the opposite tendencies (such as a capacity for ruthless predation, or a preference for immediate gratifications, or a disinclination to share). Biologists, beginning with Darwin, have long understood this. But contemporary biologists sometimes give too narrow an account of this evolutionary process, because they attempt to link selfish genes directly to unselfish behavior without explaining the intervening psychological mechanism. As I try to show in chapter 6, what evolution has selected for over countless millennia is not simply a desire to reproduce one's genes in the next generation, or even to ensure that similar genes among one's kin get reproduced, but a particular psychological orientation that has as one of its effects a preference for kin but extends to nonkin as well.

---

one thinks that abortion is defensible. Nor do I address the interesting problem of "deferred infanticide"—that is, the neglect of one child (typically a girl) in favor of another (typically a boy), leading, over several years, to wide differences in survival rates (Johannson, 1984: 463–85).

My interest in this psychological orientation grew out of my studies of crime. What most needed explanation, it seemed to me, was not why some people are criminals but why most people are not.* That they are not is all the more puzzling since the forces that may easily drive people to break the law—a desire for food, sex, wealth, and self-preservation—seem to be instinctive, not learned, while those that might restrain our appetites—self-control, sympathy, a sense of fairness—seem to be learned and not instinctive. It is easy to suppose that instinct will triumph over learning or even that, for many people, learning will never occur at all. This supposition is reinforced by the observation that every society has laws and government, whether or not they are called by those names, all apparently designed to curb our elemental, and thus our especially powerful, passions. The clear implication is that learning, culture, norms—all of the components of the social bond—are quite precarious, for they are contrivances, not instincts, created for collective but not individual advantage and maintained by creaky and uncertain institutions rather than by powerful and always-present emotions.

In my view, the restraints we acquire on the exercise of our appetites are, indeed, precarious, but not because they are rules that we imperfectly learn. As acquired by the young child, these restraints are neither rules nor wholly learned. Moreover, they are not entirely the product of the higher regions of the brain (the neocortex); in all likelihood they are to some degree the products of the more primitive parts (the limbic area). They are sensibilities whose acquisition is as much a product of our human nature as the appetites they are meant to control. The reason for their being so precarious is that sentiments are not the sole determinants of action; circumstances—the rewards, penalties, and rituals of daily life—constrain or subvert the operation of the moral sense.

Were this book an effort to explain human behavior, it would start with incentives in order to discover what we are rewarded for doing. But this is an attempt to clarify how we evaluate human behavior, and so it starts with judgments in order to discover what we are praised for doing. Almost everyone has a moral sense that is

---

* An explanation for criminality is found in *Crime and Human Nature* (1985), which I wrote with Richard J. Herrnstein. Travis Hirschi (1969) is one of the few criminologists who has attempted to explain non-crime.

The Moral Sense

evident when we speak disinterestedly about our behavior or that of others. We regularly praise and condemn other people's speech and conduct. If we cared only for our own interests, we would of course admire some behavior as efficient or clever and scorn other behavior as inefficient or obtuse, but we would hardly praise it as brave, dutiful, fair-minded, and generous or condemn it as craven, self-indulgent, one-sided, and self-seeking. Yet we use these words all the time. Of course, some words of praise or condemnation may be uttered only for self-serving public consumption, but that cannot be the whole story. For such words to reflect well on ourselves they must be taken seriously by others. If the moral sense were mere sham for everyone, then no one would be fooled by our employing moral terms, and soon such terms would drop out of daily discourse.

This book is a modest effort to supply the evidence that man has a moral sense, one that emerges as naturally as his sense of beauty or ritual (with which morality has much in common) and that will affect his behavior, though not always and in some cases not obviously. The moral "sense" exists in two meanings of the word: First, virtually everyone, beginning at a very young age, makes moral judgments that, though they may vary greatly in complexity, sophistication, and wisdom, distinguish between actions on the grounds that some are right and others wrong, and virtually everyone recognizes that for these distinctions to be persuasive to others they must be, or at least appear to be, disinterested. Second, virtually everyone, beginning at a very young age, acquires a set of social habits that we ordinarily find pleasing in others and satisfying when we practice them ourselves. There are, to be sure, some people who, again from a very young age, seem to have no regular habits that make their company pleasurable to decent people and lack any tendency to judge things as right or wrong in a disinterested way. Such people are rare, as evidenced by the special terms we have for them: the former are wild, the latter psychopathic.

How can one reconcile the existence of a moral sense with the evidence of moral depravity, immoral oppression, and amoral self-indulgence—that is, with crime, cruelty, and licentious extravagance? There is no puzzle here. The moral sense is no surer a cause of moral action than beliefs are the cause of actions generally. Behavior is the product of our senses interacting with our circumstances. But when we behave in ways that seem to violate our fundamental moral sensibilities—when we abandon children, sacrifice victims, or kill rivals—we offer reasons, and the reasons are never simply that we enjoy such acts and think that we can get away with them. The justifications we supply invariably are based on other claims, higher goods, or deferred pleasures: we need to assure a good crop, reduce suffering, produce a son who can inherit our property, or avert a plague that would devastate the community. Our moral sense requires justification for any departure from it; as circumstances change—as we learn better ways of averting plagues or producing crops—arguments that once seemed adequate begin to seem inadequate, and our behavior changes accordingly. It is this feeling that we must offer justifications for violating a moral standard that explains the difference between a standard that is purely a matter of taste ("I like chocolate ice cream") and one that is a matter of moral sensibility ("I ought not to be cruel"). If we decide to switch to vanilla ice cream, we need not justify our decision, especially by any argument that the new flavor merits our respect; if we are cruel, on the other hand, we feel obliged to justify it, usually by saying that the suffering party deserved his fate.[50]

Before the reader repeats the well-known criticisms of the idea of a moral sense, let me acknowledge that I know them also: If there is a moral sense, what is the sensory organ? If sincere people disagree about what is right and wrong, how can there be a moral sense? If a moral sense is supposed to emerge naturally, what evidence is there that human nature is sufficiently uniform so that this sense will emerge among most people in more or less the same way?

I do not think one can easily give general answers to these important questions. The truth, if it exists, is in the details. This book is about the details; it is the result of scavenging through science in order to illuminate everyday life. The scavenging was not motivated by the belief that the propositions science can affirm are akin to the rules by which we live. In fact, most of the time we do not live by "rules" at all, but by habits and sensibilities. To say the same thing in different words, I am not trying to discover "facts" that will prove "values"; I am endeavoring to uncover the evolutionary, developmental, and cultural origins of our moral habits and our moral sense. But in discovering these origins, I suspect that we will encounter uniformities; and by revealing uniformities, I think that we can better appreciate what is general, nonarbitrary, and emotionally compelling about human nature.

PART ONE

Sentiments

Sympathy

A child feels distress when it hears another child cry; the parent suggests that the first child share its toy with the second. A man winces when the hero in a motion picture is wounded, exults when he is triumphant. A woman is saddened by the sight of an abandoned kitten or a lame dog, delighted by the spectacle of a stranger's new baby. People who have just given blood feel good about themselves; people who were asked but declined feel guilty. A crowd cheers when its favorite team is victorious even though no one in the crowd is acquainted with anyone on the team and no one on the team knows who is cheering for it. In these and a thousand other ways, we are affected by the distress or pleasure of another, even if the other is a stranger, an animal, or a fictional character.

But what of it? We are affected in varying degrees by the joys and sorrows of others, but those feelings are usually short-lived and often of no consequence. Recall how we react when we learn of a great catastrophe—a flood, famine, or earthquake—that has taken tens of thousands of lives. "How terrible," we murmur, and then return to our concern of the moment, such as deciding what to wear or where to dine. Even when we witness with our own eyes a fatal accident or a serious injury, we discover that we are soon able to put it out of our minds, especially if it is soon out of sight.

Given these familiar facts, it is hardly surprising that many students of human behavior attach little significance to sympathy; to them, it is actions, not feelings, that count, and most human actions can be explained by narrow self-interest. Actions that help others more than they help ourselves are much rarer than actions that help ourselves more than they help others. Altruism is the exception, self-interest the rule. And many actions that appear altruistic turn out, on closer examination, to be nothing more than a certain kind of self-interest. We give to charity—but only because we want applause. We help needy friends—but only because we want their help in return. No doubt there are occasional acts of real altruism, as when a soldier falls on a grenade to save his comrades; but such acts are sufficiently rare that little effort need be devoted to explaining them.

Our subject here is not altruism, though examples of altruistic actions will be discussed. Rather, it is *sympathy*, by which I mean the human capacity for being affected by the feelings and experiences of others. Sometimes sympathy leads us to act altruistically; usually it does not. More often it restrains us from acting cruelly. And even when it does not inspire benevolent actions, sympathy is an important source of the moral standards by which we judge both others and ourselves. Sympathy, in other words, is both a motive and a norm.

Consider a person who makes a conspicuous gift to a hospital for blind children, earning by this charitable act the applause of others. We might discuss his motive, finally concluding that it was his desire for approval. But that is not the end of the story. It is just as important to ask why we applaud him for making his gift. Why do people approve of generous actions even when they suspect that generosity may not have been the motive? The answer, I suggest, is that most people wish to encourage in each other sentiments of sympathy; they wish to affirm the importance of this disposition by rewarding even its apparent display.

We praise people for being generous and praise them the most when their generosity is uncompensated. We reserve our highest praise for heroes who sacrifice their lives that others may live; we give at best grudging compliments to social climbers who contribute money in exchange for social reputation or business advantage. That self-interest plays some part in most benefactions and the whole part in a few is indisputable; this fact leads some cynical observers to deny that benevolence exists or deserves to be called a virtue. Charity, in this view, is merely another form of exchange subject to the same expectations of fair return that we find in the marketplace. But if that is the case, it is hard to explain why our language is filled with words designed to distinguish self-regarding from selfless acts, kind

Sympathy

from unkind persons, and heroism from bravado. If we purged our discourse of such terms, the only difference between Tiny Tim and Scrooge would be their age.

Our language is rich in such distinctions because they are necessary ones: we cannot organize our impressions or rank our judgments without attending carefully to differences in motives, however small or hard to verify. Almost all of us encourage our children to acquire other-regarding motives. We do so in part because it is useful: generous people attract more friends and better opportunities than do skinflints. But most of us also do so because we think such motives are good in themselves. We want our children not only to be praised but to be praiseworthy.

Because sympathy is sometimes wholly absent and because even when present it must struggle with self-interest on uneven terms, it is understandable that, for reasons of intellectual economy, scholars might emphasize the daily examples of egoism and minimize or ignore the rarer examples of altruism. But the same scholars train their own children to share toys, donate blood without compensation, leave tips in restaurants they never plan to visit again, and contribute money to organizations without public acknowledgment.

Sympathy as a Standard

Before he became the preeminent economist of all time, Adam Smith was the preeminent moral philosopher of his time, and his attempt to explain moral sentiments was founded on the near-universal human attribute of sympathy. How ever man may be supposed, Smith wrote, "there are evidently some principles in his nature, which interest him in the fortune of others, and render their happiness necessary to him, though he derives nothing from it except the pleasure of seeing it." One such principle is "pity or compassion, the emotion which we feel for the misery of others, when we either see it, or are made to conceive it in a very lively manner."[1]

This statement is often taken to mean that Smith believed that we have, or ought to have, a tendency to help others—that is, to be benevolent. That is almost correct, but not quite. Smith did not mean that we always feel so much distress at the plight of others that we feel obliged to alleviate it; were that the case, it would behoove us to perform endless and probably futile acts of benevolence. Indeed, were pity our chief motive, we would all soon be either paupers or busybodies. What he said was a bit more complicated: sympathy, defined as the capacity for and inclination to imagine the feelings of others, is a source—to Smith, *the* source—of human moral sentiments.

We have a natural desire to be admired by others; to be admired by them, we must please them. Since our happiness depends somewhat on the goodwill of our fellows, we naturally seek to understand what may please or offend them.[2] To do this we seek to enter into the minds and feelings of others, and we are aware that others try to grasp our own thoughts and feelings. We cannot, of course, know what others feel, and so we must imagine it.[3] Our powers of imagination are very strong; they can be aroused not only by the plight of a friend but by the flickering lights and shadows on a motion picture screen, so that we are reduced to tears by the sight of a fictitious boy looking in vain for an equally fictitious dog.

But we do not simply share the feelings we imagine others to have; we also judge them. More particularly, we judge whether the actions and feelings of another person are proportionate. A rich boy distraught at the loss of a penny arouses not sympathy but derision; a boy indifferent to the loss of a loving dog arouses not sympathy but disdain. We approve of the conduct and character of another person if, when we imagine ourselves in his position, our feelings correspond to those that we think motivate him.[4]

This sounds more complicated than it is. Suppose we see someone reacting angrily to being overcharged. We ordinarily do nothing, but we judge the other person's reactions. If we think they are appropriate, we say to ourselves something like this: "I know just how he felt! I wouldn't have paid that bill either!" If we think his reaction was too extreme, we judge differently: "He's overreacting; there's no need to get carried away." In neither case have we done anything, but that does not mean we lack sympathy. Sympathy—our sense of another's feelings and of their appropriateness given the circumstances—is the basis of our judgment. More bluntly, to sympathize *is* to judge.

Sometimes another person's situation may prompt our action. He may be injured, or he may be injuring another. How we behave will depend in part on our assessment of his motives: If he is injured, was he blameless? If he is harming another, is it for good reason? There will be, of course, many other factors that determine whether we act, some of which we shall examine later on. But even when we do not act, we judge. We say to ourselves: "He has only himself to blame," or "He shouldn't hit that child." Even when we judge but do not act we express—and thereby reaffirm—a standard of moral character.

As we grow from childhood to adulthood, we increasingly judge ourselves as we judge others. We do so at first because we imagine what others must think of our motives when they see us acting in a certain way. Since we want to be admired, we want to conform, within reason, to the expectations of others. But at some point a remarkable transformation occurs in how we judge ourselves. We desire not only to be praised, but to be praiseworthy. As Adam Smith put it, "man naturally desires, not only to be loved, but to be lovely."[5] Thus we are often embarrassed when we are praised without deserving the praise.

Just how this transformation occurs is not well understood. Smith believed it arose out of our desire to be like those we most admire. When we emulate a parent, a friend, a popular hero, or even a fictional character, we become acutely aware of the difference between merely pretending to be excellent and really being so. Up to a point we can fake honesty, courage, or generosity; but we know the difference between *really* being honest, brave, or generous and just going through the motions in order to impress other people. Smith said that at this point we are beginning to listen to the voice of an impartial spectator located within our breast; in modern terms, we begin to hear the voice of our conscience. At first we judge others; we then begin to judge ourselves as we think others judge us; finally we judge ourselves as an impartial, disinterested third party might. The importance of this last step can hardly be exaggerated, because the "man within the breast,"[6] unlike some other person, *knows* our real motives. We can fool our friends, but not ourselves.

Not that we don't try, of course. We rationalize our actions, suppress self-awareness, and drown out the whisper of conscience with impulsive actions and synthetic exuberance. But in our calmer moments, or perhaps when our lack of self-command has led to tragic consequences, we reflect bitterly on how wrong it was—and not merely how inconvenient—to have allowed our actions to be governed by the wrong motives. And even in our daily lives, there will be innumerable cases of our obeying rules, resisting temptations, and doing the honorable thing for no other reason than that we instinctively act that way and reflexively feel guilty when we don't.

Since Adam Smith wrote in 1759, the development of conscience has been the object of a good deal of study; in the chapter on duty I will try to summarize what we have learned from those inquiries. I am impressed by how well the account given by some modern scientists agrees with Smith's "prescientific" view. It may be objected, of course, that not everybody has a strong conscience. If some people do not, how can we say that a conscience-driven moral sense is natural to man? Smith, of course, was quite aware that "men differ considerably from one another," such that some "appear much less anxious about the praise-worthiness than about the praise."[7] Later we will encounter some rather grim evidence on just how free of conscience a few men can be. But what is striking to me (and presumably to Adam Smith as well) is how many people do acquire a conscience. It is an inconvenient voice at times, but it is normal to hear it, and almost everybody does so.

Insofar as they arise out of sympathy, then, our moral sentiments originate in our natural sociability. Because we like the company and desire the approval of others, we adjust our actions to conform to others' expectations. If that were the end of the matter, we might properly conclude that morality is little more than a popularity contest. But that is not the whole story. Our natural sociability leads us not only to act so as to please others but also to judge how others act toward us; and in judging them we learn to judge ourselves. We want the approval of others, but—to a degree that cannot be explained by immediate self-interest—we also want to deserve that approval. And insofar as we want to deserve it from others, we also want to deserve it from ourselves. In other words, we desire not only respect but self-respect.

Sympathy as a Motive

If sympathy merely shaped our judgments, it would be important, but it acquires even greater significance to the extent that it governs our actions. Since the 1960s, psychologists and other scholars have explored in considerable detail the circumstances under which and the degree to which feelings of sympathy lead to benevolent or altruistic actions. Their conclusions are these: Sympathy is not an

Sympathy

idle sentiment; on the contrary, it often—but not always—leads to benevolence.[8] A person who feels distress at the plight of another is more likely to help than is one who does not, though specific aspects of the situation and of the person will influence his response.

Psychologists debate whether feeling distress at the plight of another means that the sympathetic person "really wants" to help the distressed person or whether the former gets some psychic benefit (such as avoiding shame or relieving stress) from helping the latter. Though this may seem like the worst sort of academic hair-splitting, in fact it is a significant issue. Suppose that you confront a person who has collapsed on a bus. You feel distressed. If your distress is truly sympathetic, your only course of action is to help the person, unless, of course, someone else helps him first. But if all that you want to do is to relieve your sense of distress, you can get off the bus at the next stop. Out of sight, out of mind.

Some people will help, some will get off the bus, and some will do one or the other depending on the situation. Most of the evidence obtained from laboratory experiments suggests that people feeling distress prefer helping to running away.[9] Some of the research done on the street (involving staged scenes of distress) suggests that many people will move away.[10] This should not be surprising; if sympathy always or even usually led to benevolence, we would not regard benevolent action as so praiseworthy. We praise only motives that have defeated self-interest; we reserve our greatest praise for those motives that have the greatest difficulty in overcoming self-interest.

When people donate blood, offer help to a collapsed stranger, assist motorists trapped in a car, intervene to stop a crime in progress, or rescue Jews whom the Nazis want to send to a death camp, they are acting benevolently. That benevolence can have many motives, ranging from a desire to impress onlookers to sympathy for the victim.

It is difficult to know motives, especially when the relationship between motives and action is complicated by the action's costli-ness—perhaps even its danger—and the uncertainty of its results. We would not fault a person who cannot swim for not helping a drowning swimmer, nor criticize a person for not bailing out a sink-ing boat if he had only a spoon with which to bail. Much of the scholarly evidence that we have about altruism has been produced by scholars who have staged scenes that suggested to naive onlookers that some "victim" needed help. Though contrived, many of these scenes were not college-based laboratory experiments; they occurred in public places among whatever bystanders happened to be there or among people invited to an office that they could not have known was the setting for a deception.

Not surprisingly, many of these studies show that where the costs of helping are high, people are less likely to help.[11] When a person (actually an actor) collapsed on a subway car, a large proportion of the bystanders tried to help. But fewer helped when it seemed more costly: when, for example, the person apparently collapsed because he was drunk as opposed to being lame, as indicated by his carrying a cane. In the first case, it was a messy situation and in any event the "victim" had brought it on himself; in the second case, it was less likely to be messy (perhaps he just needed a hand up), and in any event it was not obviously the victim's fault. When the cane-carrying man bled from the mouth after collapsing, he received less help than when he did not; a bleeding victim, like a drunk one, created a messy situation and thus, for potential helpers, a more costly one.[12] Similarly, men were much more likely than women to help the collapsed man—it takes strength to pull up a fallen person.[13]

On the other hand, if the apparent victim experiences a catastrophic emergency, many people will help strangers even at some substantial risk to themselves and do so impulsively with little reflection on the hazards they run. In one experiment, people rushed to the aid of a man who apparently had been the victim of a serious electrical shock even though he still seemed to be in contact with the live wires.[14] A person's suffering will induce this kind of spontaneous, unreflective help when the emergency is absolutely clear and the victim wholly innocent.

Perhaps the most carefully studied aspect of helping behavior is the so-called Kitty Genovese effect, named after the 1964 incident in which no one even called the police, much less tried to help, when Genovese's cries were heard as she was being stabbed to death in a New York City neighborhood. Many of the popular commentators immediately interpreted the apparent indifference of the victim's neighbors as evidence of personal apathy, moral callousness, or urban anonymity. But in a remarkable series of experiments, Bibb Latané and J. M. Darley showed that these explanations were probably wrong.[15] They staged a number of "emergencies" in stores, offices, and Laundromats, ranging from medical problems and fire alarms to thefts and disorderly conduct. In every case, a lone bystander was more likely to help the "victim" than was a group of bystanders.

Contrary to what many had supposed, people do not seem to act on the principle that there is safety in numbers. This finding casts great doubt on the notion that altruism among strangers is always a form of reciprocity by which helpers get credit for good deeds that can later be cashed in for other rewards, such as status.[16] If altruism is really a self-interested investment in the future, then we should be more likely to help victims when others can witness the good deed. But we are less likely, it seems. When in a group we experience a social inhibition against helping, that probably derives from a diffused sense of personal responsibility. It is as if each person in a group says to himself or herself, "Maybe somebody else will do it."

There are countless ways to avoid accepting responsibility for the plight of others. One may not notice (or pretend not to notice) the plight, notice it but decide that it is the fault of the victim, or perceive it as an emergency that someone else is better able or more likely to handle. When other bystanders are present, it is easier to pretend not to notice, easier to allow others to decide if the victim is innocent or blameworthy, and easier to avoid a sense of personal responsibility. Moreover, in the company of others one risks embarrassment if one tries to help only to discover that the victim angrily rejects the help or that the emergency is not real (the alarm was false, the theft did not really occur, the commotion was staged). A wholly self-interested person, of course, would not help either in the company of others ("let somebody else bear the costs") or alone ("no one will know if I do nothing"). But persons moved by sympathy must decide when sympathetic feelings imply personal obligation, and that is more likely to occur when one stands alone confronting the plight of another. Since the first Kitty Genovese research was published, scores of other studies have been done on the effect of bystanders, and with few exceptions they all confirm the social inhibition effect.[17]

Even more compelling evidence comes from the study of events that were in fact emergencies, and ones involving the highest possible risks to both victims and onlookers. Samuel and Pearl Oliner interviewed at length more than four hundred Europeans who helped Jews avoid being sent to Nazi death camps during World War II.[18] Those chosen for the study acted without material reward and placed their own lives in danger. Though some helped only on one or a few occasions, most engaged in this risky business for several years. They did not act out of a sense of religious or ethnic kinship, for none of the rescuers was a Jew.

Some—perhaps one-sixth—acted out of sheer hatred for the Nazis, but for the vast majority the main reason seems to have been ethical: either they felt a keen sense of sympathy for the victims of the Holocaust, or they felt obliged to follow the directions of some authoritative figure, or they believed in some principle (justice, fair play) that made it wrong for anyone to be treated in this way.

About a third of the rescuers gave sympathy as their main motivation. What was distinctive about them is that in each case reported by the Oliners, it was a face-to-face meeting with a threatened Jew that lead them to act. A Polish woman was approached by a man who had escaped from a camp; his pitiable condition—shaved head, prison garb, abject attitude—moved her to help. A Polish man, interviewing women to hire as a maid, realized that one was a Jew and that if he sent her back out on the street she was likely to be arrested. Another Polish man who lived near the ghetto regularly encountered Jews desperate to slip through the barbed wire; over the years he helped twenty of them, each someone he had met on the street. A German soldier could not bring himself to shoot some captured Jews; instead, he helped them escape. A Dutch couple could not resist taking in a three-year-old boy.[19]

Rescuers driven by sympathy were moved by their firsthand encounter with human suffering rather than by abstract principle, organized campaigns, or even hatred of the Nazis. Some confessed that had they not experienced these encounters, they would have done nothing. As the Polish man hiring a maid put it, "If somebody had told me before the interviews that I was going to take a Jewish woman as my maid, I would have said he was a madman."[20] Of course empathy alone was not enough; the rescuers also had to have a sense of personal responsibility for those they encountered.[21] One wonders how many would-be rescuers did nothing because, though they had a keen sense of sympathy, they were in groups when they encountered Jews and so their sense of responsibility was diffused, much as had been the case with those who heard Kitty Genovese's cries.

The empathic rescuers were neither saints nor ideologues but ordinary people with an extraordinary willingness to alleviate suffering when they encountered it. Compared to a group of Europeans who were bystanders, the rescuers had been very close to their parents, both fathers and mothers, and had learned from them the importance of dependability, self-reliance, and caring for others. These warm familial feelings extended to others: sympathetic rescuers saw people as basically good and had many close friends.[22]

A smaller study of Christians who rescued Jews came to some of the same conclusions. The long-term rescuers were very close to their parents, one or both of whom held strong moral convictions,[23] a pattern that reappears in a study of people who were active for long periods in the civil rights movement during the 1960s. Compared to those who were only briefly involved, the fully committed activists had a warm and close relationship with one or both parents. Though there were often arguments (including arguments over whether the child should become a civil rights activist!), there was a fond respect for one another's views.[24] These findings are not precisely comparable to those of the Oliners, since the latter two studies did not distinguish between activists motivated by sympathy and those driven by duty or principle, but the general pattern of warm familial relationships is striking.

The scholarly studies of altruism have been quite useful, especially in demonstrating how many benevolent acts could not possibly have been motivated by a desire to impress others. Though our natural sociability may be the source of our sympathetic sentiments, sympathy acquires an autonomous status as a motive. These studies have one defect, however: they rest the case for sympathetic altruism entirely on the finding that some people will under some circumstances take positive steps to aid someone in need.

Yet a moment's reflection should remind us that the most common way in which sympathy guides our actions is by restraining us from inflicting harm. We often say, when confronted with an opportunity to benefit ourselves without running any risk, "That would be like taking candy from a baby." We repeat the familiar phrase to remind ourselves that taking candy from babies is wrong, however enjoyable the candy and defenseless the babies. Not only do we not take candy from them, we don't, ordinarily, disturb their sleep, inflict great pain, or tease them unmercifully. We also forbear to take advantage of adults under many circumstances when it would be easy and costless to do so. In fact, we are especially unlikely to take advantage of them if they are particularly vulnerable to being taken advantage of; if, for example, they are blind, disabled, or elderly.

THE MORAL SENSE

We praise people for genuine acts of charity or altruism but, being sensible and realistic folk, we don't expect them to be charitable or altruistic all of the time or even much of the time. But we always expect people to avoid inflicting unnecessary harm on innocent others. Someone who does not rush to the scene of every accident is not thought to be hard-hearted; someone who inflicts pain without reason, and seems to enjoy doing it, is thought monstrous.

Sympathy is often expressed by phrases that convey, not tenderness or concern, but anger and vengeance. If we see an abominable act—say, a man laughing while torturing an innocent baby—our first reaction is not likely to be an expression of sympathy for the child but rage at its tormenter; and this will be true even if it is not our child. Sympathy is often wrongly portrayed as entirely a tender sentiment: sympathetic people are sometimes described as soft, warm, or weepy. They often are; but they are much more than that, and some of the most sympathetic people have no trace of cuddliness in their temperament. Even so staunch a utilitarian as John Stuart Mill recognized this: "It is natural to resent and to repel or retaliate any harm done or attempted against ourselves or against those with whom we sympathize." Our sense of justice, he wrote, involves a desire to punish wrongdoers, even when we are not the victims, and that sense is a "spontaneous" and "natural" sentiment. A mere desire for vengeance is not a moral attitude; it becomes moral by its "subordination ... to the social sympathies, so as to wait on and obey their call."[25]

Altruism and Evolution

Behavior that is natural is behavior that is, to some degree, innate. If our willingness to help others or shun cruelty is in some sense natural, then this trait must have had some evolutionary value. Otherwise, it would have been extinguished, because its existence would have reduced the prospects of survival of those endowed with it. People who risk injury or death to help others would leave fewer offspring than those who look out only for themselves. After a few millennia, there would be few, if any, altruists left; everyone would be self-regarding. Many evolutionary biologists have puzzled at great length over what they call the paradox of altruism—namely, that helping behaviors occur even though they would appear to reduce their reproductive fitness. If I am to maintain that sympathy is natural, I must show that it has enabled the species to survive.

At this point some readers will think I am about to say something like "sympathy is genetically determined" or otherwise pronounce on the general subject of sociobiology. I know from long experience that even a hint of such an intention is enough to put people on guard, if it does not lead them to throw down the book in disgust. Patience. I am not about to argue that there is a "sympathy gene." But there must be some heritable disposition that helps us explain why sympathy is so common, as a norm if not a motive, among humans. Let us see what it might be.

The most powerful human disposition is self-preservation, and so our most elaborate and heartfelt tributes go to those who have sacrificed their lives that others might live. These tributes are rare because such heroism is rare. If we were ants or bees, however, the landscape would be littered with such monuments. Those creatures regularly work and often die that others of their kind might survive. The workers are sterile. Yet they gather food, fight enemies, and build nests so that someone else, the queen, can survive and reproduce.

Charles Darwin explained that nature favors individuals who leave the most offspring. The creatures that we see today are the descendants of those that had traits—for example, skills at hunting and mating—that made them reproductively successful in their particular environment.[26] But how can Darwin's theory explain the survival of ants, most of which cannot reproduce? (Not only have they survived, they have prospered: ants make up the most numerous species in the world.) The answer involves the notion, first advanced by William Hamilton, of inclusive fitness.[27] An individual is reproductively successful to the extent that his genes occur in the next generation, and he can assure that occurrence not only by reproducing himself but also by assisting in the reproduction of individuals who have some of his genes. The more closely related the first individual is to the second, the greater the number of the first's genes will appear in the next generation if the second individual produces offspring.

Ants in a colony (and other social insects) are genetically very similar to one another, more similar than are wolves in a pack or humans in a family. Indeed, female ants are genetically more similar to their sisters than they are to their daughters. By working selflessly to feed and defend their sisters, these female worker ants are increasing the survival of their own genes and, at the same time, the survival of the colony, albeit at the expense of their own survival.[28]

If we apply the theory of inclusive fitness to humans, it implies that we will make sacrifices for others with whom we share genes and in proportion to the degree of that sharing. It can be illustrated this way: If our sister is drowning, we should risk our life to save her if there is at least one chance in two of success, because the sister has half our genes. But trying to rescue our grandchild makes evolutionary sense only if there are three chances in four of success, because the grandchild has only one-fourth of our genes. Trying to save our grandmother, assuming that she is past childbearing age, makes no sense at all, because she can pass on none of our genes to the next generation.[29]

Of course in no particular case might we act this way. The theory only states that if the tendency to be altruistic has any genetic basis, then over a long period of time the world will come to consist of people who help only themselves and their close kin, because their offspring will be more numerous than will be the offspring of people who have drowned while trying to save their grandmothers.

This theory is consistent with the fact that, as a rule, we strive harder to protect our own children than somebody else's, that parents seem to make more sacrifices for their children than children make for their parents,* and that children are less likely to be abused by their natural parents than by their stepparents.†

But what is true in general is not the whole truth. Not only will people try to rescue their grandmothers even though they are past childbearing age, but they will also try to save their adopted children and even their dogs.

Studies of adoptive families provide no evidence that parents of adopted children are any less loving, solicitous, or protective than are

---

* Adam Smith noted that a person's sympathy is "by nature more strongly directed towards his children than towards his parents," an insight he had long before the concepts of reproductive success and inclusive fitness had been propounded (1759:6.2.1.3).

† Wilson and Daly, 1987. Moreover, the much greater abusiveness of stepparents cannot be explained by economic differences, since natural-parent and stepparent families do not, on average, differ in income (ibid., 225).

the parents of biological children. Mothers who have both an adopted and a biological child report no difference in their feelings toward them.[30] If anything, adoptive parents are more protective and less controlling than biological ones,[31] a puzzling finding if one believes that investment in child care is driven by a desire to reproduce one's genes. Adopted children report that they were loved as if they were natural children.*

Humans do not practice the hard-core altruism of ants; they practice, at best, a soft-core altruism that, though less intense, is more inclusive. Humans may not sacrifice as much for their own kin as do ants, but they sacrifice more than do ants for nonkin—adopted children, friends, neighbors, and countrymen. And in the case of people who lavish care on their pets (even to the extent of risking death to rescue a dog from a burning house), they even make sacrifices for other species.

One can attempt to solve these puzzles of affectional behavior directed toward nonkin and nonhumans while remaining within a narrow interpretation of the evolutionary perspective by advancing the notion of reciprocal altruism: we engage in altruistic acts—such as helping nonrelatives, caring for adopted children, or being affectionate toward pets—in order to impress others with our dependability and hence to increase our opportunities to have profitable exchanges with these others.[32] There is a great deal of truth in this; having a reputation for doing one's duty, living up to promises, and helping others will enhance one's own opportunities. Moral behavior is far more common when utility conspires with duty, and the strongest moral codes are invariably those that are supported by considerations of both advantage and obligation.[33]

But sometimes sentiment alone, unsupported by utility, motivates our actions, as when someone makes an anonymous benefaction or a lone bystander helps an endangered person. While anonymous giving may be relatively rare, we have already seen that generally a lone bystander is more likely to go to the aid of a threatened person than

* Triseliotis and Hill, 1990. The fact that adopted children are at greater risk than natural children for psychological problems and conduct disorders does not invalidate the argument that the former are cherished equally with the latter. Adopted children have more personality problems because their biological parents had these problems, which have a large genetic component (Cadoret, 1990; Bohmann and Sigvardsson, 1990).

a bystander who is part of a group, the opposite of what one would predict if reputation enhancement were the motive for altruistic actions.[34]

Moreover, altruism reinforced by utility must be seen in the context of a prior, dominant fact: we value human society and fear loneliness, and the greater the anxiety we experience the more we seek out the company of others.[35] We engage in acts contributing to reciprocal altruism only when we first value reciprocity, especially in its nonmaterial forms. And we value nonmaterial reciprocity only when we are affectionally dependent upon one another.

Evolutionary biology provides a powerful insight into human behavior at the level of the species, but it fares less well at the level of daily conduct. This deficiency arises in part because evolutionary biologists ordinarily do not explain how a selected trait governs behavior in particular cases.[36] Altruism is puzzling only if we do not ask what psychological mechanism governs it.

Sympathy for persons who are not offspring and creatures that are not human is a characteristic of almost all humans. Indeed, we regard as inhuman people who act as if they have no feeling for others and we criticize as insincere those who merely feign it. If sympathy is widespread, it must have been adaptive, but what was selected for was not a simple desire for reproductive success; what has been selected for is a generalized trait that both encourages reproductive fitness and stimulates sympathetic behavior. That trait, or adaptive mechanism, is *attachment* or *affiliative behavior*. The mechanisms by which such attachments form are discussed later in this book. To anticipate: humans are biologically disposed to care for their young, but, unlike some other species, what people find attractive in their own young are traits that, to some degree, are also present in other people (and even other species).

The Sources of Sympathy

The human capacity for sympathy has complex origins. It is rooted in part in a sense of kinship (and the closer the kin, the more we are inclined toward generosity); in part in those dispositions that prepare us to make sacrifices over long periods of time for highly dependent children; in part in those sensory cues that remind us of things that we find appealing about our infants (and by extension of infants generally); and in part in our capacity (itself the product of the long period of dependence that we experienced as children) to imagine and even experience, vicariously, the joys and sorrows of others.

The innate sociability of the child is the vital embryo in which a capacity for sympathy and an inclination to generosity can be found, and from which parents may help produce a sympathetic adult. Developmental psychologists have drawn a portrait of children who are most likely to help or comfort others and share things: They are sociable, competent, assertive, and sympathetic. They do not crave approval and they are not fatalists. They are typically raised by parents who combine nurturing love and consistent discipline and who themselves help others and share things.[37]

All this may strike many readers as obvious, and perhaps it is; but two things should be borne in mind. First, the evidence supporting this portrait comes from a great variety of studies—not only those based on interviews, but also ones based on observing children at play, putting them in situations in which they must make choices, and learning of their reputations among playmates. Second, until fairly recently, many scholars did not believe there was any such thing as a general disposition toward prosocial behavior. A famous set of experiments conducted on several thousand schoolchildren in the 1920s by Hugh Hartshorne and Mark May led scholars to conclude that the moral behavior of children was specific to the situation: for example, a child might be generous to a classmate in one situation but not in another.[38] Now it is certainly true, in ways that will be suggested later, that the situation determines to some degree how generous a person will be. The error Hartshorne and May made was not in pointing this out but in denying that there was any general tendency in the child that manifested itself in a variety of situations. A new analysis of their own data, as well as a host of subsequent studies, suggests very strongly that there is such a tendency—a trait, if you will—toward sympathy and generosity, strong in some people and weak or nonexistent in others.[39] And it is a trait that persists: children who seem at one age to be more generous than their peers tend to remain more generous five (and in one study, twenty-six) years later. [40]

We are here speaking of generosity spontaneously expressed. The children who behave in this way are sociable, interested in other people, well adjusted, and self-confident. Children may also act generously when asked to do so by a friend, teacher, or parent. It is not clear that this should be called generosity at all, or at least the kind that reflects a sympathetic concern for the well-being of others. Whatever it is, giving because one is asked to do so is not as clearly associated with sociability and self-confidence.

Children are by nature sociable; in the family they learn to extend sociability into generosity. Such learning requires the instruction and example of parents, other kin, and older playmates. The innate sociability of children makes them sensitive to the moods and actions of others. At first they try to control those moods and actions simply for their own pleasure; later they grasp that what pleases them may not please others, and so they act on the basis of some knowledge of the feelings of others. For most children the ability to be affected by the emotional state of others leads to a concern for the well-being of others.[41] Children learn without much instruction that their own happiness is in some ways affected by the happiness of others; with some instruction, they learn that the happiness of others can be improved by modest sacrifices in their own well-being.[42] Their own experiences and the teachings of others produce habits of action that routinely take into account the feelings of others. All this occurs early in life, before the children have understood sermons, mastered moral precepts, or read cautionary tales.

Sympathy and Similarity

A child's sympathetic habits, being formed in familial settings, may not extend much beyond those settings. We find it easiest to sympathize with people who are most like us, and accordingly, we may be most disposed to help those who are most like us. Being "alike" means being able to enter imaginatively into the other's mental state—knowing, or thinking that you know, what the other person is feeling or thinking—and being able to predict how the other will react to what you do or say. To the extent that benevolence depends on sympathy, benevolence will be bounded by our capacity for sympathy. The more people can enter into the mind of another—in academic jargon, engage in role-taking—the more likely they are to be generous to that other.[43]

Grasping the relationship between similarity and sympathy helps us resolve an apparent contradiction in much of the academic writing on altruism. Scholars regularly hold up as examples of the highest or best form of human behavior that which reflects principled moral

S y m p a t h y

reasoning, by which is meant a commitment to the equal rights of others, a generalized sense of duty, or a concern for the well-being of society as a whole.[44] But studies of children at play reveal that those living in the simplest agricultural communities are more caring of others—that is, more willing to offer help and comfort—and more willing to cooperate with one another than are ones living in more complex or modern societies.[45] Children in rural villages in Mexico, Colombia, Kenya, the Philippines, Israel, Korea, and aboriginal Australia are more cooperative with each other than those living in urban settlements in New England, Israel, Australia, Mexico, Korea, and so on.[46] The explanation offered by the investigators is that, by necessity, people living in simpler, kin-oriented societies based on subsistence agriculture place a higher value on altruism and cooperation and discourage egoism and individualism, while those living in urban, industrial cities or in villages with an extensive division of labor reward individual achievement. A key variable is the work load of the mother: the greater the burdens she has, the more she expects her children to help with household chores and, most important, with the raising of younger children.[47]

Children living in small, economically simple cultures and having strong kin ties may be more nurturant to one another than those living in large, economically complex cultures, but it is almost inconceivable that the children in the former communities will have an elaborate view of the rights and needs of people from other cultures and other places. On the contrary, the history of tribal warfare and ethnic conflict suggests that the tighter the community, the less value its members assign to the humanity of strangers.* One might suppose that there is a trade-off between the intensity and the scope of altruism among humans just as there is between humans and animal species: the more intensely we care for others, the less extensively will that caring reach. As I argue later in this chapter, that does not seem to be the case for families: it is precisely people with

---

* "Orchard Town," the New England community studied by Beatrice and John Whiting, scored very low in the degree of nurturance and helping displayed by children compared to the Philippine village of Tarong or the Kenyan village of Nyansongo. Before readers bemoan this confirmation of the worst features of competitive individualism, they should ask themselves where they would wish to live if they were to be given the task of starting a chapter of the American Civil Liberties Union, the Friends of the Earth, or the Humane Society. I doubt they would buy a ticket to Kenya or the Philippines.

the strongest and warmest attachment to their parents who are most likely to aid perfect strangers, often at great risk to themselves.

But at the level of culture as opposed to family, deeply held loyalties do appear to conflict with generously broad sentiments. In many places one helps and trusts one's own family before one helps— and certainly before one trusts—a stranger. Pierre van den Berghe has gone so far as to argue that nepotism is the basis of ethnic solidarity, a proposition that is certainly true in small, isolated cultures and may also be true in larger, diverse ones, as suggested by the efforts so many people make to find and honor some claim to common ancestry.[48] Tradition holds that Jews and Muslims are descended from Abraham, the Japanese from an Original Ancestor, and the Navajo from Changing Woman. For many people, genealogy is more than a hobby; it is a passion. Scholars who claim that ethnic identity is no more important than any other principle of stratification must dismiss as cranks those who take pride in discovering that they are descended from Charlemagne, a Mayflower Pilgrim, a Polish count, or a wayward pope. But the primordial hold that descent and ethnicity have on millions of people is neither inexplicable nor atavistic; it is the powerful—albeit sometimes perverse—legacy of familial membership, a membership that habituates all children in varying degrees to the obligations of sympathy.

Contemporary Americans are so committed to universalist, as opposed to familial, grounds for benevolence that in many aspects of our life we have made nepotism illegal. But in most parts of the world, nepotism is not only legal but customary, and in some places it is mandatory.

Likes attract likes. This is probably as true for helping behavior directed toward strangers as it is for the choice of marriage partners. When researchers posing as either a native or a foreigner asked help from people in large European cities, those appearing to be compatriots fared much better than those appearing to be foreigners. Athenians and Parisians were more likely to give correct street directions to their fellow countrymen than to a foreigner.[49] In a similar study, wallets were dropped on New York City streets, each containing a small amount of money and a local address. Attached to each wallet was a letter written either in standard English or in a way clearly indicating that the writer was a foreigner. The proportion of wallets returned to their owners was smaller for those containing a letter apparently written by a foreigner.[50] Similar experiments suggest that whites will help other whites more frequently than they will help blacks.[51]

A trivially small degree of similarity can influence the amount of helping. Suppose that you find a letter left on the sidewalk (of course, it was really planted there by a researcher). In the stamped envelope is a money order for a small amount made out to a charity; along with it is a completed public opinion poll. If the poll suggests that the person who "lost" the envelope has the same views as you, you are twice as likely to mail it than if the poll contradicts your strongly held opinion—even though mailing it costs you nothing but walking a few steps out of your way and the charitable contribution goes to some worthwhile entity.[52] If people are asked to watch a stranger receive supposedly painful electric shocks, they will display stronger physiological reactions—changes in heart and pulse rate—if they have been led to believe, falsely, that the stranger is in some way like themselves.[53] If schoolboys are told, individually and privately, that they differ in their ability to guess the correct number of dots on a screen, they will later divide money among other boys in ways that favor the boys who are most like themselves in dot-guessing abilities—even though the boys have not met as a group, the information about their dot guessing is wholly fabricated, and the money they are passing out is not their own.[54]

The evidence provided by these clever experiments will be old news to parents who have watched their children become teenagers. When very young, children fear strangers (though in differing degrees, depending on their temperament and how attached they are to their mothers). When they are adolescents, they are less fearful of strangers but more insistent on conformity among their peers. Even the smallest sign of deviance in dress, manner, or speech among teenagers can become the grounds for the cruelest forms of teasing and ostracism. Even as adults we retain a fear of strangers, especially if we live where we are likely to encounter them. The larger the city in which people live, the faster they walk and the less likely they are to make eye contact with passersby.[55] People in small towns are in fact and not just in legend more helpful than those in big cities.[56] In cities of the same size, areas where population density is the highest produce less helping behavior than areas where it is lowest.[57] The desire to be among likes is so strong that people conform to group norms simply because they are aware that they are members of a social classification—such as a political party, the supporters of a baseball team, or a collection of dot guessers—without ever coming into actual contact with one another.[58]

Tolerance and intolerance are two sides of the same coin, each growing out of the attachment we develop to family and kin.[59] One of the deepest puzzles of modern history is how so many people have been persuaded to respect the rights of unlike people and behave benevolently toward distant strangers, especially those that are, by race, religion, or culture, markedly different. Throughout much of human history, dissimilar cultures, when thrown into contact with one another, either fought savage wars or practiced cruel slavery. In chapter 9 I offer some thoughts on how these tragedies have become a bit less common—or at least less easily justified. For now, it is important to realize that humans cannot dispense with a sense of belonging to a small group. Familial and kin networks are the essential arenas in which sociability becomes sympathy and self-interest is transferred, by a pattern of reciprocal obligations, into duty and fair play. Such in-groups are necessarily defined by a process of exclusion—of strangers, foreigners, enemies—that create out-groups.

Sympathy, Responsibility, and Authority

Sympathy is a fragile and evanescent emotion. It is easily aroused but quickly forgotten; when remembered but not acted upon, its failure to produce action is easily rationalized. The sight of a lost dog or a wounded fledgling can upset us greatly even though we know that the woods are filled with lost and injured animals; but if someone takes the pet or bird away, our distress quickly dissipates. We are softened by the sight of one hungry child, but hardened by the sight of thousands. It is my experience that when there were a few homeless people begging on the streets of American cities, a passerby was probably more likely to help and certainly more likely to sympathize than when many were begging; indeed, the sight of scores of importuning people causes some onlookers to feel anger rush in to replace a waning sympathy.

How we act depends in part on our sense of personal responsibility. Adam Smith noted the difference between our passive and our active sentiments: If a man were to learn of the destruction of 100 million Chinese, he might lament their passing and speculate as to its meaning, but in a moment he would return equally to his business or leisure. But we would startle with horror at the thought of a man who in order to save the loss of his little finger would will the death of the very same number of distant Chinese.[60] If our sentiments were directed simply by our love of humanity we might feel equal anguish at both tragedies, but we do not: when the fate of others is inescapably our responsibility, we feel a greater passion, and if we do not we are held up to scorn and rebuke.

Our sense of what we are responsible for is not always, or even often, of our own making. One of the best known, and most chilling, social scientific experiments ever conducted was carried out during the 1960s by a psychologist, Stanley Milgram, than at Yale University.[61] Ordinary people, recruited by a newspaper ad offering a cash payment to those willing to participate in a "study of memory," were brought to an office where a man explained that the study was designed to determine the effects of punishment on learning. One person was to be the teacher, the other the learner. (The learner—a pleasant, middle-aged, ordinary-looking man—was in fact an amateur actor who was a confederate of Milgram's.) The learner was strapped into a chair and an electrode attached to his wrist. The teacher—the naive person recruited by the ad—was told to read aloud words to the learner to see how well he could memorize them; every time the learner made a mistake, the teacher was to administer an electrical shock, increasing in intensity. The device that controlled the shocks was a panel filled with switches, each marked with the number of volts it sent out in 15-volt increments, from 15 to 450. Lest there be any mistake about what was involved, words also appeared above the switches, ranging from SLIGHT SHOCK to DANGER—SEVERE SHOCK. Naturally, the learner made many mistakes. When he was shocked in response (of course, no shock actually occurred), he would make sounds, growing in intensity as the level of "shocks" increased. At 150 volts he would demand to be released from the experiment; at 285 volts he would utter an agonized scream. The purpose of the experiment was to discover how high a level of shock the naive subjects—male and female, young and old, of various ethnic groups and occupations—would administer.

About two-thirds went all the way to 450 volts, even as they heard the screams. The experiment was carried out under various conditions. When the teachers could see as well as hear the learner, only 40 percent went to 450 volts; when they were required to hold the learner's hand, forcing it down onto a metal plate that carried the current, "only" 30 percent went to the top of the scale. If the learner complained of a bad heart condition, it made no difference; 65 percent of the teachers still went to 450 volts. When the experiment was moved to another city, remote from Yale University and done in an office with no apparent connection to so prestigious an institution, the results were about the same.

Only two things made a big difference in the level of shocks administered: the absence of a clear authority figure and the presence of rebellious peers. If the orders were given by someone who appeared to be an ordinary man, someone recruited by the same ad that attracted the naive "teachers," or if there were two authority figures and they disagreed, very few people went to 450 volts; indeed, very few went above 150 volts. If the naive subject was part of a group whose other members rebelled (the other members were, of course, confederates of the experimenter), the level of compliance was also dramatically reduced.

Milgram concluded that when people complied with what was apparently an inhumane order, it was because their sense of responsibility had been diminished or altered: they were "only following orders." For most people, only the objections of other people like themselves (that is, like them in being "ordinary people," not "scientists") made them inclined to ignore the instructions of an authority figure.

When we need to reassure ourselves as to the propriety of following orders that require us to inflict pain on others, we denigrate the victims. It is easy to see this happening when a white police officer uses excessive force to subdue a black suspect and justifies it by calling the suspect "scum"; it is easy to see it happening when a black man, indifferent to the plight of a white truck driver lying injured on the streets of Los Angeles, calls him a racist. Melvin Lerner and others have shown that this is common in even quite ordinary situations. We often attribute to people who are just like us qualities that make them appear to deserve a fate that has befallen them. For example, an innocent student selected by lot from a class was apparently made to undergo electric shocks as part of a learning experiment. The other students watching started to devalue her. The more she appeared to suffer, the lower their estimation of her. "She didn't have to do this," they would say. "She should have complained," or "She should have tried harder."[62]

This process of denial may seem like hypocrisy or callousness, but recall that it stems from a desire to see the world as just and to rationalize our failure to rectify an injustice or our complicity in creating one. If we did not believe that justice and sympathy were important, we would not bother to denigrate the victim; we would either attack or help as our own interests required. Sympathy is not absent when we attribute qualities that excuse our indifference; the attribution is necessary to prevent a strong sense of sympathy from leading to an incapacitating feeling of helplessness.

If people were basically cruel, they would ignore or enjoy suffering, without rationalization. If they were merely hypocritical, they would pretend to care rather than admit to having devalued the victim. Being human, their moral sense requires them to manage distress by reinterpreting the situation so as to justify the cruelty or the indifference. Recall the aphorisms we use for this purpose: "As you sow, so shall you reap." "Accidents happen to people who are careless." "The sins of the father are visited on the children." "If they didn't like living that way they would do something about it."[63]

Some readers may think that many participants saw through these experiments and administered 450-volt shocks or denigrated victims just to play along. But Milgram's evidence, like that from other scholars who have done similar work with much the same results, suggests that the great majority of subjects really believed the victim was getting shocked.

But we need not leave matters with experiments. During World War II the German authorities recruited Reserve Police Battalion 101 from among men living in Hamburg. They were, as suggested by the title of Christopher Browning's compelling account, ordinary men.[64] They were not doctrinaire Nazis; they were not specially selected for their political reliability or bloodthirstiness; they had not volunteered (as had members of the SS) for the job; and they were not led by a fanatical or ruthless officer. Indeed, when the battalion was first ordered to shoot Jews in Poland, the commander offered to let any men who did not feel up to the task to step out; when a few did so he protected them from retaliation. When he gave the order to begin shooting, he wept. Nevertheless the shooting began, although initially in ways that spared women and children. Afterward the men complained bitterly about what they had been required to do. But in the months to come, the shootings continued. Ordinary men were following extraordinary orders.

No doubt the anti-Semitic propaganda with which these men had been deluged during the preceding years made it easy for them to denigrate their victims. Even so, the story of Reserve Police Battalion 101 is a chilling reminder of how weak a motive our sense of sympathy can be. It is weak precisely because it arises from the same sociability that makes us want to go along, be liked, follow orders, and win approval. Our capacity for being decent persons and one of the sources of our deepest depravity are, at root, one and the same. But the existence of depravity does not disprove the existence of sympathy; it only shows that sympathy, like love, is not enough.

Fairness

Perhaps the first moral judgment uttered by a young child is, "That's not fair!" At issue may be only the sharing of a toy or the distribution of a few pieces of candy, but implicit in those three words is a complex and profound array of claims and judgments. The child is asserting a demand ("I want") that is supported by a claim ("I own" or "I am entitled to"), modified by a recognition of competing claims ("You are entitled to"), and justified by a rule ("It ought to be my turn" or "My share should be as big as your share").

It is quite astonishing that at an early age children not only can express notions of preference, property, entitlement, and equity, but can do so in ways that in fact alter the behavior of other children. Many years later they may take a college course on moral philosophy in which they study the exquisite subtleties and verbal justifications of these concepts, but this will be long after their own conduct has been, to varying degrees, importantly shaped by the rule of fairness.

It is not difficult to give a wholly egoistic account of how such a rule might occur to a child. A toddler wants to play with a toy that another child already has. If the first child tries to take it, the second will resist. If the second child is bigger, the first will lose out. But even if the second is smaller or less determined, there will be a fuss. Fusses are unpleasant; besides, they attract the attention of parents, who will intervene, often with the result that nobody gets the toy. Moreover, the second child will sometime want a toy possessed by the first. If the first has in the past taken toys by force, he will have no plausible argument that can be used to justify, in the eyes of an intervening parent, why he should be allowed to keep what he now possesses. For all these reasons, it soon occurs to the first child that it is in his interest to enter into a tacit agreement with the second child. If both parties are to abide by it, there must be something in it for each. That something must be valuable enough to one child so that he will accept the agreement but not so much that the other child will protest it. Equal shares is the only rule that satisfies both conditions for children or roughly similar strength and determination. Following the rule of fairness, defined as equal shares, minimizes conflict to the advantage of both parties.

Something like this scenario may account for the origin of the sense of fairness, but if that were its only basis we would expect the content of the rule to change dramatically as the children got older and their relationship moved from one situation to another. A rule sustained purely by the immediate self-interest of all concerned parties would be modified substantially as the parties became significantly different in strength, skill, and determination. At age two, each child may weigh about the same, but as growth rates differ, especially as between boys and girls, soon one child might weigh half again as much as the other and, in addition, be twice as willing to use force to back up his claims. Under those circumstances, fairness defined as equal shares might well be redefined to mean "two shares for me, one for you" or even "all for me, none for you." Furthermore, a rule that makes sense when parents are watching may make little sense when they aren't. As the child's capacity for observation and reasoning increases, so also will his inclination to drive as hard a bargain as he can. Naturally he will not want to press his advantage so far that he acquires a reputation for breaking agreements—otherwise, no one will be willing to enter into any agreements with him. But subject to the constraint of being minimally trustworthy, "fairness"—or more broadly, justice—will come to mean little more than keeping one's word and honoring contracts. Children who start out observing an ethic of sharing would end up observing the ethic of the Mafia.

Indeed, toddlers do not share very often and are most likely to share when it is to their advantage (for example, to recruit a playmate for a game), in order to minimize losses (for example, to avoid or settle unpleasant fights), or when their parents are watching.[1] Rules about fairness arise in large part out of self-serving desires: to get attention, induce cooperation, or resolve disagreements.[2]

Fairness

But contrary to what one might expect if rules of sharing were simply neutral means to self-regarding ends, the commitment to fairness grows stronger as the child grows older. By the time they are in their fourth year, many children will share even when it is not in their interest to do so and even when parents are not watching. There have been a number of experiments in which four- and five-year-old children were given things they might share and were observed sharing them without any explicit direction and absent any claims by other children.

Part of the reason why sharing persists despite increasing differences in child size and reductions in adult supervision is that as children grow older they acquire a longer time horizon. (In chapter 4 I discuss how, for most of us, aging reduces impulsiveness.) Self-interest is now understood to involve future as well as immediate consequences. A child acquires, and is aware of the value of having, an investment in his reputation for fair play, much as a business firm begins to see the value over the long term of having a reputation for honest dealing and quality products. As the economist Robert Frank has pointed out, a self-interested person will often do better if he did care about fairness, not only because he will be seen by others as more likely to live up to commitments, but also because he will not be willing to settle for bad deals.[3]

And part of the reason for continued sharing may also be that in some cultures adults will stress the virtue of harmony, a virtue that obliges one to refrain from pressing too hard his claims against another, a matter to which I shall return later.

Whatever the reason, what is striking is that children begin to speak in ways that make it clear that sharing is something they *ought* to do. William Damon summarizes the studies this way:

> Virtually all [the studies] have found four-year-olds already in possession of active, flourishing conceptions of fairness. Most children at this age have firmly internalized the standard of sharing. They know that they have an obligation to share at least some part of their possessions with others on occasion. This does not mean that they always do so (as any parent can attest), but rather that they believe it is something that they ought to do in many circumstances.[4]

Whence the "ought?" How is it that a rule, useful because it leads to something one wants in some circumstances, becomes a rule that is right and desirable in itself and in many circumstances, even when it has no immediate payoff? One answer might be that children "internalize" the rule and so apply it unthinkingly and in many situations. In some sense that is undoubtedly the case, but the answer begs the question. It is tantamount to saying that the reason children apply a rule unreflectively (that is, the reason they have internalized it) is that they have internalized it. Another answer is that they apply the rule generally because they fear punishment from parents if their failure to follow it is discovered. This explanation also has some merit and was, indeed, part of the original reason that the children's wholly egoistic play came to be supplanted by more co-operative play. But this explanation, too, is incomplete, because as the child grows older parental control becomes weaker, and yet the rule—to the extent it has been implanted at all—becomes stronger. Moreover, this reason provides no account of why the parents tend to insist on the rule, even when they have but one child and thus no intrafamilial conflicts to settle. The proper question is to ask what motivates children to accept (and parents to impose) as legitimate and generally applicable a rule that often works to the child's immediate disadvantage and to feel impelled, as Damon and others have noted, to justify any departure from it.

Sharing and Sociability

The answer is the natural sociability of the child. Many decades ago, Jean Piaget concluded just this from his many hours of watching Swiss children play marbles: "The sense of justice, though naturally capable of being reinforced by precepts and practical examples of the adult, is largely independent of those influences, and requires nothing more of its development than the mutual respect and solidarity which holds among the children themselves."* Children learned marbles from each other, not from adults. The younger children were taught by the older ones; the former respected the rules because they had traditional authority, the latter because they were useful in facilitating social relations.

Years later, Judy Dunn was able to show just how early this sense

---

* Piaget, 1965:198. He went on to suggest that this sense "possesses individual or biological roots which are a necessary but not sufficient condition for its development" (318).

reveals itself. By closely observing children between the ages of eighteen and thirty-six months, Dunn found that about half of them spontaneously offered to share things, and she noted instances, familiar to every parent, of even younger babies offering a toy, pacifier, or piece of food to another person. These offerings probably reflect a desire on the part of the toddler to win approval, initiate play, or maintain contact.[5]

Around the world, children offer food as a way of establishing friendly relations even before they are able to talk.[6] This tendency to share increases with age and is accompanied by a rapid growth in the sense of what rules ought to govern play and contact. From age eighteen months on, children "understand how to hurt, comfort, or exacerbate another's pain; they understand the consequences of their hurtful actions for others and something of what is allowed or disapproved behavior in their family world; they anticipate the response of adults to their own and others' misdeeds; they differentiate between transgressions of various kinds."[7]

Out of ordinary play and interaction there emerges a fairly clear sense of rules and justifications: "principles of possession, positive justice, [and] excuses on grounds of incapacity or lack of intention."[8] These rules are not specific to particular situations but are often understood generally such that rules can be applied differently in different contexts without sacrificing the principle of the rule.

From infancy on, children court other people. Their skill and enthusiasm may differ, as may the clarity and consistency of the rules they infer from this courtship, but the process is not driven by self-interest narrowly conceived. Children (especially two-year-olds!) are learning that they have a self that is different from others, but they also are beginning to learn that their self requires the presence of others to achieve happiness. In the language of economists, children learn that utilities are interdependent—in other words, that one's happiness depends to some degree on the happiness of others—long before they can pronounce, much less spell, "interdependent." Children learn that they ought to obey certain rules because doing so pleases others; at the same time, they learn that breaking rules can be fun—up to a point—because it teases others.[9]

William Damon has made the same point by observing the words children use to justify sharing behavior. Some of their justifications are purely self-serving, such as deterrence ("I don't want to be punished") or reciprocity ("then she will give me something back"). But the most common reason is empathy: "It makes the other kid feel happy" or "I don't want my friend to cry or be sad."[10]

By the time they are in elementary school, the idea of fairness has acquired a fairly definite meaning: people should have equal shares. But once the equality principle is grasped, exceptions to it become apparent. For example, it doesn't seem right that a lazy boy should be rewarded as much as an energetic one when working on the same task. By the time they have left elementary school, children will go to great lengths to discuss and weigh competing principles for allocating things in a fair way—merit, age, need, and the like. What is most striking about this process is the way they discuss these matters almost entirely without reference to adult authority or adult rules; this is true whether they are being interviewed by adults or secretly overheard.[11] Far from expressing an internalized set of adult rules or looking furtively over their shoulders for any sign of adult power, older children discuss in sophisticated detail principles of justice that have evolved out of their own interactions. Their judgments are shaped by their membership in natural social groupings.

Such judgments, of course, are not the only things that determine action. Circumstances, incentives, and self-interest compete for control over behavior. We are all too familiar with the good child who does rotten things and with the pious adult who knows no check on his greed or lasciviousness. But it is a great mistake to suppose from these well-known facts that the principle of fairness has consequences only when it is convenient to follow its dictates.

Fairness as Equity

A vast body of research on adult behavior provides compelling evidence for the importance of fairness as a guide to how we behave. In these studies, fairness has one or more of three meanings: equity, reciprocity, and impartiality. By equity I mean what Aristotle meant by distributive justice: "what is just . . . is what is proportionate."[12] That is, things should be divided among people in proportion to their worth or merit. In modern equity theory, a division of something between two people is fair if the ratio between the first person's worth (his effort, skill, or deeds) and that person's gains (his earnings, benefits, or rewards) is the same as the ratio between the

Fairness

second person's worth and gains.* Say pay is being distributed between two workers, Ann and Matthew. Assume that both have the same skill and work equally hard, but that Ann works twice as long as Matthew. Then they are fairly treated if Ann is paid twice as much as Matthew.

This, of course, is the simplest case. Matters get much more complicated when Ann and Matthew also differ in skill and effort and more complicated yet if there is deep disagreement over whether women and men (or blacks and whites, or commoners and princes) should receive the same pay for the same work. That societies have different standards for judging worth does not mean that the fairness rule is arbitrary or merely conventional, however. Given some standard for what constitutes worth (or inputs), both the behavior and the feelings of people will change as relationships with other people become more or less fair.

In a famous set of studies done in the 1960s, various experimenters hired men to conduct interviews, paying them on a piece-rate basis. During the hiring, the "employer" (an experimenter) made clear to some men that he thought them unqualified (and hence would be overpaid for the work to be done) while saying to others that they were fully qualified (and hence would be equitably paid). The men were then sent out to work. Those who were made to feel unqualified (that is, whose skills were not worth what they were going to get in wages) produced fewer but better interviews than did the men who were given to believe that they were being fairly paid.[13] When some employees were made to feel that they were underpaid (that is, that their skills were worth more than they would earn), they produced far more interviews, but of lower quality, than did employees who believed they were fairly paid.[14]

This is not what one would expect if people were only interested

---

* Stated formally: Let I = the inputs (worth, effort, contributions) of person a or b; let O = the outputs (gains, earnings, rewards) of person a or b. Then an allocation is fair when:

$$\frac{O_a - I_a}{I_a} = \frac{O_b - I_b}{I_b}$$

(Sometimes this equation is modified to handle the mathematical problem created by negative inputs or outputs.) It can be read as saying that if the ratio between A's net outputs (or gains) and A's inputs is the same as the ratio between B's net outputs (or gains) and B's inputs, then people will judge that A and B have been fairly treated.

in maximizing their income. Both the "overpaid" and the "equitably paid" workers earned the same amount per interview completed. If getting the most money was all that mattered, both groups would try to complete as many interviews as possible and the earnings of each group would be identical. What their employer thought of them would be irrelevant. That the "overpaid" workers did less work (thereby sacrificing earnings) but did work of higher quality (thus sacrificing effort) can be explained in terms of their concern for equity. If they believed that their inputs (here, their skills) were not worth their outputs (their wages), they could eliminate the distress they felt in one of two ways—by reducing their output (earning less money) or by improving their input (doing a better job). They did both, in this and a number of other studies.[15]

The desire to be in an equitable relationship with another person can lead us to sacrifice, up to a point, our own material advantage. When people are told that they can earn more by cooperating than by working alone, they naturally cooperate. But if the pay is distributed unequally among the members of the cooperating team, many people will withdraw from the team and work alone even though they will earn less.[16]

One can test this commitment to fairness with a simple game. Called "Ultimatum," it involves two players. The first is given a sum of money—say, ten dollars—that he is to divide in any way he wishes between himself and the second player. The second player must accept or reject the offer, knowing that there will be no further offers and the two people will never play the game again. If the second player accepts, the two players divide the money in the way the first player proposed. If the second player rejects the offer, then neither player gets anything. If both players are wholly self-interested, then the first will offer the second one cent and keep $9.99 for himself, and the second player will accept the offer. After all, the second player has no choice: he either gets something or nothing, and one cent is better than nothing. The first player has no incentive to offer more than one cent, since anything more comes out of his share.

If your experience in playing Ultimatum is like that of the German economists who experimented with it, it is extremely unlikely that you will act in a rationally self-interested way. If you are the first player, you will probably propose an equal division of the money or, at worst, something like 70–30. If you are the second player you will probably reject offers that lopsidedly favor the first player, even though it means you will get nothing.[17] People are willing to forgo money in order to ensure fairness or to punish people who act unfairly—here, the "greedy" first player. In other experiments it has been shown that people prefer a more equal outcome that gives them less money to a less equal outcome that gives them more, even when the two players do not know each other, do not deal face to face, and, because they will not meet again, cannot be motivated by a desire to protect a reputation of fairness or to avoid reprisals for unfairness.*

This desire for fairness affects how people judge many everyday business decisions. It is probably the anticipation of such public reactions that helps explain why, contrary to the predictions of economic theory, the prices firms charge and the wages they pay are "sticky"—that is, they do not change as much as one would expect given changing economic conditions. In opinion surveys, people think it is unfair for a firm to lower the wages of an existing employee just because cheaper workers are now available. If, however, the present employee quits or the firm abandons its present line of work (say, painting houses) and goes into a new line (say, landscaping houses), then people feel that paying a lower wage to either a new employee or to existing employees is permissible. By the same token, if a grocery store notices that the wholesale price of peanut butter has gone up, people feel the store should not increase the retail price of the jars on its shelves but may increase the price on new jars as they arrive. It is wrong, in the public's mind, to increase the price of snow shovels just because there has been an unexpected blizzard that made everybody want to buy a shovel, but it is all right to increase the price if the hardware store has experienced higher costs.[18] Interestingly, when business executives are asked the same

---

* Kahneman, Knetsch, and Thaler, 1986a. There are many variants on this game, almost all of which produce strong evidence for a shared norm of fair distribution. Two economists, Elizabeth Hoffman and Matthew Spitzer, gave pairs of college students a choice. By a flip of a coin, one member of a pair would get to choose between receiving $12 (with the other person getting nothing) or receiving $14, provided he had agreed in advance on how to split the larger sum with the other person. A rationally self-interested person would take the $14 and agree to give $13 to himself and offer $1 to the other fellow. The other person would accept the deal, since $1 was better than nothing, his only other choice. In fact, the winner took the $14 and then split it evenly with the loser. This meant that the winner chose to earn $5 less than he would have received if he simply took the $12. The people who played this game obviously believed that a flip of a coin was not a fair way of allocating unequal benefits. (Hoffman and Spitzer, 1982, 1985).

questions, they tend to agree with the average citizen on most matters.[19]

These popular attitudes toward business transactions are, on the whole, consistent with the theory of equity. Benefits (prices or profits) should go up only if contributions (costs or effort) go up.* Sudden changes in demand for a product, the prospect of future cost increases, or the availability of cheaper labor are not good reasons for changing prices or wages because these are not considered to be the *existing* inputs (or costs) of a firm. As Arthur Okun put it in explaining why wages and prices don't change as often as economists predict, market transactions are governed by an "invisible handshake" as well as by the invisible hand.[20] Of course, some firms make these economically rational changes anyway, but there is evidence that some don't because they are sensitive to the adverse public reaction to what is perceived to be unfair dealing.[21]

It is not surprising that people are distressed when they receive less than they think is their due. What is surprising is that they often are distressed when they think they get more. An experimenter recruited people to proofread some documents for two dollars an hour. At the end they were told they had all done a good job. But when they opened their pay envelopes, some discovered that they had received exactly the pay promised, others that they had received only half the promised amount, and still others that they had earned 50 percent more than the agreed-upon fee. Not surprisingly, the underpaid workers revealed in a questionnaire that they were unhappy, but so also did the overpaid ones.[22]

People differ in how much value they attach to equity, just as they differ in how much value they attach to the good opinion of others. Very young children may offer to share, but they have little concern for fair sharing. Somewhat older children have a rudimentary sense of what constitutes a fair share: usually, equal shares. Older children and adults have a rather sophisticated view of proportionality.[23] There is some evidence that women are more likely

---

* There is one apparent inconsistency with equity theory. People object to prices going up if present costs remain the same, but do not object to prices remaining the same if costs suddenly fall. The explanation may be this: raising prices in the absence of a cost increase can only be motivated by selfishness, but failing to lower prices when costs have fallen may be justified because the lower costs could reflect greater efficiencies or technological innovation on the part of the firm, and these are contributions or inputs that merit compensation.

than men to employ the principle of equal rather than proportional shares (see chapter 8).[24]

Fairness as Reciprocity

"I helped you, so you ought to help me." When you think or say that, you are expressing the idea of reciprocity. Reciprocity is a special case of equity: it is fairness *in exchanges*. When we judge a condition as equitable or inequitable, we are comparing our situation with that of another person, whether or not we have any dealings with one another. Suppose one worker notices that he is being paid less for doing the same job than another worker even though they have identical skills and experience. The first worker feels he is being treated unfairly. That is a judgment about equity. But if the first worker helps the second fix a broken tool and later the second one refuses to help the first, the first will think that he has been treated unfairly. This is a judgment about reciprocity.

Our concern for reciprocity is evident not only in our expecting the return of favors we have bestowed but also in our distress at receiving favors we cannot return. Though some of us are happy to have anything we can get, many of us, to judge from everyday experience, are reluctant to accept large favors we know we cannot repay. "Oh, I can't let you do that" is a phrase we hear all the time from people who are otherwise quite willing to pursue their own advantage. Scientific experiments confirm this. People who, in games, give things to others without any chance of repayment are looked on as unfavorably as are people who give things conditioned on onerous repayment terms, and much less favorably than people who suggest a reasonable quid pro quo for their generosity.[25] When people have a chance to repay a favor they are more likely to ask for it than when they have no chance of repaying it.[26] The common theme of all of these findings is that we worry about accepting favors that may, in ways we cannot yet discern, imply future or burdensome obligations.

The norm of reciprocity is universal. Virtually everyone who has looked has found it in every culture for which we have the necessary information.[27] There is a good reason for this: because reciprocity is a way of rewarding somebody who has done a favor for somebody else, people have an incentive to enforce it and the means to do so (namely, withholding future favors). That means that even in a society of wholly selfish people, most favors would be reciprocated and most debts repaid.

Yet for reciprocity to be a *rule*, not just something expected or commonplace, more than mere selfish calculation is required. A powerful person could probably ignore reciprocal obligations for quite a long time and a clever person may evade them long enough to profit handsomely, if reciprocity were simply useful. Those of us watching the powerful or the clever renege on their debts would probably be indifferent to their behavior or even admire its audacity, so long as we never expected to do business with these people. But that is not how we feel; we dislike and reproach welshers even when their behavior is no skin off our nose. We *judge* these people, and by judging them affirm that we believe reciprocity is not merely useful but right. In this sense, reciprocity is a rule.

The rule requiring reciprocity is probably much like the taboo against incest. In every society, incest is rare because most people are not sexually attracted to individuals (brothers, sisters, mothers, fathers) with whom they have grown up. But there will be a few backsliders (typically, fathers lusting after their daughters). The taboo is meant to enforce the rule against the backsliders, thereby minimizing the adverse consequences of incest—the disruption of the family unit and, if incest leads to procreation, the production of biologically defective offspring. So also with reciprocity. Ordinary social interaction teaches most of us that cooperative behavior is useful and that such cooperation is impossible if every person does not do his share. A few backsliders will be so indifferent to their reputation or so inclined to maintain it by deceit or manipulation that they will cheat at every opportunity. The norm of reciprocity is instilled in us to reduce the number of backsliders.

It is easy to see how evolution would tend to select for individuals who are disposed to act reciprocally. Human existence requires cooperation; cooperation requires reciprocity. An example used by Peter Singer will make this clearer.[28] Suppose two primitive men are attacked by a sabretooth tiger. If both run, the slower of the two will be killed. If one fights and the other runs, the fighter will be killed. But if both stand and fight, the tiger will be killed. If the two men are entirely self-interested, both will run. They each will think as follows: If my buddy fights, I will live if I run. If my buddy runs, I will be killed if I fight. No matter what my buddy does, I am better off running. So I will run. Both think the same way, and so both wind up doing something that gives to each a 50–50 chance of being killed by the tiger. They would be better off if they both fought, but for that to happen, one or the other of two conditions must exist. Either they must be so committed to one another that each feels he has a duty to help the other, or they must be able to agree after a brief discussion that fighting makes them better off. For the second consideration to have any effect, they must be willing to trust the promise of the other to fight. In the first case, they do the right thing because they are altruistic, in the second because they are fair. After a few thousand encounters with sabretooth tigers, this primitive culture will probably come to consist disproportionately of people who are altruistic or fair or both. The others will have been eaten.

This example is a case of the Prisoner's Dilemma, so called because its earliest version was about two criminals, Pete and Dick, who are arrested and confined in separate cells. They cannot communicate with or make enforceable threats to each other. The dilemma exists because of the consequences of cooperating with the police by testifying against one another, or not cooperating. If neither cooperates, they get off scot free, because the police do not have enough evidence to prosecute. If both confess, they each go to jail for two years. If Pete cooperates with the police and Dick does not, Pete gets off scot free and Dick goes to jail for three years. If Dick cooperates, he gets off and Pete does three years in prison. What should they do? If neither testifies, they each go free. But for that to happen, each has to be *certain* that the other will keep mum. But neither can be certain. Pete has a powerful incentive to avoid getting three years in prison, something that will happen if Dick testifies and Pete doesn't. Dick has an equally powerful incentive to avoid the three-year term that will result if he remains silent while Pete testifies. So both confess, and both go to jail for two years.

The dilemma is not limited to crooks; it exists whenever two people can get a reward for cooperating but can get a much bigger reward for acting selfishly if each thinks the other fellow will also act selfishly. Robert Axelrod, a professor of political science at the University of Michigan, held a contest to see who could come up with the best solution for the Prisoner's Dilemma. There were fourteen entries, many submitted by world-famous scholars. The winner—the strategy that produced the highest number of cases in which Pete and Dick got off scot free—was called Tit for Tat.[29] It was very simple. Let's say that you are Pete. The first time you play the game, you should always do the "nice" thing (in this game, that means not testifying against your confederate). Then observe what Dick does. Whatever he does, you then do exactly the same thing. If he keeps mum, you keep mum. If he rats on you, you rat on him. Axelrod held his tournament a second time, attracting sixty-three entrants. Tit for Tat won again.

Axelrod's tournaments were a miniature version of how cooperative behavior probably evolved among people. There are four interesting things to remember about a Tit for Tat strategy. First, it takes time to produce a good outcome. That is, you have to play the game several times before both Pete and Dick routinely cooperate. A one-shot encounter between two people may well lead to a bad outcome, since, lacking any prior experience with each other, both may act selfishly. Second, it requires that one player start off by being nice. Even protracted encounters between two nasty people will not lead to many good outcomes. Third, it requires that bad behavior always be punished and good behavior always be rewarded. If Dick confesses after Pete has kept silent, then on the next round Pete confesses. If Dick keeps mum, then Pete keeps mum. By these moves, Pete is trying to teach Dick how he ought to behave so that they will both be better off. Finally, the good outcome emerges out of reciprocal learning and requires no central authority. Of course, if there were a central authority—a boss—capable of imposing his will, you might get a good result even faster. But that presupposes that the boss wants a good outcome for the two prisoners.

The Prisoner's Dilemma demonstrates how reciprocity can be learned so as to produce cooperative behavior. This learning is consistent with a self-interested conception of human nature—up to a point. The first limitation is one we have already noted: at least one player must start off the game by being nice (fighting the tiger, not blabbing to the police, or whatever) and always be willing to go back to being nice as soon as the other player cooperates. The other limitation becomes obvious once you ask what happens if the two players know they are not going to see each other after the game ends, *and* they know when it will end. On the last round, neither party has any further incentive to be nice. Each has an incentive to defect. For example, suppose two men know they are on their last hunt for a sabretooth tiger. If one knows that he can run faster than the other, he has an incentive to run and avoid the fight. The slower man knows this, and so he has an incentive to run, too; after all, he will surely be killed if he fights alone. But if each man has an incentive to run on the last hunt, then each has an incentive to run on the next-to-last hunt, next-to-next-to-last hunt, and so on, until nobody will be willing to fight on any hunt. What keeps them fighting together on every hunt right down to the last one is the rule. They have learned that cooperation is not only useful, it is *the right thing to do.*

Reciprocity is found in every culture because it is consistent with the sociability and the self-interest of most men. But it operates successfully in every culture because the advantages of cooperation are reinforced by the norm of reciprocity.

Fairness as Impartiality

Whenever we are judged—by jury, our boss, or our spouse—we care about whether we will prevail. That is obvious. What is less obvious is that we also care about whether we are treated impartially—that is, without prejudice and with an opportunity to present our side of the story. Imagine a person who brings suit in court. If that person cared only about his immediate material interest, his opinion of the outcome of the case would depend entirely on whether he won or lost.

Winning or losing does make a difference, but a series of studies by various scholars show that how satisfied a person is with his court experience is also, and independently, affected by his assessment of how fair it was. Tom Tyler and his colleagues have shown that convicted criminals often have a better opinion of the law and the courts when they believe that they have received a fair trial than when they receive a lenient sentence.[30] What constitutes fairness in this context often has little to do with the formal apparatus of the law and much to do with whether the parties think they got a fair hearing, by which they seemed to mean that some disinterested party heard and carefully weighed their story. This perception may explain why criminal defendants thought that plea bargaining was fairer than a courtroom trial even though the former lacks most of the rules of the latter. Other studies summarized by Tyler and E. Allan Lind come to much the same conclusion.[31]

These attitudes have real consequences for behavior. Several studies have shown that people who have been through a process they regard as fair are more likely to comply with the decision reached by that process than are those who have thought it unfair. When Craig McEwen and Richard Maiman studied six small-claims courts in Maine, they were surprised to find that the chances of a defendant paying what the court said he owed were importantly influenced by whether or not he thought he had a fair hearing; this was true independently of how much money he owed.[32] (This is no small matter, since a large fraction of small-claims defendants never pay the judgments against them.) The biggest difference in procedure in the Maine courts involved mediation versus ajudication. In some cases the defendants and plaintiffs were brought together by a mediator who urged them to negotiate a settlement; in others the two parties stood before a judge who heard their evidence and rendered a verdict. Mediation produced more compliance than ajudication. But even in the cases that went to trial, defendants who thought the judge was fair were more willing to pay what they owed, regardless of how much they owed, than were those who thought him unfair.

Fairness, Evolution, and Culture

The human sense of fairness appears to embody three related but distinct concepts. First, equity: People who are equal with respect to contributions should be equal with respect to outcomes. Second, reciprocity: People who have given something to you are entitled to something back. Third, impartiality: People who judge another person ought to be disinterested, free of favoritism, and observant of rules agreed upon in advance.

I suggest that these principles have their source in the parent-child relationship, wherein a concern for fair shares, fair play, and fair judgments arises out of the desire to bond with others. All three principles are rational in a social and revolutionary sense, in that they are useful in minimizing conflict and enhancing cooperation. At some stage in the evolution of mankind—probably a quite early one—cooperative behavior became adaptive. Groups that could readily band together to forage, hunt, and defend against predators were more likely to survive than were solitary individuals; women who could attract men who would aid them in the early years of infant nurture were more likely to survive than were those left to their own devices. And so by natural selection and sexual selection, individuals with prosocial impulses had greater reproductive success.

F a i r n e s s

Some aspects of fairness can be found in nonhuman species. Property claims are the most obvious. Even a small dog will fiercely defend its own territory (for example, its owner's front yard) against a much larger dog, but it will retreat before a small but aggressive dog if the two meet at a park where the first has no property claim. Tiny fishes will defend their patches of moss on a coral reef against the invasion not only of larger fishes but even of scuba divers.[33] Most species will defend property in the form of a piece of food; many will defend it in the sense of sexual access to a mate; and some will defend it in the sense of a feeding and mate-selection territory. But there are few cases, so far as we are aware, of animals other than humans displaying anything that we would describe as equity or reciprocity.

The human elaboration of the rules of equity and reciprocity reflects the joint operation of a social instinct and a superior intelligence. Charles Darwin described the four aspects of this process in words that can scarcely be improved upon: First, "social instincts lead an animal to take pleasure in the society of its fellows . . . and to perform certain services for them." Second, with the emergence of the higher mental faculties, "images of all past actions and motives [and, we might add, the imaginings of future actions and possibilities] would be incessantly passing through the brain of each individual." Third, after the power of language has been acquired, the wishes of every member, and especially the opinion each has of the other, can be clearly expressed. Finally, action in accordance with the opinion of others, the recollection of past actions, and the apprehension of future possibilities would quickly become habitual most of the time for most people, albeit not all of the time for any person and none of the time for some.[34]

Darwin emphasized the role of evolution, language, and sociability as the source of our sense of fairness, but it would be a mistake to omit the role of culture. Although to some, of course, culture is everything, I agree with Darwin that this surely cannot be correct. Can we imagine a culture in which people acquired and acted on the belief that equity and reciprocity were of no value? It seems most unlikely. It would require us to imagine a society in which people thought it quite acceptable for a person to be the judge in his own case: "You say that I hit you with my car? Fine; I will hear your side of the argument and then decide for both of us." It would require us to imagine a society in which a debt need not be repaid and a contract need not be fulfilled, all for no reason other than the convenience of the defaulter. Above all, it would require us to conceive of a place where such things happened and nobody argued over whether they were right or wrong.

The significance of culture, I speculate, is that it defines two features of our common disposition to value fairness. First, culture determines, within broad limits, who is equal to whom. Whether equal effort by kings and commoners, blacks and whites, or men and women should be thought of as constituting equal claims for rewards is very much a matter of custom. Second, culture determines the extent to which a concern for fairness is embodied in an abstract rule of the sort that most Western philosophers have in mind when they speak of justice. The first feature is, I think, self-evident. The second requires elaboration.

Grace Goodell, an anthropologist who has devoted several years to probing the culture of the Little Dragons—the industrialized nations of the Pacific Rim, such as Korea and Singapore—has reminded me of the extent to which people in those places (and probably in many others as well) find Western notions of justice to be excessively legalistic, depersonalized, and devoid of a vitally important sense of context. In those East Asian cultures, people certainly have a sense of reciprocity: people ought to pay their debts, and favors given are favors that ought to be returned. But this sentiment is more deeply embedded in human relationships and the sense of a right social order than it is in abstract rules or contractual commitments.[35] Goodell is not comparing the impersonal rules of the modern, industrialized, and bureaucratized West with the personal relationships of some premodern, agrarian, and organic culture; least of all is she expressing the lament of some critics of modernity that we Westerners have tragically sacrificed human relationships to abstract rules. Korea and Singapore are as modern, industrial, and bureaucratized—and competitive!—as one could imagine. Reciprocity and property count for a great deal in those places, but they count in a somewhat different way and with somewhat different consequences. Their broader, more personalistic conception of reciprocity means, for example, that precise contractual commitments count for less there than they do in the United States, or at least that complying with a contract is an obligation that is subsumed under a more general obligation to maintain a certain degree of social harmony.

Fairness and Property

Some readers may object that my argument is a not-very-subtle way of justifying inequality of condition or private possession of property. But the argument so far is not that inequality of condition is generally necessary, but only that however we judge the worth of our fellows, we will tend to consider distributions and obligations just if they are proportional to that worth.

That is how I think people make judgments, and it is different from how the famous contemporary philosopher John Rawls thinks they make them. In his theory of justice, Rawls asks us to imagine a group of rational people trying to decide on what social rules they would be willing to live by before knowing what position they would occupy in the society that would be created by these rules. In this "original position," he says, they would agree on the following principle: inequalities in wealth will be considered just only if they result in compensating benefits for everyone, and in particular for the least advantaged members of society.[36] As I understand him, everybody in Rawls's universe is averse to risk; each wants to make certain that, if he winds up on the bottom of the heap, the bottom is as attractive as possible.

But many people are in fact not averse to risk, they are risk takers; to them, a just society would be one in which inequalities in wealth were acceptable provided that the people at the top of the heap got there as a result of effort and skill. And even people who are not risk takers may endorse this position because they think it fair that rewards should be proportional to effort, even if some people lose out entirely. (These same people might also expect their church or government to take care of those who lost out.) They have this view of fairness because they recognize that people differ in talent, energy, temperament, and interests; that conflicts among such people are inevitable; and that matching, as best one can, rewards to contributions is the best way of handling that conflict.

To test this view, let us imagine a society in which property is distributed more or less equally and see why it is so and what happens when that distribution changes. Indeed, we can more than imagine such a society, we can study it.

The San are African bushmen who live in small groups, or bands, that until quite recently foraged widely through inhospitable parts of Namibia, Botswana, and Angola, hunting animals and picking edibles. Only a few simple possessions were required by their livelihood or permitted by their mobility. With few fixed places of abode, their sense of land tenure was more directed to the broad territory that they canvassed than to a specific residence that they occupied. Under these circumstances it is not surprising that most differences among people were not thought sufficiently great to warrant large differences in treatment. Food brought back to the camp was distributed equally among all, with the successful hunter having no greater claim than anyone else. Arrowheads that had killed animals did not remain as trophies of the hunter but were exchanged among other members of the band, women as well as men.[37] Contrary to what some Western observers have suggested, San life was not idyllic, nor were they quite the "harmless people" sometimes depicted: not only were the San very poor, their children (although raised in the most tender fashion) were cruel to animals, husbands (although sharing in child care) occasionally beat their wives, and adults (though they were hospitable to strangers and unfamiliar with war) committed homicides at a rate that exceeds that found in many American cities.[38]

But if not idyllic, San society was indisputably egalitarian. The weak division of labor, the need for cooperation, and the difficulty of accumulating or transporting possessions fostered the view that everyone's contribution (or in terms of equity theory, input) was roughly the same as everybody else's, and so everyone's benefits (or output) should be about the same. Culture reinforced necessity: the San engaged in ritual joking designed to deflate any claims to status or prowess.[39] Though the San are the best-known hunter-gatherer societies, there are others and once were many others and, insofar as we can tell, most tended toward an egalitarian structure.

When these peoples became settled, however, things changed. They may have acquired a sedentary life voluntarily (as when it became possible to raise crops and keep cattle), involuntarily (as when an outside power compelled them to live on reservations), or opportunistically (as when the chance arose to work for cash wages for other people). Whatever the process, the people now live in fixed abodes from whence they herd cattle, raise crops, or earn cash incomes. Living in one place requires less cooperation and permits a greater division of labor than being on the move. Cash, unlike fresh meat, can be stored and hidden. Proximity to industrial societies means that cash and crops can be exchanged for manufactured goods, not the least of which is alcohol. They can even become actors in movies such as *The Gods Must Be Crazy*. One San woman who had a part in that film used her wages to buy things that she would not share with her kin, thereby provoking a fight.[40]

Jean-Jacques Rousseau might have had the settled San mind when he wrote, with heavy sarcasm, this famous line to explain the origin of human inequality: "The first man who, having enclosed a piece of ground, bethought himself of saying, *This is mine,* and found people simple enough to believe him, was the real founder of civil society." The entire *Discourse on the Origin of Inequality* can be read as a commentary on what we know about the transition from hunter-gatherer to sedentary societies. Building huts meant acquiring property, "the source of a thousand quarrels and conflicts." Settled into those huts, the men "went abroad in search of their common subsistence" while the women "became more sedentary and accustomed themselves to mind the hut and their children." Tools become valuable and their possession possible, and so men became beholden to them and alert to the differences in status implied by differences in their ownership.[41]

The many contemporary followers of Rousseau read these words as an argument against inequality, but if anything, they are an argument against civilization, by which I mean settled living and the division of labor. Rousseau clearly preferred premodern man to modern man and opposed political society, which, arising out of the need to protect property, "bound new fetters on the poor and gave new powers to the rich; irretrievably destroyed natural liberty, fixed externally the law of property and inequality, converted clever usurpation into unalterable right, and, for the advantage of a few ambitious individuals, subjected all mankind to perpetual labour, slavery, and wretchedness."[42]

But this unhappy state of affairs did not arise because men were naturally equal; rather, it arose because the conditions of settled life forced men to recognize, act upon, and reinforce their natural inequalities, inequalities that hunter-gatherers could afford—indeed, were obliged—to overlook. In settled societies, Rousseau wrote, "equality might have been sustained, had the talents of individuals been equal." But they are not: once the division of labor took effect, "the strongest did the most work; the most skilful turned his labour to best account; the most ingenious devised methods of diminishing his labour." While all might work equally, the one would gain much while the other "could hardly support himself." Though laws may legitimate and even magnify these differences, "all the inequality which now prevails owes its strength and growth to the development of our faculties and the advance of the human mind."[43]

Equality is a special and, as it turns out, rare and precarious case of equity. Settled living, and in particular the accumulation of private property, makes equality of outcomes impossible because inequality of contributions become manifest. The task of settled societies is to devise ways of assuring that outcomes are proportional to worth, reasonably defined.

The only way to attack inequality fundamentally is to attack private property directly. Karl Marx understood this perfectly: "The theory of the Communists may be summed up in the single sentence: Abolition of private property."[44] We need not consult nearly three-quarters of a century of unhappy Soviet experience to find reasons for thinking Marx was wrong. Aristotle had long before given a crushing refutation of Socrates' argument for the common ownership of property. Aristotle's rejoinder was based on both prudential and natural concerns. Once people come together in settled communities, life gets complicated: "to live together and be partners in any human matter is difficult," especially when property is involved. (He mentions lawsuits in particular.) But holding property in common only makes matters worse. First, there will be arguments over the distribution of the income from the property: "accusations against those who can gratify themselves or take much while exerting themselves little must necessarily arise on the part of those who take less and exert themselves more." Second, people will work harder to improve something that is their own and will be indifferent to something that is everybody's. Third, "it is a very pleasant thing to help or do favors for friends," and "this requires that possession be private." Finally, and most importantly, "it makes an immense difference with respect to pleasure to consider a thing one's own." This affection for oneself and one's own is "something natural."[45]

Private property, though the enemy of equality, is the ally of equity. It gives men the motive to supply contributions of efforts and a yardstick to judge the allocation of rewards. Ownership leads to disputes, but property individually held produces fewer disputes than property commonly held. Property rights supply a basis for settling disputes that is fairer than the feasible alternative, which is brute

Fairness

force, whether that force is the mailed fist of a monarch or the velvet glove of the legislature.

Two millennia before the research of psychologists and ethologists confirmed it, Aristotle noted that having and sharing are innate human sentiments. Even among the San, babies offer things to others as a way of establishing a social bond. That they once grew up in a band that allowed few opportunities for personal possession was a consequence of the material conditions of life. That changing material conditions have permitted both private possessions and social conflict is a measure of another aspect of human nature: its acquisitiveness and love of distinction.

It has long been understood, however, that there are prudential grounds for favoring certain distributions of property over others. Though private possessions are not the enemy of equity, severe inequalities in their ownership are often the cause of political discord. Aristotle, in discussing what form of political life was best, as a practical matter, for most cities and most people, argued that a "middling possession" of wealth was best. The overly wealthy tend toward arrogance, the overly indigent toward malice; the former will be consumed by contempt, the latter by envy.[46] To recast the argument in the language of this chapter, severe inequalities distort the evaluation of contributions by both the advantaged and the disadvantaged, leading to outcomes that are unfair as judged by the natural standards of equity that develop in the household.

Lest one doubt how natural and tenacious those sentiments are, observe how both those who defend private property and those who abhor it cling alike to similar rules of fairness in circumstances where neither wealth nor talent constitute relevant measures of worth. If both are waiting in a line to buy tickets to attend the theater and someone cuts in line ahead of them, both will, I suspect, feel outrage in equal measure. Yet their outrage has no material basis, for the addition of one person to the line almost certainly will not affect their chances of entering the theater and only trivially affect their choice of seats. And neither has a property right to a seat in the theater, for neither yet owns a ticket. But each believes he has been treated unfairly, because by arriving earlier than the intruder he has made a greater contribution (however tiny the difference) and thus is entitled to a greater reward (however small the increment). But if the intruder can show that in fact he was there all night waiting for a seat, and only stepped away momentarily to get a glass of water, the two people in line behind will readily acknowledge his right to reclaim his place and will even (though less cheerfully) acknowledge the rights of his five companions, all being in the same position and all with the same prior claims. Man is a social animal, but his sociability is to an important degree distinct from that of other social creatures, owing to his propensity to regulate his conduct in a prescriptive manner.[47]

Having criticized Rawls for misjudging how people judge fairness, let me end by indicating how he and I agree. In advancing his view that moral feelings are a normal feature of human life, and indeed a precondition of people deciding on the rules by which to live, Rawls asks us to imagine a person who lacks any sense of fairness, who never acts justly except as self-interest and expediency require. If such a person existed—and as I show in chapter 5, a few do—he would be someone without ties of friendship, affection, and mutual trust and incapable of experiencing resentment and indignation.[48] Concretely, he would be someone who cut into line in front of us anytime he thought he could get away with it and who, when someone cut into line in front of him, would be upset only to the extent it materially affected his chances for a good seat. He would be less than human.

Self-Control

Parents spend much of their time trying to persuade their children that if they do not eat rich desserts they will stay slim and attractive and if they take a bitter medicine they will cure or prevent a debilitating disease. School teachers shoulder the same burden when they try to convince pupils that doing their homework now will lead in time to better grades and better jobs. Police officers and judges attempt to make adults believe that the gains from stealing a purse are not worth the risk of being caught and jailed. Doctors want smokers to forgo tobacco today in order to have a healthier life tomorrow. Dentists send notes reminding us to have our teeth cleaned, an unpleasant process, in order to avoid even more unpleasant tooth extractions in the years ahead.

We are all tempted by immediate and tangible pleasures at the price of future and uncertain rewards. Some of us succumb, some resist. Those who resist temptation take pleasure in having resisted, and may sometimes make pests of themselves by preaching to others the virtues of willpower and caution. But in what sense is self-control a virtue? Is not self-control merely a particular skill—let's call it prudence—at pursuing one's own interest, no different from having learned how to study for an exam or dress for success, and so deserving of envy, perhaps, but not of approbation? Certainly many schoolchildren think so as they taunt their fellows for being a teacher's pet or a homework grind. If self-control is useful, in what sense is it moral? Staying on your diet may make you thin, and thinness may improve your health and your appearance, but is being thin morally better than being fat? Moreover, aren't there many cases in which impulsive action is morally commendable? When an onlooker rushes to aid the victim of a mugging or an accident, the rescuer is not displaying self-control—that is, he is not calculating the net future benefit to himself and the victim; if he did that, he might well decide to stay on the sidelines. Instead, he is acting impulsively, out of either a reflexive desire to help a victim or a burst of anger at the attacker.

Yet Aristotle placed temperance high on his list of virtues and devoted an entire chapter to it.[1] By temperance he seems to have meant the habit of controlling or moderating the bodily appetites. He ranked temperance along with justice and courage as states of character that, unlike honor or friendliness, were required always and everywhere of anyone whom we would call good.[2] Why do we call the temperate person good and not merely prudent or even cunning?

To understand why, we must first understand that self-control is only a problem when one is faced with a choice between an immediate pleasure and a more distant one that is of greater value.[3] This is the problem Eve faced when she was offered an apple by the serpent in the Garden of Eden and what Ulysses faced when his boat was about to pass the place where he would hear the irresistible song of the Sirens. If Eve ate the luscious apple, she and Adam would be banished; if Ulysses drew near to the Sirens, his boat would crash on the shore. In the long run, the greater pleasure was to be had (for Eve) by staying in the Garden and (for Ulysses) by staying alive. In everyday life we face similar choices all the time: if we decline the fifth glass of beer now, we avoid the hangover tomorrow; if we go to the dentist today, we avoid tooth decay next year. These would not be difficult choices if both alternatives were presented simultaneously: if either the pleasant morning or the hangover (or the tooth cleaning and the tooth decay) would occur immediately, depending on which we chose, most of us would choose the more pleasurable alternative, and for almost everybody that would be a clear head and a painless tooth. Self-control is a problem precisely because time elapses, and so we are always comparing the immediate, easy-to-visualize pleasure of a glass of beer (or of not being in a dentist's chair) with the future, hard-to-visualize pleasure of no hangover or sound teeth.

For self-control to be virtuous, it is not enough that the more distant pleasure be greater than the more immediate one; it is also necessary that the more distant one be more praiseworthy. Most ordinary criminals are quite impulsive: they grab the purse or steal the car with little thought to the consequences and, as a result, with little effort to minimize their risks or maximize their gains. But some criminals pass up these easy targets in favor of carefully planned thefts or embezzlements that yield vastly larger sums of money and much lower chances of capture. These more professional thieves display a great deal of self-control; while we may admire the skill with which they operate, we do not regard this skill as a sign of virtue.

It is a remarkable characteristic of human society that most of the things that are best for us—that is, most likely to produce genuine and enduring happiness—require us to forgo some immediate pleasure. Success at an occupation requires study now; success at music requires practice now; success at romantic love requires courtship now; a reputation for honesty requires forgoing temptations now; the respect and affection of our grown children requires long hours and much effort devoted to their infant years. In these examples self-control is not only advantageous but also praiseworthy, because a competent worker, a skilled musical performance, a loving marriage, a reputation for honesty, and the respect of one's children are all universally praised. If these goals are good, then the character trait that is necessary for their achievement must also be good insofar as it produces these goals and not others—such as skill at stealing—that are universally condemned.

The examples given here seem quite clear; self-control in these cases is praiseworthy. But that does not answer the question of whether self-control in general is laudable. In this respect, our view of self-control is much like our opinion of sympathy: we praise people who are sympathetic to innocent victims but criticize those who are sympathetic to malevolent victimizers. Yet we are disposed to think well of people who display self-control and sympathy in general; provided they are not carried to the extreme of self-righteous asceticism or undiscriminating sentimentality, both traits strike us as, on the whole, commendable human characteristics.

The reason for this general approbation is, I think, that in general we are better off dealing with people who err in the direction of excessive self-control or sympathy than we are dealing with those who bend in the direction of excessive self-indulgence or hard-heartedness. Temperate people are more likely to keep promises, resist temptations, and reciprocate our affections than are intemperate ones; sympathetic people are more disposed to help us when we are in need and to take our feelings into account than are hard-hearted ones. Since we are usually better off dealing with temperate and sympathetic people, we praise them. What we are praising is not an abstract rule such as "Moderation in all things!" or "Love all of your enemies!" There are some actions, such as bravery, that are immoderate in the extreme and some enemies who deserve only contempt. Rather, we are praising a state of character that is disposed to moderation or sympathy. Self-control acquires moral standing in the same way that sympathy and fairness do: just as most people cannot imagine living in a society in which self-indulgence, self-centeredness, and self-dealing are the accepted standards of right conduct, so they cannot imagine living a life devoted to such principles and still calling it human.*

Because people usually praise moderation while admitting a certain affection for the occasional reckless act or impulsive gesture, we learn from family and friends to display willpower while at the same time sometimes expressing spontaneity and the capacity for surprise (because they, too, are admired, up to a point). How we learn is easily recalled from how we judge children. When they are toddlers we expect them to act instinctively; when they are young children we hold them to higher standards but still expect them to act childishly; when they become older we start telling them to put childish things behind them and act more like adults. We criticize adults who lack self-control for being childish. Growing up means in part learning to control childlike impulses because such impulses are often both self-destructive and self-centered, and society cannot exist if it is composed of self-destructive and self-centered people.

We teach self-control in countless small ways, often without

---

* We can be rather specific about why people regard self-control as admirable, even though it is sometimes carried to extremes. A group of eight-year-old London boys were assessed by psychologists, parents, and teachers to see who scored at the top of various measures of hyperactivity and impulsivity. Eight years later their police records were examined. The most impulsive boys were about twice as likely to have been convicted of a juvenile crime as the least impulsive ones. (Farrington, Loeber, and Van Kammen, 1990). The least impulsive boys may have been rigid, overly controlled, and not much fun to be around, but they were much less likely to steal things.

couching the instruction in moral language at all. An obvious example is instruction in manners.

Self-Control and Etiquette

Most cultures have devoted extraordinary efforts to developing and inculcating rules of etiquette and courtesy. From a purely utilitarian point of view, it seems inexplicable that people should insist that we eat with forks rather than with hands, wipe our mouths with napkins rather than sleeves, or address strangers as "sir" or "madam." It is not hard to imagine very different rules (which may exist in some places): certain foods ought to be eaten with spoons rather than forks or even hands in preference to either, one's mouth should be wiped on sleeves rather than napkins, and strangers should be addressed as "stranger." The precise content of such rules is conventional, that is, determined by the mores of a given society. But the insistence on having rules, whatever their exact content, seems universal and, I suspect, natural.

The universality of rules of etiquette probably reflects their value as a way of signaling the existence of self-control. Suppose how we ate food were entirely a matter of personal preference. If I were accustomed to eating with a spoon and then met someone who ate with a knife, I might suspect that the stranger waving a knife around the dinner table had some felonious intention and react accordingly. The meal would either degenerate into a fight or I would eat someplace else, alone.

According to the social historian Norbert Elias, Europeans in the late Middle Ages were accustomed to expressing their wants and emotions directly, immediately, and forcefully. Under those circumstances it was essential to have rules that would reduce the chances that innocent actions—reaching in front of another to grab a piece of meat or waving a knife around while cutting a piece of meat—might be seen as affronts or threats that would escalate into violent confrontations. Moreover, as feudalism weakened, to be replaced by a court-based aristocracy and a nascent bourgeoisie, one's social standing required confirmation by outward signs. The concept of civility and the role of the gentleman (or aristocrat) were born both to control human impulses and establish social claims. "People, forced to live with one another in a new way, became more sensitive to the impulses of others."[4] Etiquette became part of an effort, lasting several centuries, to curb self-indulgence and define social standing. Manners were taught in order to manage impulses; honor was given to those who were the most mannerly. Habits of conduct that today we take for granted required nearly three hundred years to instill, Elias suggests, from the time of Erasmus to that of Louis XIV.

A similar development can also be seen in matters of dress. Modesty is of little importance among family members living apart from other families, for numbing familiarity, incest taboos, and parental control combine to ensure that nakedness does not lead to licentiousness. We are not surprised to find that, where the climate permits, some small, primitive bands are attired, if at all, in ways that by modern standards are quite immodest. But when they come into regular contact with strangers, no such informal controls exist, and so revealing dress can elicit unwanted approaches: immodesty seems an invitation to indecency. Rules are therefore imposed requiring people to be fully covered, to undress alone or in the presence of members of the same sex, and to relieve themselves in private so that innocent acts do not convey ambiguous messages. One measure of how successfully such rules have been imposed is the greater freedom that has been acquired by both sexes, but especially women, in matters of dress. Writing in 1937, when bathing and sports attire were by modern standards positively Victorian, Elias remarked that "this change presupposes a very high standard of drive control. Only in a society in which a high degree of restraint is taken for granted, and in which women, like men, are absolutely sure that each individual is curbed by self-control and a strict code of etiquette, can bathing and sporting customs having this relative degree of freedom develop."[5] One wonders what he would have made of the bikini, nude beaches, and modern rock dances.

A display of manners and conventional attire is a signal to other people, especially to strangers, that you have self-control; you display it in small, everyday ways to assure others than it will be present in adequate degree when the stakes are much higher. The everyday display of self-control has, in any particular case, no evident moral message. You eat politely even when it would be more convenient to snatch food up and wolf it down; you put on clothes before answering the doorbell even when it would be faster to go there naked. We cannot say that wolfing down your food or answering the door unclothed are in themselves immoral actions. But we can say that the repetition of such acts will persuade others that when moral issues are front and center you do not have the state of character to restrain you from preferring your own immediate advantage over the rightful and more distant interests of others.

There are, of course, many ways other than manners and dress by which to assure people that you have an adequate degree of self-control. You can ignore the feelings of others in everyday matters and hope to persuade them when the time comes and the chips are down that you are a moderate and decent person. Contemporary American society is filled with examples suggesting that a lot of people, especially young ones, believe that these other ways are better. Standards of dress have become increasingly casual; getting "dressed up" is now something that is done only for special occasions (if that; one young man attended my son's formal wedding dressed in gym shorts and sneakers). People who dress up for other occasions—business, dinners, airplane travel—are regarded as stuffy, conventional, and probably uninteresting. While it is obvious that cultures differ in standards of everyday conduct and that any given culture may change its standards profoundly over several generations, those who too readily embrace the view that everyday conduct is a trivial and purely personal matter may be surprised to learn that they have paid too little attention to the signals they emit and so lack the trust of others when matters are neither trivial nor personal.

The Sources of Self-Control

Scholars have given far less attention to the sources of self-control than to the sources of sympathy. Many of the leading books on the development of morality in children make no reference to self-control or impulsivity, though they discuss at great length empathy and altruism.* Jerome Kagan, in his brilliant analysis of the nature of the child, explains why: Self-control "was the central criterion for morality in the early nineteenth century. But by the first decade of this century, adjustment to social demands began to replace self-control as the ideal each child was supposed to attain. Successful

---

* I find no reference to self-control in three of the best recent works on the moral development of the child, those by William Damon (1988), Tiffany Field (1990), and Jerome Kagan and Sharon Lamb (1987).

adjustment required yielding to desires for pleasure, friends, status, and wealth; hence, excessive self-control was undesirable."[6] This change did not occur everywhere. Individualistic Americans, valuing independence and self-expression, see the baby as dependent and controlled, and so encourage it to express its distinctive personality. Group-oriented Japanese, by contrast, value interdependence and self-control, and so have devoted more effort to encouraging quietude.[7]

Of course all parents value some degree of self-control in children, if over nothing more than their bowel movements and sleep habits. But self-control is today much less likely to be defined as a moral question than is sympathy or equity, even though many problems of contemporary society, including smoking, drug addiction, predatory sexuality, and much street crime are at root problems of impulsivity.

When self-control is lacking in an especially clear way, experts on child development take note. They once called the problem hyperactivity; today, the preferred term is attention deficit disorder. It has three components: inattention (failing to finish tasks, being easily distracted, not listening, not concentrating), impulsivity (acting before thinking, not waiting one's turn, unreasonably shifting from one task to another, requiring constant supervision), and hyperactivity (fidgeting, running about, restlessness, and difficulty in sitting still). Though every parent and schoolteacher has known children like this, the precise diagnosis of the pattern is not easy. Parents, teachers, and doctors often disagree as to who has the problem, and the rates at which it is thought to appear in various countries differ so greatly that one suspects (rightly, as it turns out) that different definitions are being used in different ways in different places.[8]

Whatever the difficulties in sorting out the diagnosis for most children, there is a great deal of agreement that in its extreme form attention deficit disorder increases the risk that when children become adolescents or young adults they will be poor citizens.[9] In Montreal, hyperactive children between the ages of six and twelve were followed for a dozen years. When compared to other children of the same age, sex, class, and intelligence, they were more likely to be delinquent, immature, impulsive, and poor students.[10] Four hundred boys in London were followed from an early age for over two decades; those that became delinquent differed from their law-

Self-Control

abiding colleagues by, among other things, irregular work habits and the immoderate pursuit of immediate pleasures.[11] Similar results have come from other studies.[12] Various reviews have found strong evidence of a relationship between attention deficit disorder and delinquency.[13]

Though they are at greater risk for delinquency, not all hyperactive children commit crimes. Many youngsters who are impulsive but otherwise normal with respect to intelligence, sympathy, and parental affection have no more trouble with the law than do children without attentional deficits.[14] Those who are most likely to become criminals are those who combine impulsiveness with aggressiveness and a lack of empathy.* But even among nondelinquents, hyperactive children tend to turn into adults who are restless, have difficulty holding a job or forming lasting emotional relationships, and are underachievers.[15] In one of the few studies of drug users that followed people from early childhood into adolescence, Jack and Jeanne Block found that personality characteristics apparent at ages three and four were conducive to later serious drug use. Children rated by several nursery school teachers as (among other things) fidgety, uncooperative, inattentive, unable to concentrate, and subject to rapid mood swings were much more likely than children with the opposite traits to have high rates of drug use at age fourteen.[16] Essentially the same thing was true when the child's personality as assessed at age seven was compared to drug use at age eighteen.[17]

As is true of almost all important human behaviors, impulsiveness is caused by a complex interaction of biological and environmental factors. The hyperactivity of adopted children tends to be more like that of their biological than of their adoptive parents, suggesting some degree of heritability.[18] Other studies have found that identical twins are more alike in impulsiveness than are fraternal twins.[19] Just what this heritable trait may be is far from clear. Among the leading candidates are some of the neurotransmitters (the chem-

---

* Some of the research on attention deficit disorder (ADD), especially that which attempts to predict adult misconduct from childish impulsiveness, is unreliable because the authors fail to distinguish between attention deficits and childhood misconduct. When sorted out, much adult misconduct tends to be associated, not with childhood ADD, but with childhood misconduct (Lilienfeld and Waldman, 1990; Hinshaw, 1987).

ical messengers of the brain), especially dopamine and serotonin, and the enzyme, monoamine oxidase, that flushes used neurotransmitters out of the gap between brain cells. People with low levels of monoamine oxidase (MAO) tend to be more impulsive than people with high levels of that enzyme, suggesting that the stimulation they receive from dopamine flowing from one brain cell to another is not ended by MAO.[20] Imagine a brain cell as a doorbell connected to a button. When you push the button, an electric current causes the bell to ring; when you stop pushing, a spring in the button breaks the contact and the bell stops ringing. In the brain, dopamine is the electric current and MAO is the spring. Very impulsive people have a weak spring; their bells are always ringing.

This overstimulation may explain what would otherwise seem paradoxical, namely, that hyperactive children are calmed down by consuming a stimulant such as an amphetamine. Impulsive, hyperactive children have a short attention span: they are "overstimulated" in the sense that they go rapidly and unproductively from one task to another in an effort, apparently, to find pleasure in external activity. Taking a stimulant drug increases the children's span of attention; they become more focused and less in need of frenzied activity as a source of pleasure. They are internally rather than externally aroused. Since 1937, amphetamines have been used effectively to treat attention deficit disorder.[21] This treatment is controversial because the continued use of stimulants can retard physical growth and because reducing hyperactivity in this way, while it may calm children, does little to improve their learning.[22]

The central role of dopamine in impulsiveness is underscored by what scientists have learned about the biological basis of cocaine addiction. When neurons in certain parts of the brain want to send a signal to their neighbors, they send dopamine. Ordinarily, the dopamine, after exciting the second cell, returns to the first. Cocaine blocks this return, or "re-uptake."[23] To revert to the doorbell metaphor, cocaine keeps the button pushed.

Suggestive as these findings are, they are by no means the whole story. Certain kinds of impulsiveness, such as that leading to fighting, assaults, arson, and murder, may reflect abnormally low levels of another neurotransmitter, serotonin.[24] Compulsive gamblers may be deficient in yet another chemical messenger, norepinephrine.[25]

People may differ from birth how these neurotransmitters operate, leading some to become more impulsive, excitable, fickle, quick-tempered, extravagant, and easily distracted or bored. But these tendencies do not operate in a vacuum. The family can modify biological predispositions in important ways. Using data from Scandinavia, Dr. C. Robert Cloninger and his colleagues have been able to show that after taking into account the characteristics of the biological parent, children raised by adoptive parents were importantly affected by their environment.[26] For a given genetic inheritance, children are more likely to misbehave if they were subject to lax or inconsistent discipline or grew up in an unstable family.

This fits squarely with what almost every other study of impulsivity has found, but many of these other studies are deficient in having ignored biological predispositions, leaving the impression that parents powerfully affect children but children never affect parents. In a full review of the evidence available as of 1983, Michael Rutter and Norman Garmezy concluded that impulsivity or hyperactivity was especially common among children raised in institutions instead of families and, if reared in families, among those whose mothers were "critical, disapproving, punitive, and lacking in affection."[27] But this connection was in part due to some of the children's being temperamentally hyperactive in ways that stretched their mothers' patience past the breaking point. When amphetamines were administered to overactive children, they became more orderly; as the children became easier to manage, the mothers tended to become more affectionate.[28]

Hardly anybody has carefully followed children as they grow up, observing the interaction of their temperament with their parent's care. In one of the few efforts to do so, the authors observed children at play for extended periods of time from shortly after their birth to the time they entered kindergarten, about six years later. The mothers were poor, mostly white, and mostly unmarried. The most hyperactive of these children at age six were those who, at younger ages, had been the object of frequent and inconsistent maternal interference; that is, these infants found it hard to finish any activity without the mothers' disrupting their play.[29] The baby's temperament at birth did not seem to affect this pattern, although the measures of temperament did not include any assessment of the neurobiological makeup of the children. The safest conclusion is that suggested by Rutter and Garmezy: both temperament and family are at work in a way that, for many children, leads to an "escalating cycle, in which difficult children create an interpersonal environment that serves to exacerbate their difficult temperament,"[30] a cycle that is made more common to the extent that the parents themselves share the child's impulsive disposition.

Learning Self-Control

Although breaking this cycle can be a trying experience for parents, most manage reasonably well, as shown by the fact that the majority of impulsive children do not grow up to become psychopaths, criminals, or drug addicts. Impulsive children go through a more troubled adolescence, but by the time they are adults most will have acquired enough self-control to behave in a fairly responsible manner. They will continue to show some lack of self-control—for example, they will have more car accidents, use more drugs, and do less well on written tests that require concentration—and as a consequence do somewhat less well economically.[31]

So far the best insight we have into how family life affects the self-control of children who are temperamentally hyperactive comes from the decades-long work of Emmy Werner and Ruth Smith, who followed hundreds of children as they grew up on the island of Kauai in Hawaii. The children who did the best at overcoming learning disabilities and hyperactivity were those whose parents were affectionate, consistent, and firm.[32] Similarly, data analyzed by Jack and Jeanne Block suggest that those who lacked what the Blocks called "ego control" (meaning they lacked self-control) came from conflict-ridden homes where the parents neglected their duty to instill rules and induce in the child a sense of responsibility.[33]

Happily, most children do not have attention deficit disorder; for them, learning self-control is relatively easy. It develops as a consequence of growing up. As the young child ages, he develops a more complex neural system that is better able to manage instincts, learns from experience what consequences flow from what actions, acquires from his parents a set of rules by which to predict and judge those consequences, and by watching other people begins to model his behavior on theirs. Most of us are naturally inclined to learn about consequences both because we value the good opinion of our parents and because we come to recognize that the world is arranged so that many of the most valuable experiences result from controlling our proclivity to immediate gratification. Self-control does not emerge as directly or as surely from the natural sociability of the child as does fairness, and so more parental effort must be devoted to the development of the former than the latter. Very little of a mother's time needs to be spent in encouraging the child to be aware of what is fair compared to the amount that must be devoted to getting him to do his homework, eat good food, or write a thank-you letter to his grandmother.

But we never become wholly controlled by distant consequences in preference to immediate ones. Any but the most cautious person will occasionally buy something on impulse, go off a diet, drink enough to cause a hangover, or tell the boss exactly what he thinks of him. People who never do any of these things are generally regarded as unattractive oddities and medically viewed as obsessional personalities. Some children are by nature highly averse to risk (or in Cloninger's term, harm avoidant); if that temperament is heavily reinforced by a strict parental emphasis on rules and duties, the result can be an adult who is so orderly and forward-looking as to be rigid, unhappy, obstinate, and aloof. If everyone were that way, the world would suffer from a lack of spontaneity, heroism, and entrepreneurship.

Self-control, like sympathy, is good—up to a point. Inside every person there is found a "parliament of instincts," to borrow the apt phrase of Konrad Lorenz. Self-control does battle with self-expression; the seductiveness of immediate pleasures competes with the attraction of more distant ones; the lure of what is novel contends with the comfort of what is familiar. In any large group of people, the strength of these drives is normally distributed; that is, on the average, people are neither wholly introverted nor wholly extroverted, neither avidly drawn to seeking novelty nor dully preoccupied with avoiding harms.[34]

These findings of modern personality theory would not have surprised Aristotle. Virtue, he said, is a state of character lying in the mean between two extremes; temperance lies in the mean between an excess of indulgence and a deficiency of pleasure.[35] I suspect that he might have added that any given individual is usually happiest when the balance of passions in that person roughly approximates

the distribution to be found among people generally.* He also recognized that self-control is easier for some people than for others
owing to differences in their natural dispositions.†

Most children become temperate. Most learn to look both ways
before crossing a street, to put up with medicine to cure an illness,
and to make a reasonable effort to study lessons, practice athletic
skills, or develop musical talents. Many boys—in large cities, as
many as a third—will get in trouble with the police at least once,
but by their adult years they will have acquired enough self-control
to end their criminal experiments.[36] So powerful and invariant—
over time and across cultures—is the relationship between age and
crime that it constitutes strong evidence for the view that young
people can be distinguished from older ones chiefly by their lesser
degree of self-control. And since individual crime rates, for the vast
majority of people, decline precipitously with age (beginning in the
early twenties), there is also strong evidence of a natural human
tendency to acquire greater degrees of self-control as a result of
growing up.

But no one acquires perfect self-control; for reasons already adduced, society would not want everyone to do so. And some people
acquire very little self-control. Though most adolescents who experiment with crime stop breaking the law as they become adults, a few
continue to do so at a very high rate and often despite the very low
returns to criminality and the very high probability of punishment.[37]
And some people develop a reasonable degree of self-control with
respect to most things but not with respect to all. The most important example of the last is the case of the ordinary person who
becomes addicted to gambling, smoking, drugs, food, or some other
immediate pleasure.

---

* Aristotle is often mistakenly thought to have said that moderate action is always the
right action ("moderation in all things," as some paraphrase it). This is wrong. If you encounter a man torturing a child, virtue does not consist in reproaching him moderately on
the grounds that such a mild response is the mean—that is, lies halfway between—doing
nothing and knocking him to the ground. As J. O. Urmson points out, being moderate does
not imply doing the average thing, but having a settled character that is moderate (Urmson,
1973).

† "For each of us seems to possess his type of character to some extent by nature,
since we are just, brave, prone to temperance, or have another feature, immediately
from birth" (*Nich. Ethics*:1144b4). But, Aristotle adds, natural endowments are insufficient;
habit and understanding, both acquired in the family, are necessary to enlarge and perfect
virtue.

Addiction and Morality

In Aristotle's language, most people become temperate as their natural sociability—a desire to please parents and friends—leads them to value the deferred pleasures (respect, friendship, the absence of punishment, lasting happiness) that come from subordinating their immoderate passions to moderate habits. But some people (a very few, if the small percentage of people who are career criminals and habitual drug abusers is any indication) remain intemperate with respect to all aspects of their lives, and others are incontinent with respect to some aspect of their lives.

The most dramatic example of incontinence is drug addiction, by which I mean consuming a mood-altering substance (tobacco, alcohol, drugs) at times or in amounts that the user cannot control. Some readers will deny that addiction is an example of incontinence; addicts may be intemperate, in that they prefer the pleasures of the drug to the pleasures of abstinence, but that is their business. They are not incontinent; that is, they are not consuming, because of impetuosity or a weak will, something that they know is bad for them. They are rationally consuming something that supplies pleasure or relief from psychic distress.*

There is no sure answer to this objection, but what we know of the lives of addicts makes it implausible. Most drug addicts, I conjecture, do not like their addicted state any more than most food addicts like being fat. Most smokers have tried, sometimes repeatedly, to quit smoking.[38] Drug users, when interviewed, reveal detailed knowledge of the harmful effects of drug abuse on them, their families, and their friends.[39] Alcoholics are typically filled with pain, remorse, and shame on the morning after a particularly hideous binge. Heavy users of addictive drugs discover two central facts about what they are swallowing, injecting, or inhaling: in time, a given amount of the drug produces less pleasure than did the same amount when they first started using it (doctors call this tolerance), and it becomes psychologically or physically more painful to stop using the drug the more one uses it (doctors call this dependence). Some people can consume drugs and still manage to lead a stable life,

---

* Cf. Becker and Murphy, 1988. I do not deal here with a different argument, namely, that even if people ought not to use drugs, it is their decision and society has no business trying to prevent them. I try to challenge that argument elsewhere (Wilson, 1991: ch. 12).

discharging duties to family, maintaining valued friendships, and earning a decent living, but for many tolerance and dependence lead to a situation in which the drug itself no longer supplies more pleasure, but the pain associated with not using it becomes too great to manage.* Any addict in that condition would, if he could, gladly change positions with himself in his preabuse days because, apart from whether his life has gone to pieces, addiction is no longer fun. In this sense, drug addiction is a form of incontinence: most addicts, if they could choose at one moment in time between not using the drug and being in the fully understood state of a drug addict, would reject the drug. Addiction is the result of a series of small choices (consuming a drug or smoking a cigarette at one moment in time) that provide large immediate benefits but much larger and unwanted long-term costs; by the time the costs are fully understood, the user lacks the ability to forgo the drug the next time it becomes available.[40]

In spite of the spirited policy debate over whether addiction is a disease or a crime, whether drugs should be legal or illegal, and whether addicts should be arrested, treated, or ignored, the vast majority of people persist in thinking of the more debilitating addictions as a moral problem, distinguishing among the various addictions in terms of the extent to which they made the addict less than human. Accordingly, food and nicotine addiction, though deplored on medical and aesthetic grounds, are less often regarded as a moral problem than alcohol and cocaine addiction, because while the first two may hurt the body, the latter two degrade the spirit. Not all popular judgments will be accurate at any given moment, but the standard—what is consistent with man's social nature?—remains remarkably stable. Moral judgments do not entirely settle policy issues, of course, as is evident by changing policies toward pornography and extramarital sex, both of which are regarded by large majorities as immoral but neither of which is punished by law today to the extent they once were. Public policy is shaped by considerations of prudence and feasibility as well as of morality and social

---

* Goldstein and Kalant, 1990. Smoking tobacco is a partial exception to this generalization, in that nicotine addiction does not lead to tolerance (such that it takes more and more cigarettes to produce the same level of pleasure). It does lead to a high level of dependence, however, which is why smokers, including those who fully understand the health risks, find it so difficult to quit.

obligation. As a consequence, policies change far more rapidly than do moral judgments.

People view the most important departures from self-control as moral and not simply prudential problems, and hence the investments parents make in teaching a reasonable level of self-control are regarded as among the most important of all family activities. Social conventions, ranging from the rules of etiquette through praise for hard work to the condemnation of vices, are ways of reinforcing familial commands by reminding us of our human failings. If we all took the long view and fully understood in advance the large consequences of our small choices, there would be little need for, and hence little use of, such familiar homilies as "Look before you leap," "Mind your manners," or "A penny saved is a penny earned."

Society's belief that it is important to endow rules about self-control with moral significance is challenged by evidence that some people are biologically more disposed to lack such control than others. We now know beyond much doubt that a predisposition to alcoholism is, in many people, inherited.[41] Some preliminary evidence even suggests that the gene responsible for this predisposition and its effect on the neural system have been identified.[42] In time we may learn that there is also a genetic predisposition to heroin or cocaine dependency, though as yet there are no such leads. There also exists a heritable predisposition to certain kinds of criminality, especially high rates of adult theft.[43]

Some people worry—or hope—that if science discovers a genetic basis for bad behavior, it will no longer be thought proper to punish, or perhaps even to criticize, such behavior. If addiction or criminality is to some large degree a "disease," it can no longer be a moral failing. The analogy is to mental illness, once thought to be the product of a moral defect and now understood to be an ailment with genetic and neurophysiological as well as environmental causes.

There is no doubt that alcoholism and drug addiction, like schizophrenia or depression, are diseases in the sense that they result in part from an abnormal condition of a human organ, the brain, and are responsive in some degree to medication. That is a good reason for placing the addict under the care of a physician. But addiction, unlike cancer or smallpox, is also a behavior, and the task of the physician is to induce the patient to alter that behavior. Medication can often help, but medication alone is insufficient, and even the medication requires a change in patient behavior: he or she must regularly take the pill. It is necessary to supplement the medication by changing the patient's psychic state and daily behavior; indeed, this is often a prerequisite to successful medication. He or she must acknowledge the addiction, admit that help is essential, avoid (or keep to the absolute minimum) any use of the addictive drug, and shun social settings in which the temptation to use the drug is very powerful.

Now, acting on such advice might be described simply as prudence—a useful strategy to attain a preferred goal. In a sense it is. But the goal is not simply "preferred" (in the sense that one prefers vanilla to chocolate ice cream, or being blond to being brunette). The goal is of overriding, even transcendent importance: to live life on human terms—that is, to acknowledge the obligation of one's social nature by discharging duties to family, friends, and employer, duties that rest on reciprocal affection, interdependent needs, the bonds of sympathy, and the requirements of fair play. So important is this goal that the commitment one must make to it, and the expectations other people have that the commitment will be honored, acquire a moral status. That is, while onlookers may feel sympathy for the organic infirmity that places a person at risk for addiction, failure to act in the ways required to overcome it ought to make one feel, not simply disappointed or unlucky, but ashamed. The best-known programs for aiding people in fighting addiction, such as Alcoholics Anonymous, require of the participant an admission of shame and a commitment to right conduct that are, in their intensity and justification, little different from any moral obligation.

People make rather careful and even exquisite distinctions among kinds of aberrant behavior and thus degrees of moral obligation. A diabetic must take insulin; failure to do so causes suffering for both the diabetic and his family, and so failure can lead to rebukes. But the rebukes are usually rare and generally prudential rather than moral in tone, in part because it is well understood that the patient has no desire to slip into a diabetic coma (whereas an alcoholic often wishes to have one more binge) and in part because the coma, though painful to all concerned, does not involve or cause an intentional flouting of familial or social obligations. An overweight smoker elicits somewhat more intense and less sympathetic pressure, because being overweight and smoking tobacco reflect a preference for present pleasures over long-term health. But some sympathy remains and certainly the pressure is rarely moral in tone, because the indulgences that lead to obesity and nicotine addiction do not directly or immediately interfere with familial and personal obligations. A recovering alcoholic or drug abuser who relapses into his addiction becomes less than human, inflicts pain on others, and reveals an incontinent disposition, and so we exert the strongest pressures ("If you don't stop, I'll leave you!"), all on grounds that we think, rightly, are fundamentally moral in nature ("It's not right to treat your children that way!").

So long as any behavioral change is required by an ill person, family and friends will attempt to reinforce that change by demands and expectations that become increasingly moral in nature as the intentions, time horizon, and ultimate consequences of the change imply moral relationships. This is even true of individuals with non-addictive mental illnesses, such as chronic depression. We sympathize with their plight and remind them to take their medication. But we also try to help them change their behavior because much of its is utterly self-centered—sleeping instead of working, shrugging off obligations, and ignoring the rights and needs of others. To encourage that change we adopt a tone that typically is a mixture of cajolery, exasperation, and rebuke, less moralistic than if we were dealing with a drug addict but more so than if we were dealing with an overeater.

People take self-control seriously because in routine matters it is useful and in large matters it is essential. It becomes a dimension of morality to the extent that it implicates the fundamental features of man's social nature: the respect for and the obligation toward others with whom we spend our lives or from whom we expect important benefits. For this reason, it is a profound error to say that one should not be "moralistic" or "judgmental" about the more serious addictions. Judging them morally is essential to correcting and preventing them.

Self-Control and Evolution

Since most people are not hyperactive or inordinately impulsive, one might suspect that evolution has selected for people who can take a longer view of their own interests and against those who rush headlong into every situation. Our moral approval of self-control would then reflect the fact that, on the whole, social arrangements are made better if society is composed of people who can keep their appetites under reasonable control. There is no way to prove this that I know of, but it is not implausible.

But there is another possibility. Impulsivity is common among children and adolescents; since until relatively recently, few people lived much beyond the age of thirty, one must wonder whether impulsivity at some earlier time—and in a few places or circumstances even today—conferred an evolutionary advantage. People who answered insult with insult, who fought back against any assailant without waiting for a distant government to take charge, who rushed headlong into battle against a common enemy, who plunged without hesitation into the forest in pursuit of an animal—these may have been people who at some point in mankind's development served themselves and their offspring well. As I shall indicate in chapter 9, modern society may reward self-control more than impulsivity, but modern society is, well, modern; it is a recent development that still must cope with a human animal that evolved under very different circumstances.

Duty

We usually tell the truth and keep our promises because it is useful to do so. Honesty is the best policy because it induces others to trust us, and that trust often can be turned to our advantage. We are loyal to friends and family in part because we fear losing their respect or companionship if they discover our disloyalty. We give an honest day's work mainly because diligent workers will ordinarily be paid more and promoted faster than lazy or irresponsible ones. We are more likely to give money to charity when we are applauded for doing so. We discharge many of the duties of citizenship—obeying the law, paying taxes, responding to a call to arms, observing the military code of honor—because failing to do so exposes us to punishment.

But duty—being faithful to obligations—will sometimes incline us to tell the truth even when the truth hurts and to keep promises even when honesty is a bad policy. We may admit a mistake or fault even when the costs of doing so exceed any resulting gain in trustworthiness. We may keep a promise to a dead friend or a despised rival, or anonymously, with no one at all to notice. We may be faithful to our spouse though adultery would be pleasurable and undetectable. We often have a sense of satisfaction from having given an honest day's work though no one has noticed; we sleep better knowing that, as a carpenter, we properly installed the now-hidden beams and joists. We often contribute small sums and occasionally large ones to charities with no recognition save a receipt impersonally printed out by a computer. We customarily obey the law even when the chances of detection and punishment are vanishingly small, pay our taxes when

99

the risk of an audit is virtually nonexistent, and vote in elections though the chance of our vote having any practical consequence is virtually zero. Some of us will volunteer for military service without waiting for a summons, at the cost of leaving a more comfortable and profitable civilian life for one filled with risk of death or injury. If captured by the enemy, many soldiers struggle to keep secrets and avoid collaboration even when their captors threaten pain or death.

Duty is the disposition to honor obligations even without hope of reward or fear of punishment. One reveals himself to be a moral person not merely by honoring obligations but by being disposed to honor them even when it is not in his interest to do so.

From these examples it is obvious that our motives to honor obligations are mixed and that often they involve no part of what rightly might be called fidelity. There is no way, in most cases, to estimate how frequently people act out of a sense of duty pure and simple in contrast to self-interest narrowly defined, or to measure in what degree the two kinds of motives are combined. Perhaps the easiest case is voting. In those nations, such as the United States, in which it is voluntary, it is hard to discern any practical reason for voting. To have an effect, your vote would have to make or break a tie. In the vast majority of elections, the number of votes cast is so large that the chances of any one determining the outcome is much less than the chance of the voter being struck by lightning. And voting entails burdens: going to a polling place (often on a cold or rainy day), waiting in line, and deciphering a complex ballot. Of course, one may go to the polling place for the same reason one goes to a party given on behalf of a charity: to see and be seen and to earn the respect of others by being thought a good citizen. But these social rewards for voting depend, to a large degree, on the prior understanding among the onlookers that voting is a mark of a good citizen. That is, for one to acquire status by being seen voting there must already be a widely held belief that voting is a duty. But if there is no such thing as a genuine sense of duty, it is hard to explain why people would reward one another for being dutiful, especially when, absent a sense of duty, voting is irrational. The case becomes even clearer with people who vote by absentee ballot: by sitting at home and marking their ballot, voters are deprived of any social rewards at all since no one except a computer knows that they have voted. Despite this, nearly two million Californians (about 17 percent of all voters) cast absentee ballots in 1992.

Duty and Conscience

Duty exists to the extent that people are willing to honor obligations in the absence of social rewards for doing so. Indeed, being especially dutiful can often expose a person to the charge that he or she is unsociable. We may regard as imprudent a person who is so unfailingly sympathetic as to give aid and comfort to even the most dubious supplicants, or we may regard as legalistic someone who is so scrupulously fair as to ponder endlessly over the right thing to do. But rarely would we think of them as unsocial. Still, excessively dutiful people—those who are bluntly candid, narrowly rule-abiding, or relentlessly reformist—are often regarded as unattractive. In the extreme case we depict them as obsessional personalities.

That may explain why duty is among the weaker of the moral senses. It may develop, in ways to be explained in a moment, out of an initial desire to please one's parents, but it becomes strong only to the extent that it becomes autonomous—that is, independent of the consequences that may ensue. When it is placed in competition with our natural sociability, it often loses out. We tell "little white lies" to protect the feelings of friends, we steal supplies from the office or tools from the factory when "everyone is doing it," and we fail to support a cause we otherwise like if by our support we risk becoming unpopular. On occasion we may go along with peer expectations or authoritative commands even though we have good reason to think that we are being induced to behave wrongly; recall, from chapter 2, the people recruited by Stanley Milgram to teach others by administering what they believed were strong electrical shocks.

Yet the desire to be liked rarely can extinguish altogether the sense of duty, because people who are faithful to their obligations in ways we disapprove of show us that they have a conscience, and we value people who are so inner directed that we can rely on their behaving in a certain way even when the external incentives available to them might incline them in a different direction. In fact, having a reputation for being strong willed—even being maniacally committed to some abstract principle—can work to our long-term benefit. People will often defer to our wishes if they think we will make a scene when we are expected to act contrary to a deeply held conviction, and they will often have confidence in our promises (if the promises are consistent with our principles) even when they know we will encounter many temptations to break the promise. There are business executives who prefer Mormons as employees because they believe that Mormons are more honest than gentiles.

Knowing the advantages of having a reputation for honesty, narrowly self-interested people may try to acquire one, but it is not as easy as it seems. A person may be fooled by a chance encounter, but during a continuing relationship he will usually form an accurate assessment of another person's character. For people to be impressed by your honesty, you must either be honest all of the time (in which case you will have to stop taking selfish advantage of the many opportunities for cheating, and so you might as well stop being greedy altogether), or you will have to be honest in some very conspicuous, highly dramatic fashion, such as telling the truth even when it costs a lot of money to do so. As the economist Robert Frank puts it in his excellent analysis of how we signal a reputation to others, people will accept your behavior as a sign of honesty or duty only when it would be costly to fake it.[1] If it is very costly to fake it, you can't fake it; the reputation you then earn for honesty or duty corresponds exactly to reality. You *are* dutiful.

The uneasy relationship between conscience and sociability helps explain why our sense of duty is often evoked by events that anger us. We are often aroused to act, not by our warm sympathy for the plight of a victim or our calm deliberation over what justice requires, but by our rage at somebody who seems to be "getting away with something," that is, conspicuously violating, even flouting, some obligation.

Thirty-two people who had gone to the aid of crime victims in California were studied to find out why they intervened even though they did not know the victim, often acted alone, and in almost every case suffered an injury, sometimes a serious one. These Good Samaritans stopped beatings, broke up robberies, and challenged bullies. One got a broken jaw for his trouble; another was cut by a shattered bottle. Not surprisingly, almost all the Samaritans were relatively young men who were bigger and heavier than most men their age. More surprisingly, they were not especially idealistic, and they did not speak much of their sympathy for the victims. Most acted reflexively, without deliberation. What seemed to distinguish them from similar men who did not intervene was that they were quick to anger and temperamentally aggressive.[2] When someone flagrantly and unjustifiably violates the social compact, all of us are angered to some degree; these men let their anger impel them to risky action. Conscience, in short, is not entirely a calm sentiment; it both restrains our self-interest and unleashes our indignation.

This is evident in the portrait Samuel and Pearl Oliner have painted of the gentiles who rescued Jews during World War II. As we saw in the chapter on sympathy, many of the rescuers were led to act by a face-to-face confrontation with a victim. Empathy—fellow feeling—was their chief motive. But some of the helpers, roughly a tenth, did not feel sympathy for the victims so much as they experienced anger at their oppressors; their motive was principle, animated by rage. Their relations with those they aided were more impersonal than those of their empathic colleagues. They did not wait to meet a Jew before acting; they began acting by looking for Jews to help. Suzanne, for example, helped several hundred Jews. She was not part of any organized group, did not seek out the company of others in order to win their esteem or support, and did not get involved in the lives of those whom she helped. On a psychological test she scored well below the average in empathy but well above it on a scale of social responsibility. Because she held strong views about right and wrong, she was ready to sacrifice some sociability in favor of affirming her principles. Among her friends she was disputatious; as she later put it, "we argued about everything." Her conscience made it hard for her either to ignore injustice or cultivate popularity.[3]

A reader eager to reduce all human motivation to self-interest narrowly conceived may interpret what the Good Samaritans or the Holocaust rescuers did as efforts at reputation building, but taking this view so stretches the concept of self-interest as to deprive it of any meaning. Expressing genuine indignation at an injustice and acting to set matters right at considerable cost to ourselves are not merely ways by which we signal to others our sense of duty; they are ways by which we live.

The Origins of Conscience

For about a century, the study of conscience has been chiefly the province of Freudians. In their view, the conscience is the superego, formed out of the child's strong identification with a parent; more particularly, the superego is, in Freud's words, "the heir of the Oedipus complex."[4] Every boy secretly lusts after his mother and, as a consequence, sees his father as a powerful rival. Because he cannot have his mother or overcome his father, he represses his erotic love for the former and his anger with the latter. These repressed feelings persist in his subconscious, reappearing occasionally in the form of dreams and neuroses, but at the conscious level they are replaced by a set of rules—the superego—that control his impulses. His conscience has been formed.[5]

The word that dominates Freud's account of the conscience is "repression" (*Unterdrückung*). The superego represses the boy's Oedipus complex and his natural and innate aggressiveness, obliging him to renounce revenge against his father. "Men are not gentle creatures who want to be loved," Freud wrote; they are, on the contrary, instinctively aggressive.[6] Although he is not clear on this, Freud implies that people with the strongest conscience are the most repressed: they are driven by a "cruel" superego that they come to "fear." The resulting sense of guilt can, in the extreme case, cause illness or even crime.[7] Many who have accepted Freud's theory have drawn from the idea of repression and the more unattractive features of its stronger forms the view that repression, with its connotation of victimization, is bad and ought to be overcome. Though Freud may not have intended it, Freudianism has made conscience suspect.

The continued popularity of this view is in sharp contrast to its scientific implausibility. That little boys love their mothers is indisputable; that this love is in any meaningful sense of the word erotic has never been shown and is, in fact, most unlikely. That they regard their fathers as rivals is another unsupported assumption. That conscience is the result of repression is a useful thing to believe if you would like to free yourself of the constraints of conscience—conscience becomes a "hang-up" that prevents you from "realizing yourself." But no one has shown, and indeed it cannot be shown, that young children have more or less of a conscience if their early "libidinal" experiences—with sleeping, breast feeding, and toilet training—are systematically altered. Babies that sleep with their mothers are as able to develop a conscience as those that sleep alone; toddlers subjected to early toilet training will acquire a conscience, but so will those who are left to become toilet trained on their own.[8]

A book-length review of studies that tested the scientific validity of Freud's theories, written by scholars who were by no means hostile to his ideas, concluded, with respect to the formation of the superego, that whatever oedipal conflict a boy may experience, it is not

D u t y

resolved because his fear of his father leads him to identify with that awesome figure. On the contrary, boys are more likely to develop a masculine personality and acquire strong moral standards when they have a loving and nurturant rather than a threatening or fear-inspiring father.[9]

There is another, much more straightforward account of the origins of conscience. Conscience, like sympathy, fairness, and self-control, arises not out of repressed lust and rage but out of our innate desire for attachment, and thus it acquires its strongest development when those attachments are the strongest. People with the strongest conscience will be not those with the most powerfully repressed aggressiveness but those with the most powerfully developed affiliation. That conclusion is consistent with the evidence that undermines the Freudian oedipal theory: attachment, not fear, is associated with later moral development. Just as we are predisposed to develop a good ear for the voices of others as they judge our actions, so also are we disposed to develop one for that inner voice by which we judge our own actions. When we disappoint other people by acting immorally, we feel shame; when we disappoint ourselves by failing to honor an obligation, we feel guilt. Since the sanctions that others can impose on us are more numerous and, in most cases, more powerful than those we impose on ourselves, we ordinarily fear shame more than guilt.[10]

An explanation for the development of a conscience has been proposed by Hans J. Eysenck.[11] To him, it is a conditioned reflex. Put as crudely as possible, we feel the pang of conscience when we act (or fail to act) in a certain way for the same reason that Pavlov's dog salivated when it heard a bell ring. Recall why the dog salivated at the sound of a bell. Originally it, like all dogs, salivated when it was shown a juicy morsel of meat. Pavlov began ringing a bell every time the meat was shown; soon, the dog salivated at either the bell or the meat, even though there was no reward (a dog can't eat the sound of a bell ringing). The dog had been conditioned to react to a stimulus in a certain way—unthinkingly, automatically.

People also develop an automatic, unthinking reaction to objects and events. We can be frightened by a fire or a spider and ever after get nervous in the presence of a flame or a bug. We can be punished by a parent for telling a lie or stealing a cookie; if the punishment is consistent enough we will get nervous when lying or stealing, *even when there is no chance of detection.* The same thing can happen with rewards. Suppose that every time the national anthem is played, a young boy is told by his father to stand up, place his hand over his heart, and "act proud." It will not be long before the boy feels a tingle of pleasure every time he hears the opening bars of the "Star Spangled Banner," *even when he hears it on the radio and no one will notice whether or not he stands up.* Or suppose that every time the Boston Celtics win a basketball game, there is a celebration in a child's home, with extra cookies passed out to everyone. Ordinarily the child will grow up a Celtics fan and continue to feel elation at victories and depression in defeat *even when alone or sitting with friends who much prefer the New York Knicks.*

The italics in the last paragraph draw attention to the fact that a conditioned reflex produces pleasure or pain without regard to consequences. It doesn't make much difference whether the lie is detected, you are observed standing at attention, or friends join you in celebrating a Celtics victory. A conditioned reflex is the product of a different kind of learning than that by which we master riding a bicycle, pleasing a friend, or earning a living. Eysenck suggests that ordinary learning—what psychologists call operant conditioning—involves the central nervous system. We modify how we think, memorize bits of information, and adopt certain habits of action. Classical conditioning is different; it involves the autonomic nervous system—a set of glands, muscles, and neurons that, among other things, makes our heart beat, lungs expand, and palms sweat.*

The machines popularly called lie detectors are devices that measure the operation of the heart, lungs, and sweat glands. The machines can't, of course, distinguish between a lie and the truth; that is why their operators prefer to call them polygraphs. But they can measure changes in our autonomic nervous system. Without getting into the debate over whether these measured changes are good indicators of a person's truthfulness, it is worth noting that most people do undergo involuntary bodily reactions when they tell a lie. If

---

*Classical conditioning is an important illustration of one mechanism whereby a conscience is formed, precisely because its effects seem not to depend on whether one's bad behavior is or is not detected. But such conditioning may not be the only way in which we acquire a conscience. We can also learn to feel guilty when we violate a self-imposed rule. For example, we can feel guilty when we break our diet by eating an ice cream cone even though no one has ever rewarded us for going on a diet and nothing bad has ever happened to us after we have eaten ice cream. I regard conscience as an indisputable fact but its formation as poorly understood.

there were no such thing as a conscience, that would not occur. Everybody would be able to defeat the lie detector every time.

Some people can beat it all the time. That is because they have no involuntary reactions to lying; they are psychopaths. A psychopath is not a lunatic suffering from disabling delusions or an obviously neurotic person displaying phobias and anxieties; rather, he or she is an outwardly normal person with an apparently logical mind who happens to be an emotional cipher. Hiding behind what Hervey Cleckley called "the mask of sanity," the psychopath is the extreme case of the nonsocial personality, someone for whom the ordinary emotions of life have no meaning.[12] Psychopaths lie without compunction, injure without remorse, and cheat with little fear of detection. Wholly self-centered and unaware of the emotional needs of others, they are, in the fullest sense of the term, unsocial. They can mimic feelings without experiencing them. If man were simply the pure calculator that some economists and game theories imagine, this is what he would be.

Much of what we know about conscience has been learned by studying those who have none, that is, by investigating psychopaths. In general, psychopaths are hard to condition. When most people hear a tone that is then followed by a painful electric shock, they quickly learn to associate the tone with the shock. Their apprehension can be gauged by measuring changes in the rate at which their skin conducts electricity. Robert Hare found that ordinary people became very apprehensive after just a few experiences with the tone-shock sequence, but psychopaths became far less apprehensive.[13] In another experiment, he had subjects watch the numbers one through twelve appear in sequence on a dial. They were told that when the number eight appeared, they would get a painful shock. The autonomic nervous system of the normal subjects reacted strongly to the steady progression of digits, indicating considerable anxiety as soon as the first few appeared. But the skin response of the psychopathic subjects barely changed until just before the number eight appeared, and even then it changed only slightly.[14] Other scientists have produced similar findings.[15] Hare and others have concluded from this that the psychopath does not readily develop a fearful response to an event. He may take steps to avoid unpleasant things, but he does not internalize his fear and hence does not acquire a conscience.

Accompanying this inability to internalize anxieties is the psychopath's difficulty in entering imaginatively into the emotional state of someone else.[16] A test measuring role-taking ability developed by Harrison Gough can predict with some accuracy who will and will not become a serious delinquent, independently of a person's social class.[17] In addition, psychopaths are often thrill seekers, not simply because they discount the bad things that may happen to them if they take risks, but because they are underaroused: that is, their emotional void leaves them bored and restless. Knowing little of true feelings, they cannot rely on their own feelings to supply them with much satisfaction, and so they seek it out from dangerous activities, wild parties, and an agitated quest for excitement.[18]

By turning these findings upside down we can depict the features of men and women that dispose us to acquire a conscience. We are fully social beings: we have genuine emotions and can sense the emotional state of others. We are not so greatly in need of excitement that we are inclined to treat others as objects designed for our amusement. We judge others and expect to be judged by them. In time we acquire the disposition to judge our own behavior through the eyes of a disinterested spectator, what Adam Smith called "the man within the breast."[19] We acquire this internal spectator from others; eager to earn praise and avoid blame, we adjust our actions accordingly. To a degree that varies among individuals, but to some degree in almost all of us, we develop a visceral reaction to the actions that we contemplate, experiencing internally and automatically the prospect of praise or blame, whether or not it will actually occur. Of special importance is fear: our memory of unpleasant consequences begins to arouse our apprehension even when no consequences may occur. In this way our conscience is shaped. The stronger the conscience the more distant and uncertain the prospects that it will illuminate.

A sense of duty—a strong conscience—is not the product of repressed feelings of lust or rage directed at parents, but of precisely the opposite. Compared to bystanders, the gentiles who rescued Jews out of a sense of duty were particularly close to their parents. Suzanne described her family as emotionally "very close," as did Louisa, another highly principled rescuer. Both women recalled growing up in families that combined love with an emphasis on accepting personal responsibility and taking one's obligations seriously. But it would be a mistake to suppose that these women were taking great risks simply to please their parents. On the contrary; they had so internalized their principles that Suzanne did not tell her parents what she intended to do until after she had begun, and Louisa ignored her mother's urgings that she take care of her own children rather than run risks on behalf of someone else's.[20]

The case of Suzanne and Louisa has much in common with accounts of social activists. Campus radicals and civil rights leaders during the 1960s were hardly in rebellion against their parents: they were taking parental values seriously, behaving in ways that were consistent with, albeit often more extreme than, what they had learned at home.[21] In time journalistic talk of a "generation gap" was replaced with a far more accurate account of radical students following in the footsteps of radical parents, earning for themselves the label "red-diaper babies." We now know that conservative activists are quite similar to their leftist counterparts in at least this regard: for both groups, a politics of principle represents a continuation of, not a break with, parental attitudes.* This is true not only in the United States but around the world. After analyzing the opinions of university students in eleven nations in 1969–70, Otto Klineberg was struck by the fact that "so many students express a feeling of closeness to their parents rather than conflict."[22]

Of course, the motives for public action will usually be more complex than those for private beliefs. When people are watching, a sense of principled obligation may be reinforced by (and in some cases play second fiddle to) a desire for power or status, a desire that can only be realized when the right opportunity presents itself. Social movements often founder on a struggle for influence among rival leaders or are corrupted by one leader's inability to distinguish between his follower's duty to a cause and their duty to him. In speaking of activists, it is important to distinguish the sense of duty (which leads people to act on principles) from the love of power (which leads them to manipulate principles).†

---

*Braungart and Braungart, 1990. For some reason, conservative activists tend to report having had less intensely political families than do leftist militants. Right-wing students sometimes politicized their parents rather than the other way around. But there was no rebellion.

† The study of student activists in the New Left by Stanley Rothman and S. Robert Lichter (1982) is in large measure a study of young people who had the most extreme views during the 1960s; they scored at least one standard deviation above the mean on a "New Left Ideology" test. Not surprisingly, the need for power among this group was high. Rothman and Lichter offer a Freudian explanation of this need, but their data can as easily be interpreted in non-Freudian terms. The radical activists described their parents as being emotionally

THE MORAL SENSE

Because we only see duty performed when it is performed publicly, it is easy for us to conclude cynically that self-serving motives and not public-regarding ones are all that matter. We seem to take a perverse pride in finding clay feet on all our heroes and scandals among all our saints, perhaps because we wish to justify our own inaction or compromises, perhaps because we are suspicious that fidelity, being the most fragile moral sense, cannot survive without social reinforcement. We will acknowledge that it may be duty that leads people to vote, contribute small sums to charity, or honor promises that are not greatly inconveniencing, but in all these cases the costs are low. But how often, we may ask, will people act as their duty requires when the costs are high and the social support weak? Are not the Suzannes and Louisas of this world so rare as to offer no proof of the general existence of a strongly felt sense of duty?

Duty and Honor in Near Isolation

Consider the plight of a soldier taken captive by a ruthless enemy. The soldier has been taught not to divulge secrets; his captors want him to tell everything and even to collaborate by denouncing his own country. The former is armed with his sense of duty, the latter with an array of excruciating physical and psychological tortures. The soldier is held in an isolation cell. What will he do?

We need not speculate, for we have a lengthy account about what some members of the armed forces did under exactly these circumstances. Admiral James B. Stockdale has left a compelling memoir of his eight years as a prisoner of war (POW) in North Vietnam from 1965 to 1973 and of what he saw of his fellow Americans who shared his fate.* The prisoners were not a random sample of the citizenry—they were mostly young male pilots. But neither were they distinctive for having either strong political ideologies or deep religious convictions. They were middle Americans who had chosen a military profession. Though the prisoners were not unusual,

---

distant and their upbringing as being coldly permissive. There is not much evidence here of activists suffering from an excessively cruel conscience instilled by an overly authoritarian father; on the contrary, political extremism in this group was associated with uncaring parents who were permissive, not out of fondness, but out of indifference.

*Stockdale, 1984; Stockdale and Stockdale, 1990. Though my analysis draws entirely on the experience of American POWs, I am not suggesting that this was a distinctively American reaction. I am confident that POWs from many other nations would behave in a similar fashion.

their captors were. Unlike the Germans who captured Allied airmen in World War II, the North Vietnamese did not treat their prisoners as men who had to be warehoused, at some expense and inconvenience, until the war's end; instead, they treated them as valuable political assets to be exploited for military and propaganda advantage. That meant inducing the prisoners to divulge operational secrets and, most importantly, to make statements critical of the United States' participation in the Vietnam War.

To that end, the prisoners were isolated from one another, denied decent food or care, interrogated, beaten, and tortured. The standard torture was "the ropes," a process in which a prisoner's arms are pulled up behind his back while his head is forced down toward the floor. The pain is excruciating, a compound of slow suffocation because the lungs are no longer able to expand, dislocation of the shoulder joints as the arms are pulled in an unnatural direction, and constriction of the blood supply to the extremities. To end the ordeal, one had to say "I submit" and give proof of the submission by writing a statement that either revealed military secrets or denounced American military policy. Failure to conform meant another session with the ropes. No one could hold out indefinitely; sooner or later, everyone submitted. And rarely would one statement suffice; the captors wanted more, with additional details and stronger denunciations. Stockdale endured the ropes fourteen times and signed many statements, as did other prisoners. It was not a question of hanging tough for a few weeks or months, and then being ignored by the captors. The pressure was relentless and endless. Several prisoners died.

Such circumstances make the question, "What does duty require?," a matter of life and death. Consider the question from the point of view of a person rationally interested in his own well-being. "I am wholly at the mercy of captors who will stop at nothing to get what they want. I have been here for a few years and may be here for many more. There is a good chance I will die here and no one will know when or how. I am alone: I have no cell mate and I am tortured out of sight and hearing of my fellow prisoners. If I sign a statement denouncing my country, chances are it won't be believed back home; moreover, everybody who is tortured will eventually sign. Why, then, endure long, agonizing rounds of torture before doing what they will make me and others do anyway? All of the relevant incentives are under the control of my captors, virtually none under the control of my buddies. Therefore, it is reasonable to capitulate whenever asked."

Hardly any captives decided the matter that way. Almost all resisted, endured much torture, and submitted only after they felt themselves to be at death's door. Why?

The answer Stockdale gives is that these men held out because they were able to establish, albeit remotely and tenuously, a connection with their fellow prisoners. The POW "must somehow communicate with his fellows" and "together they must establish a viable set of rules and regulations to live by."[23] The North Vietnamese sensed this and went to great lengths to prevent communication from occurring and any organization from forming. It is for this reason that the men were held in solitary confinement, often for years at a time, and severely punished for attempting to get in touch with their comrades. Despite these measures, messages were exchanged by a system of tapping on cell walls using a code similar to that used by the inmates in the Soviet prisons as depicted in Arthur Koestler's powerful novel about the Moscow show trials, *Darkness at Noon.*[24]

The tapped messages were used to establish a chain of command and promulgate rules. The rules were not an imposition but a response to a demand: the captives had to know what was expected of them. Since they were being forced to write and say things that they did not believe, they desperately needed to know what was right and what was wrong *under these circumstances.* They could not be told, "Endure the torture"; the torture was unbearable. They could not be told, "Each man must decide for himself how long to hold out"; they would not accept individual decisions so long as there was any possibility of a collective one. What they could be told, and asked to be told, was an answer to the question "What should I take torture for?" The rules developed in the Hanoi prison where Stockdale was held, and where he was the senior American officer, set forth the lines that should not be crossed without enduring significant torture. As he was later to put it, "we ordered men to [undergo] torture."[25] The rules may seem odd to readers accustomed to thinking of these dramas in terms of secrets that must be protected. They were: Do not bow to your captors in public. Make no broadcasts on behalf of the enemy. Admit no crimes in your confessions. If we are ever rescued, don't kiss the captors good-bye. Unity over self.[26] These were not rules that could never be broken; but they could be broken only if the prisoner was first tortured.

D u t y

Duty in this extreme case meant honoring an obligation to behave under duress in a way that signified how much the prisoners valued their comrades and how little they valued their captors. The key rule was unity over self. Fidelity arose out of a social connection and could be defined and preserved only by keeping that connection alive, however tenuously and indirectly and however trivial or even nonexistent were the actual social rewards for fidelity. A tiny and remote chance that one would be honored intangibly by one's comrades was more valuable than a high and immediate chance that one would be rewarded materially by one's enemies. Expressing the matter this way retains the appearance of a utilitarian calculation while showing how hollow such calculations can be when honor is at stake. When guilt and fear are one's only emotions, fear can be tolerated more easily if guilt can be overcome, and that in turn requires some signs, however faint, that one is not alone and that one's comrades, however distant, share a set of rules by which guilt can be assessed.[27]

This is not the same as saying that people want to be liked and will endure much pain to earn that affection. There were very few collaborators among the American prisoners in Hanoi; one who did collaborate was one who mistook popularity for respect. When this officer's defection became known, Stockdale asked a mutual acquaintance to explain it. "It drives him crazy if he is not liked," the acquaintance said. "He [the defector] tends to grovel and ingratiate himself before others."[28] In time the defector rejoined the tapping network of American prisoners and stopped making tape recordings for the enemy. But his comrades still resented him, not because of the political or military damage he might have done (which was probably slight), but for his betrayal of a code of conduct.

Fidelity under extreme conditions was also evident among many of the inmates of Nazi concentration camps. For many years the prevailing view, at least among English-speaking observers, seems to have been that of Bruno Bettelheim. In his book, *The Informed Heart*, Bettelheim argued that the absolute terror of the concentration camp reduced virtually all of the prisoners to a childlike dependence on their captors, leading, in its final stages, to an actual identification with them.[29] Driven by a desperate desire to survive, prisoners found their "conscience" soon transformed into obedience to the dictates of their captors.

But a newer, more discriminating view has begun to supplant this. Among its best expositors is Anna Pawelczynska, a woman who was active in the Resistance and, as a consequence, was arrested and sent to Auschwitz-Birkenau. There she found, as had Bettelheim in the Buchenwald camp, that some prisoners, typically the most brutal and unbalanced, were given authority over their fellow inmates, authority they took pleasure in exercising.[30] There were countless examples of prisoners, faced with imminent death, treating one another callously or even violently, and almost everyone became desensitized to the sights and smells of death. Viewed generally and from the moral perspective of an outsider, the camps, by methodically killing people through starvation, beatings, and asphyxiation, succeeded in reducing the inmates to savagery.

But on closer examination distinctions become apparent. The scope of obligations was narrowed, but obligations remained. In the event two persons became lovers, other inmates felt obliged to protect them from discovery. Husbands and wives ran great risks to help one another or at least to learn of one another's fate. A resistance movement arose inside the camp that tried, with modest success, to make life difficult for the guards. The scale of moral obligation was diminished but not obliterated; the commands of the ordinary moral sense were greatly revised but not wholly repudiated. Being in the resistance movement may have only marginally increased one's chances for survival, but its chief benefit was, in Pawelczynska's words, to become "a complete human person, doing battle with criminals," and not just a hunted animal. The principles of fairness and sympathy and self-command continued to be valued among people, even though under the conditions at Auschwitz they could receive only the feeblest expression. To the extent they could be stated at all, they took the form of following this rule: "Do not harm your neighbor and, if at all possible, save him." The result was nothing grand, just "small, stubborn, and laughable daily heroism in the face of misery."[31]

Duty, Self, and Society

The capacity of people in the most extreme circumstances to express and act upon conceptions of duty and honor suggests that these sentiments do not arise merely out of natural sociability. In general, a strong attachment to one's parents aids the emergence of a personal moral code that governs behavior even without external rewards. But that is not the whole story. People not only reason with others, they reason with themselves. We argue with our mothers about whether we should pick up our room, but we also argue with ourselves about whether we should keep a friend's secret or return a lost toy. Conscience is not simply imposed on us; it is in part something we impose on ourselves as we think through what it means to be human and on what terms we can live with ourselves.

Suppose Admiral Stockdale had been the only American prisoner in Hanoi. It would have been harder for him to resist the demands of his captors; he might have yielded sooner to "the ropes"; he might have said more after he yielded. But I suspect that he would still have resisted, still felt it necessary for his own self-respect to endure some suffering before any capitulation.

Happily, few of us ever have our sense of duty put to the kinds of tests endured by the inmates of a Hanoi prison or an Auschwitz concentration camp. Typically, we must only decide whether to keep a promise when it is inconvenient to do so, vote when we would prefer to stay home, or conceal some of our income from the tax collector when we know the deception will be undetectable. Since many of us at one time or another have broken a promise, failed to vote, and cheated the tax collector, we are aware of how fragile the sense of duty can be when the competing incentives have even a modest value. Indeed, it may be that our fidelity is greatest when the rewards for defecting are the greatest, provided only that it is clear that those who offer rewards such as a cessation of torture are outsiders without any moral claim to our obedience.

Duty is the way by which people cope with the free-rider problem in the absence of coercion. The free-rider problem occurs when someone can enjoy the benefits of some policy without paying his share of its cost. For example, if a person can jump undetected over the turnstile at a subway stop, he can travel without paying; he is literally a free rider. Moreover, he can justify his cheating by reminding himself that his being on the subway car in no way adds to the cost of operating the transit system. "What I did wasn't really wrong," he says to himself, "because it didn't cost anybody anything."

But of course it would cost everybody a great deal if everybody did it. The only way to ensure that everybody doesn't do this is either to have a foolproof system for enforcing fare collections or to rely on people's sense of duty. The managers of subway systems know that the sense of duty is too weak to depend on, and so they install gates, guards, and ticket takers. Similarly, the national government does not rely on voluntary contributions to support the armed services; it knows that, since everybody will benefit from national defense whether or not they contribute to its expenses, no one will have an incentive to contribute. Coercion—that is, the imposition of taxes— becomes necessary.

There are many kinds of free-rider problems that are not so easily solved by coercion, however. Voting is the obvious case. The government could make it compulsory (as has been done in Italy and Australia), but it could not safely impose a significant penalty on nonvoters without risking being turned out of office. Voting, therefore, is almost everywhere voluntary; where compulsory, the compulsion is not systematically applied. Democratic nations rely on the sense of duty reinforced by social pressure, a pressure that can be effective only if the sense of duty is widely shared.

Where there is a drought, the mayor or governor usually asks people to conserve water voluntarily. But a person who does so by taking shorter showers or not washing the dishes very often is behaving irrationally. His conservation will not add materially to the water supply available to others, nor will the water he saves be available to him later on. Conservation in a single household makes no sense for either that household or the community as a whole. Yet, many people practice conservation. Of course, if the drought is severe enough, the government will give everyone a material incentive to conserve by raising water rates. What is astonishing is that many people conserve even in the absence of higher rates. Some part of this conservation is enforced socially by the criticism of neighbors who see you washing your car, but much of what conservers do, such as taking short showers, is visible to no one.

Public radio and television stations in the United States are supported in part by voluntary contributions from people who could see or hear the programs even if they didn't contribute. In Los Angeles, over three hundred thousand people (roughly one-eighth of all viewing households) contribute to KCET, a public television station, each year. In San Francisco, one-sixth of all viewers contribute.[32]

Two scholars set out to measure how common it is for people to invest money in some group enterprise when they could get a higher return by investing in an individual one. In one experiment, people were asked to choose, alone and without knowing how others would choose, between investing money in an individual project that would earn them a certain amount of money and investing the same amount in a group enterprise that would benefit everybody, in this case, a project, such as a hi-fi set, that could be enjoyed by everyone living in a college dormitory. More people invested their money in the group project (that they would enjoy whether they paid for it or not) than invested in projects that would benefit them individually. In the twelve versions of this experiment, only one group of subjects clearly preferred to be free riders by shunning the group project—graduate students in economics.[33]

We know rather little about the personality traits or familial experiences of people who vote, conserve, and contribute. Social scientists, with their penchant for sociological explanations,* point out that voters, conservers, and contributors tend to come from the better off, more educated classes. I conjecture that, whatever their class background, people who have a sense of duty strong enough to make them act "irrationally" (but usefully from the point of view of society) when faced with free-rider problems have experienced, as children, a stronger level of conditioning at the hands of affectionate parents who defined obligations and emphasized the need to honor them.

---

*The penchant has, I think, two sources: convenience and ideology. Socioeconomic characteristics are easier to measure than personality traits or child-rearing techniques, and social scientists are overrepresented among those who believe that the social environment, especially the class structure, is of decisive importance in explaining human behavior.

PART TWO

Sources

The Social Animal

Man is by nature a social animal. Our moral nature grows directly out of our social nature. We express sympathy for the plight of others both because we value their company (and so wish to convince them of our companionable qualities) and because we can feel the pain of others even when not in their company. We learn to apply the standard of fairness both because we want to find a cost-minimizing strategy for managing joint activities (such as playing with the same toy) and because we think that the distribution of things ought to reflect the worth of each beneficiary. We acquire some measure of self-control both because we value the good opinion of others and because we value our own self-esteem. We act on a sense of duty both prudently, out of a desire for the praise of others, and reflexively, in response to an inner command that, though once spoken by others, now speaks of its own accord and in its own voice.

The attentive reader will have noticed that in explaining the virtues in the paragraph above I have combined more or less self-regarding motives with more or less other-regarding ones. The former include the desire for human company, for keeping unpleasant quarrels to a minimum, and for appearing attractive or praiseworthy in the eyes of others. The latter include feeling the pain of others, taking into account the worth of others, having a good opinion of ourselves, and responding reflexively to an inner voice. The motives that shape our morality all arise from our social nature, but some are chiefly means to an end (for example, given my desire for the company of others, how can I best and most cheaply acquire it?) while others express a conviction about what those ends ought to be.

Social scientists, out of a desire for theoretical elegance, disciplinary loyalty, or empirical simplicity, sometimes seize upon one set of motives to the exclusion of the other. For some, especially many anthropologists, man is the product of culture, symbols, and roles. He is embedded in familial and communal ties and acquires his identity from a web of relationships that is endowed with meaning by tradition and ritual; culture determines the meanings he assigns to the world about him. Man has no nature other than an ability to acquire a culture. Clifford Geertz has put it, in his words, "most bluntly": "there is no such thing as a human nature independent of culture."[1] For other scholars, notably psychologists and economists, man has a nature and it is a calculating one. He seeks to advance his own interests by finding the most economical ways of getting more of whatever he desires. To rescue this statement from tautological banality, it is necessary to specify what his "interests" are. Though in principle they could be anything, in practice they tend to be his material interest—self-preservation, wealth, and things for which wealth can readily be exchanged.

Each view is partially correct. At the level of ritual and religion, man seems capable of acquiring the most diverse cultures. Can there be anything of importance that is universally true of mankind if the ancient Aztecs could exult while "lifting pulsing hearts torn from the live chests of human sacrifices toward the heavens,"[2] while ancient Christians found equal religious satisfaction in stoically awaiting the lion's fangs in a Roman arena? Geertz thinks not and so urges upon us the task of studying in great detail the cultural particularities—indeed, the oddities—of mankind.

At the same time, whatever the culture, man certainly will seek his advantage. So far as I know, no one ever had to be taught to prefer food to hunger, wealth to poverty, or praise to blame. (Some people can be taught not to prefer those things, and so we find a few who will go on hunger strikes or live ascetic lives; but this requires very powerful teachings and highly receptive pupils.) No matter what the religious ritual, people everywhere, so far as we know, tend to consume more of valued things when the price goes down and less when it goes up.

These two perspectives are, in my view, incomplete. To believers in culture, "man is social"; to students of self-interest, "man is an animal." To me, "man is a social animal" who struggles to reconcile the partially warring parts of his universally occurring nature—the desire for survival and sustenance with the desire for companionship and approval.* And not just a social animal by accident, but a social animal by nature—that is, as the consequence of biological predispositions selected for over eons of evolutionary history.

Given the human infant's need for prolonged postpartum care, the survival of our species has required that evolution select for two things—the parent's willingness to provide care and the infant's capacity to elicit it. The evidence for the former can be found in the most obvious facts of everyday life. The evidence for the latter is more easily overlooked, and thus bears stating.

Sociability

Newborn babies engage in rudimentary social activity before they are taught it. They root, suck, and express distress at the sound of other babies crying. They prefer human sounds to other sounds, female sounds to male ones, and maternal sounds to other female sounds.[3] This prosocial behavior is not learned. Infants born blind will smile though they have never seen a smile; infants born both deaf and blind will laugh during play, though they have never heard laughter, and frown when angry, though they have never seen a frown.[4]

An infant will imitate several facial and hand gestures within two weeks of birth and some gestures within thirty-two hours of birth. Since this finding is controversial in some quarters, let me pause and explain why I find the evidence persuasive. Andrew Meltzoff, a psychologist at the University of Washington, did the original experiment. Face to face with infants ranging in age from twelve to twenty-one days, he would stick out his tongue, protrude his lips, open his mouth, and wiggle his fingers. At a rate much higher than chance,

---

*Geertz acknowledges that at some level there are universal tendencies in mankind, but dismisses them as relatively unimportant compared to the culturally transmitted habits and rituals of life: "That everywhere people mate and produce children, have some sense of mine and thine, and protect themselves in some fashion from rain and sun are neither false nor, from some points of view, unimportant; but they are hardly very much help in drawing a portrait of man that will be [anything more than a] cartoon" (1973:40). Perhaps these facts are not very important for "drawing a portrait of man," but they are all-important for understanding the moral nature of man. For that purpose, anything else, even a thick description of a Balinese cock fight, is a cartoon.

the infants would do likewise.[5] Though unlikely, it was possible that the infants might have learned this behavior, and so a few years later Meltzoff repeated the experiment with infants less than seventy-two hours old. (One was only forty-two *minutes* old.) The infants imitated the mouth openings and the tongue protrusions. It is impossible to explain this imitation on the basis of learning.[6] It might be possible, however, that the infants are not imitating adults but displaying some kind of purely reflexive behavior* similar to baby birds opening their mouths when the mother approaches with food.[7] In another experiment, Meltzoff got infants less than three days old to rotate their heads and stick out their tongues after he did likewise.[8] While it does not disprove the "pure reflex" explanation, this experiment, together with all of the others, casts great doubt upon it. One would have to believe that babies innately stick out tongues, open mouths, protrude lips, and move fingers right after an adult has done these things but for some reason other than as an effort to imitate the adult.

At least five of the universal human facial expressions—those expressing happiness, sadness, surprise, interest, and disgust—can be observed in the newborn child.[9] Within two weeks infants will reach for a presented object and will cry at the sound of another baby crying, but not at the recorded sound of their own crying.[10] Between the ages of three and six months, the baby will enjoy gazing into the eyes of its parent. Provided the mother does not try to overdo making eye contact, the baby will act as if it were fascinated with the mother's face.[11] Soon it will smile when it is smiled at. Within six months babies can tell the difference between the face of a friendly and an unfriendly adult.[12]

Within two years the prosocial behaviors of children become obvious. They will show off things that they are carrying and ask for a response ("Look at this!"), share things or activities with others, help others do things, and bring things or offer consolation to people in distress.†

---

*Technically, not a reflex but a "fixed action pattern" produced by an "innate releasing mechanism."

†Radke-Yarrow et al., 1983:481. Mothers also behave in distinctive ways toward children whatever their cultural background. For example, whether they are right-handed or left-handed, the vast majority of mothers carry their infants on the left side. It is almost inconceivable that this is a learned behavior (Trevathan, 1987:158–66).

The Social Animal

My argument—that humans are disposed to be social before they learn what sociability is all about—is consistent with a large number of studies showing that even nonhuman animals are disposed to learn some things in preference to others. Now, this will not be big news to dog owners. Labrador retrievers rarely need to be taught to fetch; they are bred to fetch and will bring you things whether you reward them for it or not. Terriers certainly need not be taught to dig up the backyard, and their owners have learned how hard it is to teach them not to do it.

Despite this common knowledge, some behavioral psychologists once viewed animals as entities that all learned in pretty much the same way: that is, by associating a certain stimulus with a certain response. In principle, anything an animal valued could reward (and thus reinforce) behavior, and anything it disliked could penalize (and thus extinguish) behavior. If you fed a rat flavored water and simultaneously made it nauseous (by bombarding it with X rays), the rat would soon learn to avoid drinking the water. In fact, it would avoid drinking even if it didn't start to feel nauseous until an hour or more had elapsed since drinking the flavored water. But now suppose that you gave the rat, not radiation-induced nausea, but an electrical shock when it drank the flavored water. The rat would *not* learn to stop drinking. Something in it tells it that drinking can make it nauseous, but that drinking cannot produce an electrical shock. It is prepared, biologically, to learn some things but not others; it is as if there were a voice in it that said after it got sick, "It must have been something I ate."[13]

Martin E. P. Seligman has called this the "sauce béarnaise effect." He developed a strong aversion to the sauce when he became sick some hours after eating it on a filet mignon. But he did not develop an aversion to the meat, or to the plates it was served on, or to his wife (who was at the table while he was eating), or to *Tristan und Isolde,* the opera he was listening to while he ate. He associated nausea with what he ate, and in particular with what was unusual about what he ate.[14] (In fact, it wasn't the sauce that made him sick at all, it was the flu. Never mind. He still lost his taste for béarnaise.)

Young children can be conditioned to be fearful of caterpillars but not of opera glasses.[15] Something in them prepares them to believe that creepy, furry things might be harmful but odd, glass-and-plastic devices probably are not. Unrelated boys and girls raised together from infancy will not form romantic bonds; unrelated boys and girls who first meet in adolescence form such bonds rather easily.[16] Children are prepared to treat opposite-sex children with whom they live at certain ages as siblings, not as love objects, whether or not they are in fact siblings. This preparedness is what enforces the taboo against incest and makes it so unlikely the boys and girls raised together in an Israeli kibbutz will later marry.

The natural sociability of children is, I think, an example of preparedness. Infants and young children are prepared, biologically, for sociability. Babies bond to humans who make eye contact, whether or not they supply food.[17] Some abused children remain attached to abusive parents, even denying the abuse.[18] The desire for attachment is so strong that it is extremely difficult to extinguish even with the use of the most severe punishments.

Evolution has selected for attachment behavior in all species that nurture their young after birth. That behavior is especially strong among humans because the human infant requires such a long period of nurturance. It takes years of parental care for the human brain to develop sufficiently to make complex intellectual activities possible—for example, figuring out the theory of evolution.

Theories of natural selection and inclusive fitness explain why caring for one's own young has been adaptive—that is, useful—for the human species. People who care for their young leave more young behind than those who do not; to the extent parental care is under genetic control, caring parents reproduce their genes in the next generation at higher rates than do uncaring ones. Evolution has thus rewarded ("selected for") people who were biologically predisposed to spend endless hours on the uncompensated, "irrational" task of tending their offspring. Had it not, there would soon have been no offspring to care for, and I would not be writing this book and you would not be reading it.

Having explained the adaptive function of parental care, many evolutionary biologists regard the story as over. Any remaining questions can be answered by referring back to the adaptive mechanisms—reproductive success and inclusive fitness. If moral behavior needs to be explained, the explanation will involve some application of the adaptive mechanisms, and so we are treated to heated debates as to whether or under what circumstances altruism or reciprocity make evolutionary sense—that is, how these behaviors might or might not spread in a population.

But the story is not over. What evolution selects for is not *be-*

havior, whether moral or otherwise; it only selects for *mechanisms* that produce a behavior or predispose an animal to it.[19] Failing to ask what psychological mechanism produces moral behavior makes it impossible to understand such behavior.

The mechanism underlying human moral conduct is the desire for attachment or affiliation. That desire is evident in the instinctively prosocial behavior of the newborn infant and in the instinctively caring response that parents make to that behavior. It is all the more remarkable because not only does the infant initiate social contacts by exchanging glances, coos, and smiles, but it also makes demands—many of them insistent, some of them unpleasant—on those who respond to its initiatives. There must be something about a baby that provides a signal or cue (in evolutionary jargon a "releaser") that elicits the parental response. One such signal that stimulates the affectional response in adults is kinship. In this respect we are no different from countless species of birds. But another is cuteness, by which I mean any set of traits that leads us to judge an organism as delightfully attractive. Mankind, as well as many nonhuman primates, seem to respond to certain cues in ways that suggest that they share a more or less common definition of cuteness: eyes large relative to the skull, chubby cheeks and a rounded chin, awkward movements, a cuddly epidermis, small size, and a distinctive smell.[20] Nonparents as well as parents respond to these cues, and the response extends beyond the human infant to other creatures with the same infantile traits. Scientists have not, in my view, taken the concept of "cute" sufficiently seriously, which is odd considering how often humans use the word.

A remarkable illustration of the value we attach to certain traits that imply sociability is the way in which mankind has become attached to animals. Some of those attachments can be explained on purely utilitarian grounds: horses transport us, cows feed us, some dogs protect us. But no one has yet found a practical use for a cat that won't catch mice—and many won't—yet cats have been domesticated at least since the second millennium before Christ, and in Egypt killing them was once a capital offense. Today the proportion of cats kept because they perform a useful service must be vanishingly small. (One of my cats hunts mice, the other won't. I cherish them equally.) The proportion of dogs kept for protection may be significant, but judging from the vast numbers of small dogs that constitute no threat to anyone and large dogs (like my Labrador) that *could* be a threat but refuse, dog ownership must also have little practical value in most cases.

What most pets provide is companionship. That truism conceals a fascinating fact. Pet owners (and people generally) share a more or less common definition of companionship, one that derives from the characteristics of the human infant. These characteristics are of two sorts: having a baby-like appearance (big eyes, round features, a cuddly epidermis) and displaying playful affection. Several scholars have commented on the tendency not only to acquire as pets animals with these childlike qualities, but also to breed these traits into animals and to make considerable sacrifices on their behalf.[21] There is very little in a theory of inclusive fitness that explains such devotion, yet the mystery disappears if what evolution has selected for is a disposition to attachment.

Attachment, thus triggered, is the mechanism out of which sociability emerges, and sociability, in turn, is the state in which moral understandings are shaped. But the attachment instinct in humans will not be as precise in its effect on behavior as the social instinct is among ants. Having a complex brain almost guarantees that for man the effect of any predisposition will be diffuse. One reason is that the human brain makes possible not only complex actions but also our imagining such actions.

The predisposition to attachment operates through an elaborate central nervous system and is embedded in the evocative symbols of language. Not surprisingly, it imperfectly discriminates between parents and parent substitutes, is evoked by adoptive as well as by natural infants, extends to creatures that have just a few of the characteristics of the human infant, and embraces not only family but kin, sometimes nonkin, and often other species, such as pets. The result is what we saw in the chapter on sympathy: people care not only for their own children but also for their adopted ones; they think that the care of children is an obligation all parents must shoulder; they take pleasure in the delights of children they see but do not know and feel pain at the suffering of children they neither see nor know but only hear about.

If a purely behavioral theory of psychological development were correct, the infant's constant demands for attention followed by the parent's (typically, the mother's) nearly constant responses would lead to the development of an utterly self-centered rather than an other-regarding character. The narrowly behavioral theory is that actions that are rewarded will be repeated. In this view, responding to demands for food, fondling, and rocking with food, fondling, and rocking would produce a selfish, dependent child. That is, indeed, what John B. Watson argued in 1928 when he advised mothers to feed their children on schedule, not on demand, and "never to hug and kiss them, never let them sit in your lap." Such views received the imprimatur of the Children's Bureau of the United States Department of Labor.[22] Millions of mothers who had never heard of Professor Watson went on indulging their infants and, miraculously, those infants became perfectly decent adults. In time the mothers who had read Professor Watson figured that out and threw his book away. The human infant is programmed, we now know, to develop in certain ways; its behavior will differ depending on the developmental stage it has reached. In the early stages rewarding its demands does not simply reinforce those demands and cause them to be repeated; rather, the "rewards" (by which is meant food, care, and affection) simply enable the child to grow into its next stage.

Parents respond in kind to these displays of sociability, reciprocating the baby's smiles, sounds, and glances with smiles, sounds, and glances of their own. Typically the mother and father find this exchange rewarding, and hence it persists. But parenthood, like infancy, is not shaped entirely by the mutual exchange of rewards, as is evident to anyone who has compared the appearance of a newborn with that of a six-month-old infant. Whereas the latter is indisputably appealing, the former often looks (to nonparents) more like a worm than a human. Parents, especially mothers, are predisposed to become attached to their offspring, even at a time—indeed, especially at the time—when the offspring are most vulnerable and least appealing.*

Parents who have experienced the "terrible twos"—the year in which children become defiant or rebellious—often forget that this is the same period during which the child is converting prosocial

---

*I do not here take a position on the argument between those who claim that there is an instinctive maternal response that appears immediately after birth and those who argue that this response often does not appear immediately but emerges, for many mothers, slowly over the course of a few weeks. Though this has been much debated by scholars (cf. Bornstein, 1989; Magnus, 1980), I regard the dispute as irrelevant to my larger point.

behavior into moral judgments. Rebellion and character formation occur simultaneously because having a moral sense first requires having a sense of self. Unless a child first grasps that he is different from others, he can neither make claims for himself nor recognize the claims of others. The tug-of-war between making claims for self and acknowledging the claims of others is exactly what makes this stage of life so tumultuous.

What is striking about the newer findings of child psychologists is that the emergence of a moral sense occurs before the child has acquired much in the way of a language. The rudiments of moral action—a regard for the well-being of others and anxiety at having failed to perform according to a standard—are present well before anything like moral reasoning could occur.[23] If mankind were not by nature social, if morality had to be written on a blank slate wholly by means of instruction, then it would not emerge until well after language had been acquired so that concepts could be understood, and by that time it would probably be too late. If the child's mind were truly a blank slate, it would probably remain, at least with respect to important matters, blank forever.

Indeed, the acquisition of language itself, rather than a necessary precursor of moral action, is itself a manifestation of the natural sociability of mankind. If language were merely a tool to be acquired once its utility were understood, its acquisition would surely be a far more uncertain and precarious process than in fact it is. All human infants learn language completely, they do so at about the same time (between the eighteenth and twenty-eighth months of life), and they do so without anything like training as the term would be used by a professional teacher. Indeed, they learn despite their parents talking baby talk or even nonsense to them.[24] By the age of three, a child will be using a complex grammar and be able to invent new languages (play languages) that obey grammatical principles they have never heard, and they will do so in accord with certain deep grammatical structures that produce certain uniformities in language across cultures.[25]

This view of how a moral sense emerges was stated with utmost clarity by Charles Darwin a century before developmental psychologists began to gather data that confirmed it. The third chapter of *The Descent of Man* is about the moral sense, and the key passage is this: "Any animal whatever, endowed with well-marked social instincts, would inevitably acquire a moral sense or conscience, as soon as its intellectual powers had become as well-developed, or nearly as well-developed, as in man."*

This is so, Darwin went on to say, for four reasons. First, social instincts will lead a creature to take pleasure in the company of its fellows and do certain services for them. It will even lead to what we call sympathy, as is clear from the fact that most social animals confine most of their helping behavior to kin. This limitation implies that a social creature more readily grasps, identifies with, or is moved by (the choice of phrases I leave to the reader) the needs and companionship of those other creatures that are like it and with which it has enjoyed a long association.

Second, as the mental faculties become highly developed, man (and to a lesser degree, manlike animals) can recall past actions, reflect on them and the motives for them, and as a consequence experience a sense of dissatisfaction from having failed to act when action was required. Third, with the advent of language the wishes of others can be expressed and there can occur discussions as to how each ought to act. Finally, the repetition of social acts in accord with one's own instincts, as modified by the expressed preferences of others, will lead to the development of habits that are, for most of us, the fundamental basis of moral life.

Before Darwin, Adam Smith had attempted to base the moral sentiments on sympathy. While he agreed with Smith's view up to a point, Darwin saw that sympathy was not the sole foundation of moral conduct. For one thing, there are certain moral impulses, such as fairness and duty, the exercise of which does not depend on feeling compassion for others. For another, sympathy is aroused far more powerfully by a beloved person than by a passing stranger; while this explains why moral actions begin in familial settings and extend at first to family members, it does not explain how people come to assign value to the well-being of people they scarcely know or have never met or why people will often do their duty toward someone whose unpleasant manner elicits in us no sympathy whatsoever.

---

*Darwin, 1871:71–72. On the same page, Darwin chides John Stuart Mill and others for saying that moral feelings are entirely learned during each individual's lifetime. Since social feelings are instinctive in lower animals, "why should they not be so in man?" And since moral feelings arise out of social instincts, the notion that the former are solely the product of learning is "at least extremely improbable" (71, note 5).

Fairness and duty can arise out of sociability even when sympathy is absent, and sympathy can extend to nonkin. These things are possible because sociability not only makes possible but animates the kind of family life in which people can learn at a very early age that play requires fair play, that if help is expected help must be offered, and that pleasant feelings come from observing certain rituals and pangs of fear or remorse are felt if they are omitted or degraded.

The obvious challenge to this view of morality arising out of infant-parent attachments and early habits of play and instruction is this: Why, for any given individual, should moral dispositions win out over selfish ones? The human animal may be social by nature, but he is still an animal. One of his strongest emotions is fear of violent death; almost as strong is his appetite for food and drink. Satisfying these drives should dominate all other considerations.

The answer begins with the central fact of social life—namely, that it is orderly. Everyday life for most people most of the time is not characterized by war, criminality, or ruthless exploitation, but by more or less peaceable encounters in homes, on the streets, and in public places. If we are all driven by self-interest, this calm and orderly public life must be the result of either some powerful contrivance—a strong government, an occupying army—or a delicate equilibrium of individual interests sustained by the need for mutual forbearance in order to permit individual aggrandizement. But neither explanation can be true for more than short periods of time. With respect to the first, the governors and the occupiers would themselves face the problem of maintaining order in their own ranks; with respect to the second, it would usually be in everybody's interest to cheat whenever they thought they could get away with it, which would be much of the time.

In fact, most people are peaceable most of the time, long before they experience the constraint of government or the interdependency of the market. Sociability dominates in man because individuals have evolved in ways that place their most self-centered instincts under some kind of higher control. The success families have in socializing their children would be impossible if it were not for both the prosocial instincts of the infant and the central nervous system's favoring of society-regarding impulses.

If the essential elements of social behavior—such as the infant's distress call when it is separated from its mother and the mother's response when she hears those calls—had to be learned or were produced by the higher and later-to-evolve parts of the brain (such as the neocortex), then it would be difficult to imagine how the species could have survived. Long before a neocortex had appeared and thus enabled a creature to learn complex social behaviors, infants would have had no way to signal distress and parents no inclination to respond. And if somehow only the higher parts of the brain were involved in sociability, they would often be overridden by the more urgent, primitive demands of fear, hunger, sex, and anger.

No one is quite sure how the human brain ensures that animal impulses are kept in reasonable check by social ones, but a plausible theory, consistent with such experimental evidence as we have, is the following: The oldest part of the brain, the limbic system, is the source of much instinctive behavior—not only the instinct to eat, breathe, and move, but also to build nests, defend territory, and emit distress calls. The separation call is perhaps the most primitive sound made by mammals and, because it serves to maintain contact between infants and their mothers, the most important. A particular part of the limbic area, the cingulate gyrus, "appears to be involved in feeling and expressive states conducive to sociability and the procreation of the species."[26] Various mammals, such as birds, will mate, breed, build nests, rear their young, respond to distress calls and engage in play, all without having a functioning neocortex but never without having a limbic area.

This theory suggests that many of our self-seeking impulses can be kept on a short leash by some of our more social ones because both derive from the oldest, most "primitive" part of our nervous system. Put another way, sociability does not require a modern brain and may not even require (although it can be advanced by) language. Mating, rearing a child, and defending it against predators may express some of the more "primitive"—that is, the more instinctive—aspects of our nature.

Individual Differences

People differ, and many observers will argue that the differences are more important than the similarities. Some people are sociable, some are not. The former may acquire a moral self, but the latter may not, or may acquire a different one. Some of us are more impulsive or aggressive than others, and so some of us present a greater challenge to parental control and find it harder to learn or to act on the necessary rules of human society. Moreover, these individual differences have, to some degree, a genetic basis; this means not only that people are different, but also that the differences are ineradicable. Responding to that objection is a difficult matter. I want to acknowledge human differences while arguing for an underlying similarity with respect to the central fact that shapes our moral sense: sociability.

Beneath the apparently endless variety of human personalities are a few major factors. Just as boxes, though they come in countless shapes and sizes, can be described for the most part by just three dimensions—height, width, and depth—so also do personalities, though they take on a myriad of forms, seem to vary chiefly along three dimensions. Their names and details vary depending on the scholar describing them. Here I will use the formulation of Hans J. Eysenck; though other psychologists state matters somewhat differently, most are describing quite similar things.[27] His three factors are:

> *Extroversion-introversion.* People who are highly extroverted are sociable, lively, active, assertive, carefree, venturesome, dominant, and sensation-seeking; those who are introverted tend to have the opposite traits.
>
> *Neuroticism.* People who are neurotic tend to be anxious, shy, moody, depressed, tense, and emotional and to have strong guilt feelings and low self-esteem. People scoring at the opposite end of this scale are described as emotionally stable.
>
> *Psychoticism.* People scoring high on this scale (which does not necessarily mean that they are "psychotic" in the sense of mentally ill) tend to be cold, aggressive, impersonal, egocentric, antisocial, tough-minded, and lacking in empathy. People scoring low on this scale are said to have ego control.

These dimensions of human personality can be derived from any number of different tests, they appear, so far as we know, in all cultures, and they tend to be quite stable within a given person over long periods of time.[28] Obviously, having a personality trait explains nothing by itself. If somebody is a lively, carefree, fun-seeking party-goer, we can call him extroverted, but we cannot then say that his being extroverted explains why at parties he is a lively, carefree fun-seeker. However, if there are biological, biochemical, or other factors that produce a given personality type, then knowledge of those factors and the way in which they shape human personalities can provide us with ways of explaining behavior.

A good deal of evidence suggests that certain aspects of personality, and these three aspects in particular, are to some significant degree genetically determined.[29] Individuals differ in the extent to which they initiate or respond to human contact, and hence they probably differ in the extent to which their capacity for sympathy will be enlarged and extended by parental influences. We know from the study of twins and of adopted children that much but not all of the personality differences among people—their tendency to be introverts or extroverts, for example—are inherited.[30] Like personality and intelligence, a disposition to altruism may have some heritable component.[31] This possibility is reinforced by the impressive findings of Thomas Bouchard and his colleagues at the University of Minnesota, who, having carefully examined more than one hundred pairs of twins who were separated in infancy and reared apart, concluded that there was a heritable influence even on such attitudes as religiosity.[32]

These studies usually have measured personality traits by means of paper-and-pencil tests, and so we cannot be certain how important such characteristics, heritable or not, may be for actual behavior. One of Bouchard's associates in Minnesota has conducted a remarkable experiment suggesting that heritable individual differences actually influence cooperative behavior. Nancy Segal asked about fifty pairs of twins ranging in age from six to eleven and having similar IQs to solve a simple puzzle. Almost all of the identical (i.e., monozygotic) twins completed the puzzle within the allowed time limit; fewer than half of the fraternal (i.e., dizygotic) twins did so. Age, gender, and intelligence had no effect on this dramatic difference. What did have an effect was that the identical twins were much more likely than the fraternal ones to cooperate with each other. The former were more likely than the latter to look at each other's work, exchange supportive glances, and encourage one another, and they were less likely to make aggressive physical gestures.[33] Cooperatively solving puzzles is not quite the same thing as acting generously on behalf of another, but neither are they unrelated: in intimate settings, a generous spirit facilitates a cooperative undertaking, and the spirit may be the most generous when the people are most alike.[34]

One possible interpretation of Segal's study is that we are more disposed to cooperate with people who are most like us because the perceived similarities make us both more interested in the other person and more confident that we can predict the other's reactions to our actions. When we are very similar—identical, in the case of monozygotic twins—cooperation is the greatest because the cues as to one another's sociability are the most numerous and persuasive.

Some temperamental differences follow ethnic or racial lines. For example, when a comparison was made between Caucasian and Chinese newborn infants of the same gender and born to mothers matched for age, income, and medical care, the Caucasian babies cried more, were harder to control, and blinked longer when confronted with a bright light. When a cloth was passed over their noses, the Caucasian babies pushed it away, while the Chinese babies adapted to it by breathing through their mouths.[35] These differences may help explain why some infants (and the average infants within certain groups) may later differ in extroversion, introversion, and other dimensions of personality, but none of these differences materially alters the essential prosocial behaviors of the newborn.

Scientists are beginning to discover the mechanisms by which a person's biological endowment is expressed in his temperament. Consider extroversion.* As we saw in chapter 4, a growing body of evidence suggests that persons scoring high in extroversion, and especially in sensation seeking, have low levels of an enzyme, monoamine oxidase (MAO), and of a neurotransmitter, serotonin.[36] For example, when some Swedish physicians measured the amount of MAO in the blood of over one thousand eighteen-year-old boys, those with low levels of MAO were more impulsive and more inter-

---

*I offer here a vastly simplified version of a complex chemical story. Monoamine oxidase comes in two forms, A and B. Both forms are found in the brain cells; only MAO B is found in blood platelets. In humans, the amount of MAO A cannot be measured directly, but the amount of MAO B can. When we say that sensation-seeking extroverts have low levels of MAO, we are saying that they have low levels of blood MAO B, which we assume is indicative of low levels of both forms in the brain. Similarly, we cannot directly measure the amount of serotonin in the human brain (serotonin is also found in the bloodstream, but serotonin levels in the brain and blood are not necessarily correlated). We can measure, however, the amount of a metabolite of serotonin, 5-HIAA, found in the spinal fluid. When we say that sensation-seeking extroverts are deficient in serotonin, we are actually saying that they are deficient in 5-HIAA. MAO and serotonin are linked: the former oxidizes the latter into 5-HIAA after the serotonin has done its work as a neurotransmitter. Thus we would expect the level of each to be correlated: the less MAO, the less the amount of serotonin that can be oxidized into 5-HIAA. Sensation seekers are low in both.

ested in seeking out excitement than were high-MAO boys. The low-MAO boys who also had lower than average intelligence were the most at risk: they were more likely than any other group to abuse alcohol and drugs and to reveal various psychological problems.[37] When American college students with very different levels of MAO were followed for two years, those with extremely low levels of MAO were more likely to have dropped out of school and to have had an unstable job record.[38] The amount of MAO in a person is, for the most part, genetically determined; the amount of serotonin may be.[*]

At the opposite end of the scale are people who are shy and inhibited. Where extroverted children seek out the unfamiliar, inhibited ones shun it; where the former are eager for excitement, the latter are fearful of it. The shy child will be slow to approach unknown people or objects, will cling to his parents when in an unfamiliar setting, and stop playing or talking when a novel event occurs. Extreme inhibition, like extreme sensation seeking, is a biological predisposition. Allison Rosenberg and Jerome Kagan have shown that most very inhibited Caucasian children have blue eyes while most very uninhibited ones have brown eyes.[39] Of course it is not the blueness of one's eyes that causes extreme shyness; rather, eye color is a biological marker of a complex biochemical condition in the body that affects temperament.

Children with an excitable, sensation-seeking temperament may be harder to raise than those with placid or very inhibited dispositions. We have already seen how highly impulsive or sensation-seeking children may find it harder to learn self-control, and we have speculated about the biochemical factors that may contribute to impulsivity. Plausible as this speculation may be, we know surprisingly little about how temperament affects child rearing or the acquisition of moral habits. An important attempt to explain this connection was carried out by Alexander Thomas and Stella Chess, who classified newborn babies into "easy," "difficult," and "slow to warm up." They followed these children for several years and found that about 70 percent of the difficult babies, but only 18 percent of the easy ones, developed behavioral problems serious enough to require psychiatric attention.[40] But from the standpoint of moral de-

---

[*]Oxenstierna et al., 1986. The level of serotonin (actually, its metabolite, 5-HIAA) in the human spinal fluid has been used to predict recidivism among impulsive fire setters and violent offenders three years after their release from prison (Virkkunen et al., 1989).

velopment, it is hard to know what to make of these maternal reports or the later problems. An easy child can become a spoiled monster and a difficult one a moral visionary; people can have behavioral problems and still understand and act in a considerate and fair-minded fashion.

The reason for our ignorance is this: it is very difficult to measure in babies those aspects of temperament that are likely to affect moral development. All parents are aware that babies differ. Some infants are active, noisy, and fussy while others are passive, calm, quiet, and malleable. But it is not clear that these moods are indicators of an underlying sociability. We have good reason to think that tempera-ment is significantly under genetic control, but apart from the more extreme forms of inhibition and extroversion, the child's tempera-ment does not appear in an easily recognized form until the child is past infancy.* The delayed appearance of personality means that it is difficult to decide how much of a difference in a child's conduct is the result of problems the child created for the parent and how much the result of problems the parents foisted on the child.

By the time children are past infancy, such tests of temperament become a bit more reliable, and by the adolescent years they become even more reliable. As the tests get better and better, they seem to distinguish between people who easily or quickly learn from experi-ence and those who learn slowly or with great difficulty. For example, many scholars have long known that there is some biological basis for criminality, but they have been unable to specify what causes this heritable tendency. Some have thought that criminals are under-aroused: that is, they seek excitement because their own psychic state does not supply much, and they find it harder to learn from experience. A normal person does not need endless exciting experi-ences to find happiness; an abnormal person does. A normal person who is given an electrical shock immediately after seeing a bright light quickly learns to be apprehensive if he sees the bright light again; an abnormal personality can see the bright light repeatedly without becoming nervous by the prospect of the shock.[41]

To test this theory, some psychologists examined the level of

---

*The reader may wonder how scientists can know that a behavior is genetically influ-enced if it is invisible in infants. The answer is that heritability is determined by comparing adult identical twins with adult fraternal twins and by comparing the behavior of adopted children with that of their natural and adoptive parents.

arousal of about one hundred fifteen-year-old English schoolboys. They did this by measuring their heart rate, how readily their skin conducted electricity, and their brain wave patterns. Nine years later, when the boys were twenty-four, the psychologists looked up their criminal records. Those who had been convicted of a serious crime were much more likely to have had as teenagers a slow heart rate, lower skin conductance, and a distinctive pattern of brain waves.[42] These findings are consistent with the view that the source of moral sentiments is human sociability: people who are underaroused are less sensitive to the behavior of others and learn less easily from their contact with others.

Commonalities

Most people are neither underaroused, thereby requiring constant external stimulation, nor excessively shy, thereby shunning such stimuli. Most people take subtle cues from their environment, and they learn from those cues. Most people, in short, are sociable. (Only 17 percent of the English schoolboys were convicted of a crime and typically were convicted only once; only a tiny fraction were repeat offenders.) The vast majority of infants are born with a social nature that ensures their ready participation in the process of moral habituation. One of the reasons that so much research has been devoted to temperamental differences among people is that these differences are departures from a norm. We are fascinated by the highly extroverted or very shy person because he is uncommon. Moreover, though there is clearly a biological basis for these temperamental differences, the behavior of children as they grow up tends to converge toward the norm. For example, when Jerome Kagan followed his very shy infants for several years, he found that about half of them by age seven no longer were very inhibited (though, of course, very few had become extroverted).[43]

No infant needs to learn to assert its own needs; it cries when it is hungry or in distress. Until recently, many psychologists assumed it had to learn everything else; we now know, however, that most infants bring to their own rearing a keen sensitivity to the distress of others. As early as ten months of age, toddlers react visibly to signs of distress in others, often becoming agitated; when they are one and a half years old they seek to do something to alleviate the other's distress; by the time they are two years old they verbally sympathize, offer toys, make suggestions, and look for help.[44] Though these youngsters are no doubt expressing some learned reactions to distress, they seem prepared to learn those things. It is obvious that infants are biologically inclined to seek attention; it may also be that they are biologically inclined to give it.[45]

This innate sensitivity to the feelings of others—a sensitivity that, to be sure, varies among individuals—is so powerful that it makes us grasp not only the feelings of friends and family members but also those of some strangers, many fictional characters, and even animals. We wince when the motion picture hero is threatened and exult when he is triumphant; we are disturbed by the sight of a wounded dog and pleased by the sight of someone else's baby.

Sociability is a two-edged sword: it is the source not only of our moral sentiments but also of our concern for reputation and respect. Our tendency to judge others is accompanied by the constant awareness that others are judging us. We are wounded when we are slighted and offended when unfairly criticized, not only when people do these things to our face but even when we learn of these offenses indirectly and from strangers who are in no position to affect our daily lives or means of livelihood. Scarcely a waking hour passes when we do not wonder how we appear in the eyes of others. Because we want to be liked, we sometimes join in a crowd's assault on an innocent person. Because we want to be admired, we sometimes cheat in order to acquire prestige for ourselves. Because we want to be thought a reliable comrade, we sometimes obey leaders who order us to commit atrocities. It is the rare individual who can honestly say to himself, "I care nothing for what anybody else thinks of me," and the few who can say this are often rather unattractive people. Our sociability generates our moral sense and then places us in countless positions where its expression is muffled or distorted. That is the human predicament. To be fully human is to recognize this predicament and to take advantage of our calmer, more detached moments to reflect on the moral components of our social sentiments so that we might find our way out of it.

Families

The child, as Richard Shweder has put it, is an intuitive moralist.[1] His tendency to moralize comes from his desire to socialize, but moralizing does not reflect simply a desire to please; were that the case, we would act only in ways that made us popular and praise the actions of others only if they pleased us. The human passion to moralize—that is, to judge the actions and motives of others as worthy or unworthy—reflects something deeper in our nature than just a penchant for approval, important as that is. If it is true that we are *intuitive* moralists, we must spontaneously organize our judgments into something approximating moral categories.

That we do this is evident from the fact that, beginning at an early age, children can tell the difference between moral and nonmoral issues. That is to say, when asked whether it is all right to do something even if there is no rule against it, children draw distinctions between actions that are always wrong (for example, lying, stealing, and unprovoked hitting) and things that are wrong only when there are rules against it (for example, boys entering the girl's bathroom, not going to school every day, or staring at someone while they undress.)[2] Moreover, there are some things that young children regard as wrong whether they are middle-class residents of Hyde Park, Illinois, or Hindus living in the Indian village of Bhubaneswar. These include breaking a promise, stealing flowers, kicking a harmless animal, and destroying another's property.*

---

*Shweder, Mahapatra, and Miller, 1987:61. These findings bear on the difficult question

141

In ways that we do not fully understand, nature has prepared us for making distinctions and organizing judgments. What we learn from our interaction with families and friends builds on that prepared ground, developing, shaping, modifying, or in some cases deforming it, but never quite supplanting it. Many accounts of our moral sense begin with the process of learning, as if morality were wholly a product of learning, the result of parents teaching children moral rules that the parents had already learned. Few developmental psychologists believe this anymore, but some readers may; indeed, in talking with other parents about their children's faults, I am struck by how often—indeed, how nearly universally—these adults ask, rhetorically if not sincerely, what it is that "they did wrong." Modern scholars would advise parents not to take full blame for their children's failures or full credit for their successes; the child brings more than most parents know to this relationship, as would be evident if the parents listened to children, even very young ones, talking with one another about their own behavior. Much of this conversation is a series of exchanges about how things should be judged—is this fair or unfair, right or wrong?—and these judgments are based as much on moral standards the children are evolving as on moral rules the parents have inculcated.

Parents' inclination to explain their children's moral qualities exclusively by reference to how they were trained reflects how deeply we all have fallen under the spell of psychoanalysis and the more extreme forms of behavioral psychology. Sigmund Freud taught us to believe that morality was rooted in the feelings of guilt we acquired from hav-

---

of what rules of conduct are universally thought to be morally binding—that is, unalterably obligatory for all persons similarly situated, whether or not there is a law requiring the action—and what rules are recognized to be merely conventional. The most important recent research on this has been done by Richard Shweder at the University of Chicago and Elliot Turiel at the University of California, Berkeley. They both find that some rules are universally held to be morally binding, but differ over whether people generally recognize the difference between a moral and a conventional rule and over whether the two kinds of rules are learned in different ways. Shweder and his colleagues argue that in many cultures people give moral status to rules of dress, food, and ritual that in the United States, with its individualistic culture, are regarded as conventions (ibid.). Elliot Turiel and his colleagues disagree, arguing that properly designed studies reveal a clear understanding of the difference between what is moral and what is conventional in Korea, Nigeria, and Indonesia (Turiel, Killen, and Helwig, 1987). For my purposes, the disagreements between the two groups are much less important than their agreement. What both find to be morally binding everywhere are those rules governing the fundamental conflicts of everyday, intimate life—keeping promises, respecting property, acting fairly, and avoiding unprovoked assaults—that have been the subject of earlier chapters in this book.

ing had our sexual and aggressive instincts repressed and turned back on ourselves by the commands of civilization.[3] To him, we become moral by thwarting our strongest drives. B. F. Skinner taught us to believe that "morality" was a conditioned response, no different from any other behavior learned by adjusting what we did to the consequences of doing it. To him, we become "moral" in the same way that we learn to drive a car.[4] To Freud, human nature was antisocial and aggressive; to Skinner, it was neutral and malleable. To Freud, the key learning experience was the management of the oedipal drive; to Skinner, it was one's adaptation to rewards and penalties. To Freud, morality was what civilization required and enforced; to Skinner, "morality" (he did not think the word meant anything important) was a conditioned response to certain reinforcers that were accompanied by someone shouting "Good!" or "Bad!" Different as these two views were in so many respects, they were alike in one central regard: neither assigned any positive role to the child and neither thought of morality as involving a disinterested capacity to judge others. To both, morality was impressed on the child by society. For all the difference it made, people might as well have been Labrador retrievers.

It is easy to make either of two mistakes: to suppose that the child is a blank slate or to think he is a miniature adult. While some people ignore the child's proclivity to moralize and strain to find rules to cover every eventuality, others take that proclivity to be so deserving of respect as to require nothing of the parents than to help the child discover his naturally good self. Though the human infant is a remarkably resilient creature, protected by redundant systems from many kinds of misfortune, it is vulnerable to the excesses of both rule-obsessed and laissez-faire parents.

Just how vulnerable is not clear, however. Though the sillier forms of Freudian or behavioral child psychology may have lost their appeal, most of us still think that the family makes the child. As the twig is bent, so grows the tree, and we fathers and mothers are the twig benders. But behavioral geneticists have been amassing information from studies of identical twins reared apart and of children raised in adoptive families that casts doubt on just how much of a difference the family makes in forming the child's character. The evidence reviewed in the preceding chapter might be summarized, with only slight exaggeration, in this way: for many intellectual aptitudes and personality traits, children growing up in the same family turn out to be very different—so different, indeed, that one must wonder whether parents make any difference at all.

They do make a difference, but in a far more complex way than once was thought. How parents raise their children probably does not determine the broad dimensions of the latter's personality: children turn out to be extroverted or introverted, neurotic or stable, with little regard for how they were raised.[5] But child rearing may well affect how likely they are to act aggressively toward others or to flout flagrantly or defiantly the essential rules of everyday life.[6] Personality may not be produced by parental training, but some aspects of morality—for example, the understanding of moral rules that shape the boundaries within which the moral sense operates—will be. That training, however, should not be thought of simply as the general child-rearing style of the mother and father. We often characterize parents as being warm or cold, tolerant or rule-oriented, and suppose that these global qualities have an equal effect on all their children. But they don't. The shared family environment—the aspects of family life that affect all the children—may be far less important than the particular and unique experiences of each child within the family, what scientists call, somewhat clumsily, the nonshared environment.

These two hints from recent research—that families may have an effect more on morality than on personality and that this effect may involve differences in the way individual children are treated—are quite consistent with the view that children are intuitive moralists. An intuitive moralist will always be comparing how he is treated with how his brother or sister is treated, judging the treatment as fair or unfair and reacting accordingly. Now, it is impossible—literally impossible—for parents to treat two children exactly alike (with the possible exception of two identical twins). Even if the children are of the same sex, they will usually differ in age and almost certainly in temperament, intelligence, and aptitude. It would be ludicrous to speak to a one-year-old as one speaks to a three-year-old, and it would be pointless to treat a child gifted at reading the same as one treats a child who hates reading and is not very good at it but is skilled at assembling puzzles or throwing a ball. And though we may wish to give equal attention to both a cuddly, obedient child and a restless, obstinate one, we know that we cannot. Every parent of more than one child is acutely aware of these differences and of the difficulty (and sometimes the heartbreak) of trying to manage them. Each child is observing and learning from these differences, with the result that some important part of his character is being formed by the judgments he makes about the differences he experiences.[7]

What this means for how the child will turn out is not well understood. Psychologists have spent more time studying families "as a whole" than the particular experiences of individual children within families, and they have relied more on "objective" observations of parent-child interactions than on the subjective reactions of the participants in those interactions. Indeed, it may be that how the child turns out is inherently indeterminate (that is, unpredictable) because we shall never be able to observe, much less assess, the net effect of individual experiences and individual reactions to them. Novelists may do a better job of explaining character formation than social scientists.

Bonding

But social scientists have made some headway. The single most important discovery has been the importance to the child of having a strong and affectionate bond to the parents, especially to the mother. John Bowlby's pioneering accounts of the importance of a secure attachment were followed by studies, many done by Mary Ainsworth and her students, designed to measure that bond and estimate the effects of its strength or weakness.[8] There is some controversy over how this measurement is done and what the measure implies, but relatively little over the importance of what is being measured—the mother-child bond.*

Obviously both the mother and the baby might influence how strongly and securely the two are attached. A fussy, irritable baby might elicit less warmth from the mother; a distracted, insensitive mother might prevent even a cuddly baby from becoming bonded.

---

*Attachment is usually measured by the Strange Situation test: A toddler playing in an unfamiliar room is repeatedly separated for a few minutes from his mother and then reunited. Sometimes a stranger is present, sometimes not. Observers note how the child reacts to his mother upon reunion, classifying him into one of three (sometimes four) main groups: *attached* children seek out the mother's company and, after a friendly reunion, resume playing; *avoidant* children resist a reunion; *resistant* children are ambivalent about the reunion, seeking out the mother but displaying anger and distress. (A fourth possible group, *disorganized* children, engage in chaotic, disoriented behavior.) The chief difficulty with the Strange Situation test is that it produces somewhat different results in different cultures, possibly because children in those places become attached to their mothers in ways other than what is common in the United States and possibly because innate differences in infant temperament cause attached children to react differently to separation (Lamb et al., 1985: ch. 11).

THE MORAL SENSE

By the same token, a caring mother might lead even a fussy baby to feel secure, while a cuddly baby might lead even a cold mother into a strong bond. The debate among psychologists over the relative importance of maternal care and infant temperament is a spirited one, with no consensus yet in sight.*

There is less disagreement about the larger implications of attachment. Whether wholly the result of maternal behavior or partially the consequence of infant temperament, a strong early bond—the kind that produces a secure child—seems to be associated with a strong bond several years later and to produce more sociable behavior.[9] Securely attached children are more self-reliant, curious, and involved, and they get along better with playmates than their less securely attached comrades.[10] By contrast, children who at age one year were insecurely attached turned out, three or four years later, to be overrepresented among children who had behavior problems in school.[11] The children with the weakest bonds to their parents—those who had been the victims of child abuse—tended either to avoid people or to react to the distress of others with fear, anger, or hostility.[12] Of special importance is the fact that securely attached children show greater empathy than do avoidant children, probably because, having experienced empathy themselves, they have a greater capacity to display it toward others.† Though the distribution of

---

*Scholars that argue for the importance of temperament include Jerome Kagan (1982), Jay Belsky (Belsky and Rovine, 1987; Fish and Belsky, 1991), Susan Crockenberg (1986), and H. H. Goldsmith and Jennifer Alansky (1987). This view is hotly disputed by L. Alan Sroufe (1983, 1985), among others. As with most examples of the debate over nature versus nurture, there is a tendency of both sides to write as if only one or the other factor were important and to cite evidence most supportive of the preferred position. In their calmer moments, most of the protagonists understand that in all likelihood both factors are at work. Even Sroufe, the most adamant defender of pure attachment theory, after writing that "there is *no* evidence that observed differences at or near birth . . . predict later behavior" concedes on the next page that infants "probably do differ in temperament, and such differences probably influence certain aspects of behavior" (Sroufe, 1983:70–71). As we have seen, twin studies show that there are very large, heritable differences in temperament. It would be astonishing if none of these affected the child-mother bond.

†Sroufe, 1983:63. Attachment does not inoculate children against all problems nor does its absence invariably put them at risk, in part because parents sometimes change how they treat their children and in part because other forces are at work. Despite their firm belief in the power of attachment, Sroufe and his colleagues showed that the peer competence and emotional health of at-risk children who were in the early grammar school grades were better predicted by general home conditions three years earlier than by how they had performed in the Strange Situation Test (Sroufe, Egeland, and Kreutzer, 1990).

Families

attachment patterns among infants differs across cultures, the positive relationship between secure attachment and sociable behavior
seems universal.[13]

All this may strike the reader as the rediscovery of the obvious:
babies who are loved and attended to do better than those who are
unloved or ignored. But it is hardly obvious. Consider the alternative
theory: if you are always picking up, caring for, or otherwise responding to the baby, it will become spoiled, dependent, and whiny. Some
people believe that if you reward behavior it will be repeated, and
infer from this general truth the particular claim that if you pick up
a crying baby, it will always cry; if you play with a fussy baby, it will
always fuss. Not so. The natural sociability of the child inclines it to
acquire greater autonomy and confidence, not greater dependence
and manipulativeness, when its desire for attachment is met with an
equivalent response from its parent.

This is the great paradox of attachment: bonding will occur even
when bonding is not rewarded with food; bonding, once it has occurred, will persist despite punishment; and bonded children will
become more independent, not more dependent. Many readers will
recall Harry Harlow's famous experiments with rhesus monkeys in
which he showed that infants would bond to terry-cloth dolls as well
as to their own mothers.[14] Most readers will remember stories of
abused children who became more, not less, attached to their parents. Those stories are confirmed by a great deal of evidence.[15] It is
clear from these facts that bonding is driven by powerful biological
forces and is not simply the result of a greedy organism doing whatever will enable it to get fed.

And bonding may have powerful biological consequences as well.
It is possible that highly nurturant mothers who play with and talk
to their babies a great deal during the first few weeks of life may
actually be altering their child's central nervous system. We know
that rats handled during infancy experience changes in the structure
and even the size of their brains, changes that last a lifetime.[16] We
cannot be certain that this happens with human infants, but we do
know that touching and handling very low birth weight, premature
infants increases the rate at which they gain weight, improves their
alertness, and increases their activity. In one study, stimulated babies
gained half again as much weight as did a control group of similar,
but unstimulated ones, even though both groups ate the same
amount of food.[17] These changes in weight and activity may well

have been accompanied by changes in brain structure or neural systems. The human is born with many more brain cells than survive; the ones that are preserved are, in all probability, the ones that are used.*

The relationship between sociability and morality should, by now, be evident. One would assume, therefore, that securely attached children, as they grow older, will develop a moral sense more easily than will be the case for insecurely attached ones. Unfortunately, no one has followed children from birth to adulthood to find out how important early bonding is to later morality. But the assumption is consistent with what little we know about the tendency of children with strong bonds to their mothers to be concerned about and try to help other children in distress.

Let us be clear about what is going on here. It is probably not the case that a secure child simply acquires a moral sense. More likely, secure children are confident and easy to be with, and so they elicit confidence-building and friendly reactions from others. Insecure children handle their frustrated instinct for bonding by exaggerated behavior, displaying either anger and aloofness or an off-putting demand for attention. Other people find these to be unattractive qualities, and so treat the child warily, coldly, or inconsistently. This reaction confirms the child's view of the world—that it is unfriendly, cold, or undependable—and this confirmation inclines the child to act in what it takes to be a rational way: by ignoring, attacking, or manipulating others.[18]

Training

As the parent of every two-year-old child knows, bonding is not enough. For the child's own safety and the parent's peace of mind, rules must be stated and enforced. The parent must decide which actions of the child will be rewarded and which punished, what constitutes an appropriate reward or penalty, and how consistently the parental reaction will follow upon the child's actions. At this point, the insights of behavioral psychologists become especially important.

---

*Gary Kraemer (1992) offers some intriguing speculations on the psychobiological basis of attachment. A similar theory is presented by Mary Carlson, Felton Earls, and Richard D. Todd (1988).

Families

Those insights are a refined version of common sense. Most rewarded behaviors are repeated, particularly if the rewards are infallibly and consistently delivered. But if the rewards are big enough and the effort to get them modest enough, even occasional rewards will produce repetitive behavior. Suppose that you walked by a coin-operated telephone every day. Three times in one month you found a quarter in it. It is likely that you will start looking in the phone every day for many days, even if you don't find a quarter most of the time. If you were to find ten dollars once every year, you would probably go out of your way to inspect it daily. (That is one reason people operate slot machines in casinos.) Much the same thing is true of penalties.

A parent wants the child to follow certain rules. Small rewards, such as compliments, or small penalties, such as rebukes, tend to lead to rule following, provided these reinforcements are consistently given. But suppose the child really wants something, such as candy on a shopping trip or a chance to watch television when at home, that the mother thinks is inappropriate. Suppose she usually ignores the request, while occasionally saying yes and occasionally slapping the child for pestering her. The child cannot learn a rule from this, other than that he has been entered in a lottery in which he sometimes wins big (free candy), sometimes loses (the slap), but usually is ignored. The best strategy for playing this lottery is to nag his mother all of the time. Not only is the child not learning the rule the mother wants him to learn (that there is a right and wrong time for eating candy or watching television—in short, that self-control is desirable), but several other bad things will happen as well. The mother will think, wrongly, that she has an out-of-control child; in fact, she has failed to understand the different effects that consistent and inconsistent responses have on behavior. An observer may think, wrongly, that the slaps have caused defiant behavior; in fact, it is the erratic use of either rewards or penalties, and not the particular reinforcement used, that has caused the misconduct. Or the observer may conclude, wrongly, that the child should get to eat candy more often because a little candy never hurt anybody; in fact, the issue is not how much candy a child eats, but whether the child is learning to control his appetites.

Diana Baumrind at the University of California at Berkeley has shown that neither love alone nor rules alone are sufficient for inculcating good behavior. By closely observing children at play and dealing with their parents, she was able to sort out the children's manner of play and link it with the parents' child-rearing practices and then show how those practices affected children's behavior several years later.

Parents who were cold and aloof but who controlled their children closely (what she called the "authoritarian mode") had children who tended to be withdrawn and passive. Parents who were warm but lax in enforcing rules (what she called the "permissive mode") had children who tended to lack self-control; they were self-indulgent or spoiled. If the parents were both warm and very controlling (what she called the "authoritative mode"), the children were most likely to be sociable, cooperative, and self-reliant, especially if the authoritative mode was accompanied by careful explanations of the reasons for various rules.[19] Baumrind's families were almost all upper middle class and well educated, but much the same pattern has been observed among more ordinary children.[20] Moreover, there is abundant support for the view that a warm and affectionate bond combined with consistent and judicious discipline is found among families with few, if any, delinquent children, while the opposite familial ethos—parental neglect or coldness coupled with inconsistent and unjustifiably harsh discipline—is a characteristic of families with seriously delinquent offspring.[21]

All this may sound quite sensible, even commonplace, to contemporary Americans. But not long ago child psychologists were warning us about the harmful effects of discipline, some even suggesting that "undemocratic" families would produce authoritarian children.[22] Naive Freudians feared that restraints would impede psychosexual development or create dependent, unassertive adults. But the child is not a robot. An obedient child does not automatically become a conformist adult, because the child is an active, evaluating partner in the process of growing up. He imparts meaning to the behavior of others, an ability that increases with age. Children soon learn to tell the difference between parents who care for them, whatever rule they enforce, and parents who either regard them as a nuisance to be avoided or an object to be exploited.[23] The notion that one cannot become an independent, self-assertive adult unless one was allowed to be an independent, self-assertive child is an intellectual fad that careful research has all but destroyed.

Much of what a child learns about the moral status and practical consequences of behavior is not "learned" in any formal sense at all.

That is, he does not come by all of these beliefs and standards because his own behavior has been rewarded or punished by his parents; he acquires some of them simply by observing the behavior of others. Children imitate what they see others doing. This process has been called observational learning by the psychologists, such as Albert Bandura, who pioneered in its study.[24] As we saw in the preceding chapter, rudimentary forms of imitation may begin as early as the first few weeks of life; as they grow older, children develop the ability and inclination to imitate increasingly complex activities. Because of that ability, many people worry that watching violent television programs will make children behave violently.[25] These worries are often exaggerated, because they fail to take into account both the child's ability, as it ages, to distinguish between fantasy and reality and its awareness that what happens to Wile E. Coyote in a cartoon or to Arnold Schwarzenegger in a motion picture is different from what happens to real people in real life. Observational learning almost surely has its greatest effect in real life, not in fantasy life. Moreover, we don't know how long the effects of single observations last (most experiments test the effects over very short periods of time) or how important it is that the person whose behavior is imitated be a parent, a sibling, or a close friend as opposed to a casual acquaintance or a movie hero.[26] Finally, social-learning theorists tend to neglect the extent to which a child is biologically prepared to imitate some actions more than others.

But even allowing for these uncertainties, there can be little doubt that we learn a lot about how we ought to behave from watching others, especially others to whom we are strongly attached. Our tendency to imitate has probably been very important for the survival of the species. To see why, imagine that human beings learned only what they were formally taught. To inculcate any habit or rule, a parent would have to reward the right behavior and punish the wrong one when each appeared. This would be an immensely difficult and time-consuming task; it is hard to imagine mankind surviving for tens of thousands of years if parents had to have the skill, persistence, and good luck sufficient to teach every rule of right conduct the same way they might teach the multiplication tables. Doing the right thing, practically and morally, is so important for survival that these tendencies must be rapidly acquired, and that can only happen if children are biologically disposed to imitate behavior and learn the underlying rules of that behavior directly, by observation, and without formal instruction or the receipt of rewards and penalties.[27]

Rights versus Duties

Some people argue that the balance we Westerners (or we Americans) have struck between nurturance and control is not the only, and perhaps not the best, strategy for developing in children a strong moral sense. These critics point out that enforcing and explaining rules is a method of child rearing geared to producing independent, self-reliant adults, each equipped with an internal compass that will ensure a reasonable degree of self-control and a principled commitment to fairness. That may be appropriate for a competitive, individualistic culture such as our own. But there is another kind of culture for which a different style of child rearing is appropriate, and this alternative may be preferable.

The other kind of culture is one that emphasizes the group over the individual, obligations over rights, and helping over fairness. Some liberal critics of American society find examples of such cultures among smaller, more primitive societies (the San of the Kalahari are a favorite example), while some conservative critics take Japan as their alternative. Both sets of critics agree in describing these other cultures as being much more child-centered and family-oriented than ours, but whereas liberal critics point to mutual aid as the chief benefit, conservative ones point to low crime rates and economic competitiveness as the happy result.

There is no doubt that in some places the infant remains in closer contact with its mother for longer periods of time and with less attention to discipline or control than is the case in this country. Melvin Konner has remarked on how different infant-care arrangements are across cultures and how little effect on psychological well-being these differences seem to have.[28] A !Kung San baby is continuously in its mother's company, is nursed by her on demand for up to four years, and is not the object of much toilet training. By the standards of American followers of Dr. Spock, the !Kung baby is hopelessly spoiled. By contrast, in the Israeli kibbutz babies sleep in an infant house and, though frequently visited by their parents, they soon enter into a planned course of training, schooling, and chores based on communal principles. By the standards of the !Kung, the kibbutz child seems cruelly abandoned. Some Russian infants are swaddled, and Navajo babies are bound onto cradleboards. In rural Guatemala infants stay close to their mothers but in darkened huts where there is not much talking. Japanese mothers sleep with their babies, apart from their husbands; American mothers sleep with their husbands, apart from their babies. Japanese infants are greatly indulged; the orderly social discipline that so impresses American visitors does not begin until the child is considerably along in years, much older than are American children when they experience similar rules.

Despite these differences, the majority of babies in all cultures where tests have been done seem securely attached to their mothers.[29] Infant sociability and maternal affection are such universally powerful forces that, although local cultures may modify infant-mother relations, the consequences of those differences for human bonding seem rather small. If culture were the all-powerful source of human character that some imagine it to be, then cultural differences would cause bonding differences to a greater extent than seems to be the case. Of course, it is always possible that cultural effects appear much later, after bonding has occurred and in spite of an apparent similarity in the degree of attachment. I am not aware of any studies that systematically test that possibility. One bit of negative evidence is worth pondering, however. Though infants in Japan and Israeli kibbutzim experience radically different mother-children relations, the rates at which Japanese and Israeli become delinquent or enter into criminal careers are similar, and almost equally low.

But though bonding can occur under a variety of circumstances, and though almost all children acquire a moral sense, the expression of that sense may differ depending on the child's temperament and how it is raised. That, of course, is what critics of American child-rearing practices have in mind when they point to the more nurturant and communal aspects of family life in other societies. In many primitive cultures, children help raise other children more than is the case here, and so a sense of mutual obligation may be heightened by the fact of mutual dependency. In Japan the child is taught interdependence (*amae*) rather than independence. Though indulged as an infant, the indulgence is designed to so strengthen the mother-child bond that the child will attach a very high value to pleasing her and, through her, the family. Among the ways the child expresses that value is to honor the father, cooperate with others, and avoid bringing shame on the family. When Japanese parents or teachers wish to correct children, they often resort to ridicule.[30] The fear of shame and the need for approval is reinforced by these means, although the inclination toward introversion, inhibition, and wariness probably reflects in part some inborn tendencies that lend themselves to (and are magnified by) inhibition-promoting child-rearing practices.[31]

These differences in temperament and child-rearing almost surely make a difference in what components of the moral sense receive greatest emphasis. But what kind of difference? On this matter, the closest students of Japan are by no means in agreement. George De Vos argues that the Japanese child is made so dependent on the family and the approval of its mother that it learns to internalize its aggressive impulses, submerge its individuality, and develop a keen sensitivity to insults or slights.[32] Robert Smith does not deny De Vos's account of child rearing, but claims that Japanese values still allow a substantial scope for individuality provided it does not threaten group cohesion. The Japanese adult is not the product of an inordinate sense of guilt and dependency, but of a finely honed desire for self-control.[33]

Where authorities differ, amateurs are wise to move cautiously. Let me suggest this as a tentative argument. We need not settle the argument between guilt and self-command as the source of a distinctive national character, much less the deeper issue (to which neither De Vos nor Smith speaks), namely, the existence of a heritable tendency toward group affiliation. It is enough to suggest that wherever children learn mutual dependency and family obligation, they are learning to give highest priority to self-control and the sense of duty. When, as in the United States and other societies with a more individualistic and democratic family culture, children learn independence and self-expression, they are learning to give highest priority to sympathy and a sense of fair play. The need to take care of each other and to help raise children requires of a child that he or she subordinate a desire for fun to the requirements of helping; in short, they require self-control. When the family is the primary source of social approval and ridicule is used to control misconduct, the fear of being shamed leads to a strong sense of honor. When, by contrast, the children from an early age are encouraged to engage in play with others outside the family, to develop their own personalities, and to make their own decisions, they will acquire a strong stake in peer-defined and peer-enforced rules of fairness (else the play will quickly get out of hand) and will greatly value the good opinion of peers and so come to be sensitive to the moods of others.

If this argument is true, it has some rather large implications. A willingness to extend to other people—especially to people who are very different from oneself—the same fundamental respect one extends to friends requires that one believe that people, as people, are entitled to understanding and fair play. This means that in the more individualistic child-rearing cultures, where sympathy and fairness are dominant concerns, one will find the greatest deference to universalistic standards of justice. These standards will be the enemies of familial and neighborhood control: people who believe that there are universal rules based on equal respect will also believe that they are entitled to be autonomous, independent individuals who have the right to do as they wish so long as it does not hurt anyone else.

On the other hand, a preference for preserving the honor of the family, avoiding shame, and meeting obligations is consistent with the view that people are not individuals but members of distinct social units—kinship systems, local communities, racial and ethnic groups—that are as inward-looking and group-serving as one's own. In Japan, child-rearing patterns and cultural patterns combine to limit personal loyalty to the immediate group. Not only obligation but even communication with persons outside the family or the work group is much more limited than what Americans are accustomed to. Karl Zinsmeister reports that elderly Japanese are only half as likely as their American counterparts to have daily conversations with their neighbors.[34] Within the core group—the family and the workplace—cooperation and etiquette are paramount; outside that group, the devil can take the hindmost.

Honor is not a universalistic standard but a particular one; people valuing it will value it even at the expense of others, with no sense that some rule has been violated. Honor and self-control can even be seen as a mark of superiority; those displaying it are civilized, those lacking it, barbarians. In chapter 9 I look at some possible explanations for the rise of individualistic and communal emphases in the moral sense.

Culture, of course, is a compound of ancient lore, religious belief, customary practice, and economic necessity. More communal or group-oriented child-rearing techniques, whatever the cultural endorsement they receive, may grow out of the family's need for survival. When from an early age !Kung children care for one another and take on adult chores, it is in part because any other arrangement would spell disaster for a family living a subsistence life in a harsh environment. There are no funds with which to hire baby-sitters or pay day-care fees and no television sets to provide passive amusement for restless children.

What this may mean is suggested by a remarkable study of the impact of economic adversity on American families. Glen Elder examined the lives of children whose families had been hit by the Great Depression. Almost everybody was affected by this calamity, but some suffered more than others. He compared how adolescent children behaved in families that were the most deprived (their incomes fell by more than 35 percent) with those that were the least deprived (their incomes fell by less). In both social classes, but particularly in the better-off one, children in the hardest-hit families began playing adult roles—the girls taking on domestic chores, the boys seeking paid work—to a much greater extent than was true of families that were less hard hit. As a result of having assumed, at an early age, adult responsibilities, these teenagers, and especially the boys, were later rated by their teachers as having grown up faster, become more self-reliant, and learned better to control their impulsiveness than was the case of the children from the least disadvantaged families. When they became adults, they were more family-centered.* Urie Bronfenbrenner, the child psychologist, summarized Elder's discovery with a phrase from Shakespeare's As You Like It: "sweet are the uses of adversity."[35]

Hardly anyone favors adversity as a social policy, however much it may encourage self-control and a sense of duty. But it is worth recognizing that a free lunch is no more available in moral development than it is in economic policy. Prosperity is the ally of freedom, and among the consequences of freedom are the opportunities people acquire to express themselves. For better or for worse, enhanced freedom and prosperity permit young people to postpone for a long time—in contemporary America, well into their twenties—the need to accept adult responsibilities.

*Elder, 1974. Other data examined by Elder and R. C. Rockwell suggest that adversity had this beneficial effect only on boys who were adolescents during the depression; those who were children when disaster struck did not benefit from the experience, presumably because they were too young to assume those adult roles that enhanced moral development (Elder and Rockwell, 1978). But Elder's families lived in cities; had they lived on farms where even young children can assume some adult duties, the results might have been different.

Thus far I have been writing about "normal" family experiences; that is, about how most children experience their familial world, given their innate desire to make sense of it and their inescapable tendency to judge it. There are differences among what most children experience, differences that, in conjunction with their temperaments, may incline them to assign a slightly higher value to self-control, or duty, or sympathy. These small individual differences might make a large collective difference in how people treat strangers and compatriots or how orderly they are in school. But so long as the child's evolving moral sense is met by a compatible parental response—so long, that is, as its desire for affection is met by affection and its openness to learning is met by teaching that is consistent and principled—then the fundamental moralizing instincts of the child will flourish, and differences among children will be relatively modest.

Troubled Families

But for some children, the child's desire to make sense of his world is met by parental behavior that is senseless: his need for affection is spurned, his responsiveness to rewards is met by inconsistent rewards, and his desire for reasons is greeted by silence or inexplicable reasons. In these conditions, the child's moral sense is placed at risk. The criminological literature is filled with studies that portray the potentially harmful effects of cold, broken, erratic, and discordant family lives.[36] I say "potentially harmful" because many of these studies do not investigate the child's own contribution to these outcomes in those cases where it is innately resistant to learning, unresponsive to affection, or lacking in the capacity for conscience or self-control.

There is no mystery here; almost everybody can describe, without benefit of having studied the matter, the characteristics of a bad family. What deserves comment is not that such families exist but that they are so rare. Suppose that families were machines assembled without much instruction by amateurs, often illiterate ones, out of whatever materials happened to be handy. Suppose that we knew what we wanted the machines to produce—people with a decent moral sense and a willingness to act on that sense most of the time. What fraction of these machines would we expect to malfunction and produce people with no moral sense and little proclivity to act on whatever sense they had? A quarter? A third? Most of them? In fact, the proportion that turn out to be real lemons is astonishingly small: only about 6 percent of teenage boys and a much smaller fraction of girls growing up in families get involved in serious and protracted criminality.[37] Perhaps a few percent more get involved but don't get caught. But even making generous allowances for hidden criminality, the fraction of children who fail morally is probably far smaller than the fraction of automobiles that fail mechanically. Part of the reason, of course, is that society doesn't leave matters entirely in familial hands; it has self-protection and control mechanisms—teachers, bosses, and police officers. But part of the reason is that family processes do not much depend on invention, self-discovery, written instructions, or educated people; they depend on instincts, mutual attraction, and organic relationships.

These instincts were forged by millennia of natural selection. Parents that would not care for the offspring had few surviving offspring; parents that cared badly for them did not do much better. What nature was selecting for, of course, was not simply skill at reproduction, but skill at parenting. Natural selection is an imperfect force, and so some incompetent or uncaring parents will produce children who survive and perpetuate their unhappy legacy. But the selection process has been powerful enough to produce one indisputable outcome: the family is a universal human institution.

In virtually every society into which historians or anthropologists have inquired, one finds people living together on the basis of kinship ties and having responsibility for raising children. The kinship ties invariably imply restrictions on who has sexual access to whom; the child-care responsibilities invariably imply both economic and noneconomic obligations.[38] And in virtually every society, the family is defined by marriage; that is, by a publicly announced contract that makes legitimate the sexual union of a man and a woman. Even in societies where men and women have relatively unrestricted sexual access to one another beginning at an early age, marriage is still the basis for family formation. It is desired by the partners and expected by society.[39] Marriage, is short, is not simply a way of legitimizing sex, and so it cannot be dispensed with just because sexual activity need not be made legitimate. Marriage exists because people must take responsibility for child care and assume economic obligations. Marriage, and thus the family that it defines, is a commitment.

The conditions under which child care occurs have changed in modern times. At one time and in many places, children were valuable. Having more children in order to gather food, herd or hunt animals, care for elderly parents, and maintain dynastic claims made sense. Families were large. Today in most industrialized parts of the world children make little economic or dynastic sense. Moreover, the cost of raising them has gone up. Children still need parents, but parents don't need children. Happily, the predispositions to attachment for which evolution has selected are so powerful as to operate even in the absence of economic incentive.

But powerful as they are, the expression of these instincts has been modified by contemporary circumstances. When children have less economic value, then, at the margin, fewer children will be produced, marriage (and childbearing) will be postponed, and more marriages will end in divorce. And those children who are produced will be raised, at the margin, in ways that reflect their higher opportunity cost. Some will be neglected and others will be cared for in ways that minimize the parental cost in personal freedom, extra income, or career opportunities. In the United States, the average white parents spend ten hours per week less time with their children than they did in 1960; the decline in parental investment in children has been even greater for black parents.[40]

This raises the explosive question of nonparental child care, or, as it is phrased in the United States, the day-care debate. It is all but impossible to write dispassionately about this issue and still be taken seriously, because so many participants are so charged with personal emotion and political ideology that any conclusion will be rejected out of hand by one group of partisans or the other. Moreover, the evidence on the enduring effects of nonparental care on the moral development of the child is scanty, and much of what exists is inconsistent or inconclusive. This inconsistency is hardly surprising, since "nonparental care" includes everything from children raised by grandmothers or next-door neighbors to those raised in profit-oriented kiddie corrals, with university-based day-care centers somewhere in between. In addition, the child brings a personality to day care just as he brings it to his own family; separating out what the child contributes to moral development from what professional caregivers contribute is no easy matter.

The early view of most developmental psychologists was that day care (here defined as infant care in a center or group facility) had no adverse effects on the child's attachment to the mother or later social development.[41] The conclusion fit well with the belief that women in general and mothers in particular had been unreasonably excluded from the workplace. Beginning in the mid-1980s, however, some warnings were heard. One of these came from a scholar, Jay Belsky at Pennsylvania State University, who had changed his mind. Once having said that there was no harm in day care, he now said that there may be some harm under some circumstances. In a widely reported 1988 article, he reviewed all of the studies measuring the effect of nonmaternal care on attachment and social development and concluded that, subject to many caveats, "entry into [day] care in the first year of life for 20 hours or more per week is a 'risk factor' for the development of insecure attachment in infancy and heightened aggressiveness, noncompliance, and withdrawal in the preschool and early school years."[42] By "risk factor" he meant that the child in day care was somewhat more likely to experience these adverse outcomes than a similar child under parental care, especially if the day care was not of high quality.

What had changed between 1978 and 1988? One thing was the simple accumulation of evidence. Another was the shift in research focus away from high-quality, often university-based day-care centers to more common, and often lower-quality, centers. But more or better evidence did not prevent a firestorm from descending on Belsky's head. Some critics attacked him politically, while others argued with him on scientific grounds: the evidence is less clear than he suggested, the experience of children in cultures where nonparental care is common is good, and whatever ill effects exist (if any) do not last.[43]

Sorting out these competing claims is difficult. One argument is indisputable: the evidence is inconsistent. But inconsistent evidence should not be interpreted as meaning "no cause for concern"; rather, it means that there is reason to believe that under some circumstances—circumstances not yet well understood—day care in the first year is associated with impaired social development, and not just for children in poor day-care centers. But even if it were true that the only problems were with low-quality day care, this is not a reassuring finding, because it is impossible as a practical matter to prevent low-quality providers from operating; indeed, the more common day care becomes, the higher the probability that any given provider will be of low quality.* The view that the harmful effects, if any, of day care do not persist cannot be sustained, because there have been scarcely any long-term studies of child development in which the quality of infant care has been carefully assessed.

That children can be raised effectively by people other than their parents in certain cultures is almost surely correct. As we have already seen, there is an extraordinary variety in infant-care arrangements around the world. Fathers, aunts, grandmothers, brothers and sisters, and even more distant kin can play very large roles in child rearing, with no obvious ill effect. But it is hard to know what to make of this variety, for the cultural understandings and economic conditions that make group care possible in some places cannot be exported to countries with very different understandings and conditions. A good example are the problems, to be discussed in chapter 8, experienced by single, teenage mothers in American cities. Teenage American women often do not make very good mothers. But around the world millions of teenage women become mothers and raise perfectly splendid children. The difference is the context in which a teenage woman becomes pregnant. Where the teenager is married, lives in an extended family, and is part of a supportive village or tribal network, her youth probably makes little difference. Put the same teenager alone in a public housing project with no husband, few kin, and a hostile neighborhood environment, and the results will be quite different. So also with nonparental care of children: what works in a communal culture may not work at all in a radically individualistic one, and what works in an individualistic culture for middle-class children embedded in a rich array of supportive services may not work for lower-class children lacking such services.†

The importance of the family will remain beyond dispute no matter how the debate on day care turns out. Not even the scholars most convinced by the studies that claim to find no harmful effects in group care doubt that nurturant and controlling families are important to the well-being of the child.

---

*The reasons why organizations producing low-visibility, hard-to-measure services (such as policing, schooling, or day care) are likely to have major quality-control problems are set forth in my book *Bureaucracy* (Wilson, 1989).

†If interpretations of the studies on day care are controversial, those on the effects of maternal employment are even more so. To see how different scholars come to different conclusions from the same facts, contrast the study by Jay Belsky and David Eggebeen (1991) with that by Kathleen McCartney and Saul Rosenthal (1991).

Yet families shape our lives far beyond the years of nurturance and training. We live in families during our youth, but are part of families forever. Families are more than nurseries, and growing up involves more than getting into bigger clothing sizes. The family is not simply a nest, it is a polity—an arena in which conflicts occur and must be managed. Family members love and quarrel, share and sulk, please and disappoint. Members who are lovable at one stage in their lives are hard to love at others; activities that are enjoyable on some occasions are a bore or a burden at others; hopes that are occasionally realized compete with those that are frequently dashed. A woman who at one time is an indulgent mother may later become a medical burden, a brother whose teasing reduces his young sister to tears may later become her friend and protector.

The moral education that families supply to us does not cease with the end of childhood, but for all we scholars know about this continuing saga it might as well not exist. That the more complex aspects of family life have escaped scholarly attention is rather remarkable, considering that the shelves of our libraries are filled with novels about families, daytime television programs consist almost entirely of dramas about family relationships, and the everyday discourse of most people is about the triumphs, tragedies, and tedium of family life.

Families are the world in which we shape and manage our emotions. Love is one of those emotions, but family life is not simply about love; in many societies families are formed without romantic love as the chief motive, and in every society some families are strong without their members displaying much affection for one another at all. Families perform all sorts of functions—supplying sex, managing production, educating children, supervising property, allocating patrimonies, and (historically of the greatest importance) negotiating relations with kin. As we bemoan what we take to be the breakdown of the modern family, we would do well to recall the words of the anthropologist Robin Fox, who observes, after surveying the extraordinary variety of functions that families must perform, "what is remarkable about so fragile an institution is that it works at all."[44]

In the process of serving, however imperfectly, all of these functions, the family becomes a world that does far more than socialize babies and thus has far greater moral and practical significance than one would suppose from reading those texts on child development that stop when the child begins adolescence. The family is a continuous locus of reciprocal obligations that constitute an unending school for moral instruction. Like a marriage, a family is a commitment, one that places heavy burdens on its members, burdens that the experience of history has shown must nevertheless be shouldered if people are to be happy and society is to prosper. These burdens may be light and bearing them can be a joy, or they may be heavy and bearing them can be an affliction. Whichever is the case, one can no more choose to take the joy and ignore the afflictions than one can choose to live a life that is both solitary and happy.

G. K. Chesterton put the continuing significance of the family this way:

> Of course the family is a good institution because it is uncongenial. It is wholesome precisely because it contains so many divergences and varieties. It is . . . like a little kingdom, and like most other little kingdoms, is generally in a state of something resembling anarchy. . . . Aunt Elizabeth is unreasonable, like mankind. Papa is excitable, like mankind. Our youngest brother is mischievous, like mankind. Grandpa is stupid, like the world; he is old, like the world.[45]

We learn to cope with the people of this world because we learn to cope with the members of our family. Those who flee the family flee the world; bereft of the former's affection, tutelage, and challenges, they are unprepared for the latter's tests, judgments, and demands.

Gender

Nature has played a cruel trick on humankind. It has made males essential for reproduction but next to useless for nurturance. Yet if the child is to do more than survive—if it is to grow up in an orderly and safe environment and be part of an elaborate and useful culture—it must be part of a community. For such a complex social organization to develop, men must be induced to provide resources and act cooperatively, if for no other reason than to prevent their quarrelsomeness from leading to a war of all against all. Living in a community requires of them sympathy, prudence, and above all, commitment.

Unfortunately, when men are born they are on average much less amenable to socialization than women. Compared to their sisters, men are born neurologically less advanced: they are four to six weeks less well developed and thus, correspondingly, more in need of care.[1] They are more likely to be hyperactive, autistic, color-blind, left-handed, and prone to learning disorders.[2] If they are born prematurely with a very low birth weight, boys will suffer more harm and display more conduct problems than premature girls.[3] Boys can't even sing as well; males are less likely to sing in tune than females.[4] If the mother used alcohol or drugs, a male infant is more likely to be adversely affected than a female one.[5] If raised in a discordant or broken family, boys suffer more adverse consequences than do girls.[6]

Men are more aggressive than women. Though child-rearing practices may intensify or moderate this difference, the difference will persist and almost surely rests on biological factors. In every

165

known society, men are more likely than women to play roughly, drive recklessly, fight physically, and assault ruthlessly, and these differences appear early in life.[7] Some people with a romanticized notion of primitive cultures imagine that before men were corrupted by civilization they lived in harmony with one another, but this was scarcely the case. One review of the archaeological evidence suggests that in the state of nature, about one-quarter of all the human males died in fights, a rate of violent death that is about the same as the anthropologist Napoleon Chagnon found to be true among Yᶐno-mamö men now living in the Amazon basin.[8]

The neurochemical basis of the greater aggressiveness of human males is not well understood, but a growing body of evidence implicates hormones (such as testosterone), enzymes (such as mono-amine oxidase), and neurotransmitters (such as serotonin).* As they grow up, men are much more likely than women to cause trouble in school, to be alcoholics or drug addicts, and to commit crimes.[9] Though some aspects of the human personality change as people grow up, aggression in males is least likely to change, at least through adolescence.[10]

It is not hard to explain why women care for their infants; without the female breast the child would perish. If there ever existed women who lacked the inclination to nourish their offspring, those offspring would have died. To the extent that that inclination is genetic, nature would have selected for women who cared for their children. But men have been less important for the survival of the child. Though it would have been helpful had they gathered food while the mothers nursed, females living where fruits, nuts, and vegetables were naturally available could often collect enough food to meet at least their minimal requirements. Among many primates this continues to be the case. That men are not essential for infant care under all circumstances is suggested by the fact that today, and possibly for many millennia, men are less likely than women to invest

---

*Males, especially younger ones, have significantly higher levels of testosterone and lower levels of platelet monoamine oxidase than do women or older males, conditions that are heritable and associated with higher levels of impulsivity and aggressiveness (Eysenck, 1990; Bridge et al., 1985; Olweus et al., 1988). Some accidents of nature such as the fetal andro-genization of female infants and pseudohermaphroditism among male infants, provide data showing that biological endowment is at least as important as child rearing in explaining gender differences in many forms of behavior, including aggression (Imperato-McGinley et al., 1979; Earhardt and Baker, 1974).

in child care, and despite that reluctance the human race has survived.

No woman needs to be reminded of the fact that men are less likely than women to get up when the baby cries, feed it, or fret over its moods and needs. Infidelity is more common among men than women.[11] (Men also have more premarital sexual intercourse and with a greater variety of partners than do women.)[12] Single-parent households, a large, growing, and worrisome feature of modern life, are, in the vast majority of cases, female-headed households. In this regard the human male is very much like most other male primates. Among most mammals, the male contributes little to offspring development beyond his sperm and, in some cases, defense against rivals and predators. Since human infants require a long period of care after birth, a central problem for women living anywhere but in the most nurturant environments is to find ways of inducing the male to supply the resources necessary to make this care possible.

Because resources are scarce, it is to the mother's advantage if the father will supply her and her alone. In this regard mankind does not manage to do as well as many species of birds. Monogamous pair bonding is common to quail and uncommon to mankind. Among human societies monogamy is the rule in only a minority of cases (roughly 17 percent); polygyny—that is, one husband taking more than one wife—is far more common.[13] And even in monogamous societies, infidelity is widespread. By contrast, polyandry—that is, a wife taking more than one husband—is vanishingly rare. (Of course, even in polygynous societies, most men will invest in child care to some degree.) The high rates of divorce and separation with which we are all too familiar provide ample evidence that humans have not yet figured out how to solve a problem that quail and wolves have solved without reading a single book.

It seems clear that Mother Nature would much prefer to produce only girls, because she does such a poor job of producing boys. Her preferences are quite clear in this regard: all fetuses begin as females; only in the third month of gestation does masculinization begin. And when it does begin, it sometimes is a process prone to error, leading to all manner of deficiencies and abnormalities. Not only do men have a shorter life expectancy than women, a fact that might be explained by their more violent tendencies, but the higher mortality rate appears almost from the beginning: male fetuses are more likely than female ones to die in utero, and male infants have a higher death rate than female infants.* Having invented the male, Mother Nature doesn't quite know what to do with him. It is as if she had suddenly realized, too late, what every student of biology now knows: asexual reproduction is far more efficient than sexual reproduction. But now we are stuck with men who are likely to be both troublesome and vulnerable.

At one time the traits that we judge to be troublesome may have been useful and those that we take to be vulnerabilities may have been irrelevancies. When prehistoric man hunted for wild animals, aggressiveness and even hyperactivity were adaptive. Even after he had settled into sedentary communities, aggression and physical activity were useful if, as was often the case, his communities were threatened by enemies. That he might be color-blind, have a speech defect, or be dyslexic was of little importance. Evolution has selected for traits in males that have aided them in hunting and in competition with other males for access to females, but at the price of reduced longevity.[14]

Even though evolution has equipped men with traits that make them good hunters but not necessarily good fathers, most men who father children will aid in their care. In this respect, the human male is more like a bird, wolf, or butterfly than he is like many other primates.[15] Most male baboons do not invest much in caring for their offspring; male humans invest substantially. As a consequence, family life among humans is not only possible but even commonplace.

Why? Why should a man, who can in a few moments conceive a fetus that will grow in the mother's belly and be dependent on the mother for food for many months after its birth, stick around to care for it? And why should he even forsake other women, along with the sexual opportunities they can offer, to cling to the mother alone? If the principle of evolution is reproductive fitness—that is, selection for creatures that maximize the number of genes they reproduce in the next generation—then evolution ought to select for the genes of

---

*McMillen, 1979; Trivers, 1985:306. The higher death rate of males is probably a consequence, at every age, of the presence of the male sex hormone. Castrated male cats live much longer than intact ones, and not simply because they fight less (Hamilton, Hamilton, and Mestler, 1985). Among humans, eunuchs outlive intact males (Hamilton and Mestler, 1969).

those males who produce the largest number of offspring. That would mean selecting for the most promiscuous males, and under those circumstances, family life would be next to impossible.

Sexual Selection

The chief answer to this puzzle is female choice. Females who nurture their young for extended periods will, on the average, prefer to mate with males who are likely to aid in that nurture for a long period of time. In species that do not require extended infant care, the female will pair with the male that makes the most impressive display of size, strength, plumage, coloration, or territorial defense.* In these cases the female is selecting mates whose vigor creates the best prospects for the survival of offspring even when the female alone must provide the care after birth. Selection for these traits, however, does not make possible an elaborate social life. But in other species, and notably among humans, females will select mates that seem not only vigorous but inclined to make long-term investments in child care.

Just why the human female, unlike many primate females, should have begun to select for dependability is unclear. But having done so, males biologically disposed to share in nurturance began to have a reproductive advantage.† The result of female choice is evident in what we observe in males today. Despite the difficulty in socializing young ones, adult males usually respond warmly to

---

*The female choice model has been suggested by Mark Ridley (1978) as an explanation for paternal care among various animal species, but he was frank to admit that there was not much evidence for it among the lower life forms. More recently Robert Trivers has supplied some additional evidence, as among female African weaverbirds who, before bonding, inspect the elaborate nests built by males, rejecting those who build poorly and selecting those who build well (Trivers, 1985:249–56; 1972:171–72).

† I am aware that some forms of male investment in child care may result, not from females having selected nurturant males, but from males wishing to maximize the number and fecundity of their offspring. In the latter case, the male is managing a tradeoff between impregnating as many females as possible and helping ensure the survival of the results of those impregnations. Time devoted to survival is time taken away from impregnation. For many nonhuman males, and possibly for some human ones, there is an optimal strategy that produces the maximum number of surviving offspring. I am indebted to Robert Boyd for pointing this out to me. In my view, the kind of human male investment that we now see, and have seen through most of recorded history, reflects a disposition to nurture one's kind, however small the number, and not to maximize the total number of offspring.

infants. Many if not most men find fathering, and not just insem-
inating, to be a rewarding activity; they respond instinctively and
with compassion to the sight, sounds, and touch of their offspring.[16]

Though as a group men invest far more heavily in child care than
do, for example, male rhesus monkeys, individual men vary greatly in
this disposition. As a result, the choice of mate made by (or for)
women will be based on a careful evaluation of the suitability of
various men. When the choice is left to the women, it typically
occurs after a long period of courtship in which men are tested in
various ways for loyalty and affection; sometimes sexual favors are
granted or withheld on the basis of evidence that the man will be a
good father—that is, will be dependable, caring, and monogamous.
When the choice is made by the bride's family, much the same
evaluation occurs, though with less emphasis on affection and more
on reputation, wealth, status, and other signs of both having a capacity for support and being embedded in a network of social obligations that will guarantee support (but perhaps not fidelity).

Courtship is a way of testing commitment. If the woman is
sexually easy, the value of the test will be lessened, as the man will
have less of an incentive to produce evidence of commitment in
order to acquire sexual access. If the man is deceitful, he may be able
to fool a woman into thinking that commitment is assured when in
fact it is not. Since individuals differ in these respects, the process is
imperfect. Its imperfection has supplied the themes of thousands of
years of songs, plays, and stories that give expression to the continuing differences between the sexes.

The songs and stories portray women who want commitment
coping with men who want action. In modern times the signal of
commitment is romantic love: if the man is sensitive to the woman's
feelings and caring of her needs and responses, his expression of
those feelings is taken to be a sign of an enduring emotional investment. But romance can be feigned or be a short-lived prelude to sex.
Love is the currency; women hope it is an asset that will be invested,
but men may treat it merely as the price of consumption. Female
choice—in Darwin's terms, sexual selection—has shaped the evolutionary development of men, but without making men like women.
As a result, one would expect the moral development of men and
women to differ.

Gender and Culture

Some of that difference will be shaped by the way in which a society's culture and economic system makes certain traits more adaptive than others. Mary Maxwell West and Melvin J. Konner illustrate this by sketching the differences in styles of fathering in five non-industrial cultures.[17] Hunter-gatherers, such as the !Kung San bushmen of Africa, and fishermen, such as the Lesu of Melanesia, can feed themselves without constant labor and do not depend on possessing capital stocks (such as cattle) that must be defended against rival tribes. Women supply some of the food by their own foraging or gardening. Neither finding food supplies nor protecting land or cattle are full-time preoccupations, freeing men to spend time with their families. Family life in these places tends to be monogamous, and the men are deeply involved in child care. They often hold and fondle their children, who are indulged by both parents.

By contrast, the Bedouins of the Arabian desert raise cattle, and the Thonga in South Africa practice both farming and herding. They have both cattle and land to protect, as well as the cash income that those stocks generate. Fighting is commonplace, both within the group and among rival groups. In this warrior culture, fierceness and bravery are highly valued, leading to a strong emphasis on male authority and heavy discipline. Men remain aloof from their children and often mistreat their wives. Subsistence living based on scarce capital assets, it would appear, reduces male involvement in child care and rewards male aggressiveness.*

This explanation of the warrior culture also appears in Robert Edgerton's comparison of four East African tribes, the members of which were divided between areas where the economy rested on either farming or herding. Both groups had capital stocks to protect, but the pastoralists were most at risk from raids by rival tribes endeavoring to steal their cattle. Accordingly, the pastoralists were more militaristic, more given to direct expressions of aggression, and more inclined to respect central authority than were the farmers, who tended instead to secrecy, caution, indirect action, mutual

---

*In the fifth case, the villagers of Sondup'o in Korea practice large-scale, intensive agriculture, and father-child relations are intermediate between the harshness of the Thonga-Bedouin and the warmth of the !Kung-Lesu.

suspicion, and jealousy. Such evidence as Edgerton gathered on male dominance and aloofness showed that both traits were clearly stronger among the pastoralists than among the farmers. In one tribe, the Kamba of Kenya, the antagonism between men and women was especially acute. A male Kamba herder stressed the need to show that men were "always superior" to women and that he was entitled to "come and go as he pleases" and to buy, sell, and beat his wife. The women described their husbands as "never affectionate" and not involved in rearing children. Though the women professed to accept this as a natural state of affairs, many revealed a smoldering antagonism that they expressed indirectly by means of witchcraft directed against the men.[18]

Modern society presents an especially complex challenge to the task of socializing males. Industrialization and the division of labor improve the standard of living while moving production out of the household. As the standard of living rises, improvements in diet reduce the age at which women can conceive and thus the age at which they first give birth. Contraception separates sexuality from procreation. The father's role in child care is reduced because he spends more time away from home. For most men aggression is no longer adaptive, because capital stocks are now conserved and managed by bureaucratic processes that require conformity and technical competence more than boldness and physical prowess. But while they are no longer adaptive, aggressive impulses are still present. The rise of large cities weakens kinship controls on such aggression, brings groups with different standards of conduct into close contact, and multiplies opportunities for violent exchanges.

These circumstances require of society that it invent and enforce rules to regulate aggression among men and to ensure that they care for the children they beget and the wives they take. Legal codes take on great importance but are rarely sufficient. In Anglo-Saxon countries, the control of male behavior since the eighteenth century (at least) has required the preachings of the church, the discipline of the factory, and the supervision of the temperance society.

During the nineteenth century, these informal methods of control reached their greatest strength; we in the United States and Great Britain refer to these teachings as "Victorian morality." As applied to male behavior, that morality was, in essence, the code of the gentleman. The invention of the "gentleman" constituted the emergence of a society-wide definition of proper behavior to replace the premodern definitions enforced by kinship groupings and the feudal definitions enforced by the aristocracy.

The requirements of gentlemanly behavior included everything from table manners and the obligation to play games fairly to one's responsibilities toward ladies and one's duty to country. So successful were these moral exhortations and codes of gentility that, so far as we can tell, both alcohol abuse and crime rates declined in England and America during a period—the second half of the nineteenth century—characterized by rapid urbanization, massive immigration, and the beginnings of industrialization. Though not without its oft-remarked hypocrisies and its heavy reliance on a double standard governing male and female conduct, the code of the gentleman was the most successful extralegal mechanism ever invented for adapting male behavior to the requirements of modern life.[19]

In those places where the moral code was weak, the legal system impotent, and bureaucratic structures absent, the warrior culture often emerged. If large numbers of unmarried young men were thrown together outside of the control mechanisms of the conventional economic system, they would reduce their investment in family life or child care in favor of using their physical prowess to acquire and defend free-floating forms of wealth.

One example is the discovery of gold in remote areas. There were two American gold rushes in the midnineteenth century, the famous one in California and a lesser-known one in Appalachia. The former attracted single males whose life, devoted to acquisition and defense in an area beyond the reach of the law, came close to the Hobbesian state of nature: solitary, poor, nasty, brutish, and short. Sixteen thousand people died in the California mining camps, victims of disease, murder, and insanity.[20] Such family life as existed was male-dominated, with little paternal investment in child care. The Appalachia gold rush, by contrast, attracted Cornish miners who arrived with their families and soon became part of well-organized mining companies. Owing, it would seem, to the combined effect of familial bonds and bureaucratic constraints, the North Carolina gold rush produced relatively little violence.*

---

*Glass, 1984. I am indebted to Professor David Courtwright of the University of North Florida for calling my attention to the gold rush literature.

Marauding male gangs have excited fear for as long as man has lived in cities. From time to time we forget that young men in groups are always a potential challenge to social order, and so we are surprised when they appear in places that we think of as tranquil and civilized. We are astonished to learn of football gangs tearing apart trains, pubs, and athletic grounds in stately, sedate England. England? Supposedly, people there are utterly civil, with violent crime scarcely a problem and daily life moving in the orderly, class-ridden, but polite tempos of *Masterpiece Theatre*. What terrible thing—poverty? alienation? despair?—could produce football riots in England?

This idealized view of England can only be sustained if one forgets that in every society, a certain small fraction of young males will have an inordinate taste for violence and a low degree of self-control. What is striking about England and other civilized places is not that there are young thugs, but that in some places they organize themselves into gangs. England, contrary to popular belief, has a rate of burglary and robbery not much different from that in the United States.[21] But whereas American gangs are found chiefly among the inner-city poor and are territorially based, British gangs are found chiefly among football (in American terminology, soccer) supporters and are not territorial. They go to every game, traveling by bus, rail, or plane, trashing these conveyances along the way and spoiling for a good fight. Bill Burford's horrifying account of these gangs—or "firms," as they call themselves—does not depict unemployed, disenfranchised youth searching for meaning; it depicts young men of the sort always found overrepresented among the criminal classes—thrill seekers with a predisposition to alcoholism and violence, young toughs who *enjoy the fight*.[22] What is surprising is not that they exist but that they manage to sustain a modicum of organization, with captains and lieutenants, and that the physical conditions of British athletic grounds (or in American terms, stadiums) contribute to their sense of being a caged minority. That these gangs are intensely patriotic, singing "Rule Britannia" while destroying property and assaulting women, is not at all surprising; men in groups define sharply, however implausibly, the boundaries within which someone is either in or out.

Lionel Tiger's well-known book *Men in Groups* suggests the evolutionary origins and social functions of such behavior: it derives from the need for males to hunt, defend, and attack.[23] Much of the history of civilization can be thought of as an effort to adapt these male dispositions to contemporary needs by restricting aggression or channeling it into appropriate channels. That adaptation has often required extraordinary measures, such as hunting rituals, rites of passage, athletic contests, military discipline, guild apprenticeships, or industrial authority. (By contrast, one almost never reads of equivalent rituals, authority systems, or fraternal rules employed to socialize women, in part because they have often been confined to a subordinate status and in part because the realities of childbirth and child care provide an automatic process of socialization.) Modern society, with its rapid technological change, intense division of labor, and ambiguous allocation of social roles, frequently leaves some men out, with their aggressive predispositions either uncontrolled or undirected. Gangs are one result.

Matters get worse when the gangs can earn profits from illegal alcohol and drug distribution systems. Prohibiting the sale of certain commodities provides economic opportunities in which young males have a comparative advantage, and this in turn leads to the emergence of a warrior culture that underinvests in family life. Economic activity is separated from family maintenance and organized around capital that can be seized by predation. In these warrior societies, today as in the past, status among males is largely determined by physical combat and sexual conquest. Women can no longer control male behavior by requiring monogamous commitment in exchange for sexual access. Moreover, since women can, through contraception or abortion, control their reproductive rate, what once was a moral obligation gives way to a utilitarian calculation. The obligation was: "She is going to have a kid, and so I must marry her." The utilitarian calculation is: "If she wants to have the kid when she doesn't have to, then raising it is her problem." As a result, the children are raised apart from their fathers.

Among male animals generally, and perhaps among male humans as well, the more a male engages in promiscuous sexuality and intraspecies fighting, the less he invests in caring for his offspring. But the reverse is also true: the less he invests in caring for offspring, the more he is disposed to compete, violently if need be, with others for sexual access to a large number of women.[24] A culture that does not succeed in inducing its males to care for their offspring not only produces children that lack adequate care but also creates an environment that rewards predatory sexuality.

Gender and Family

Although men and women come together out of natural attraction, it is not clear why a household—that is, an enduring and cohesive family—should be the result. If the household is, as Aristotle put it, "the partnership constituted by nature for [the needs of] daily life,"[25] what is there in nature that produces not simply sex but partnership? We know why men and women come together, but what keeps them together? Unless we can explain that, we cannot explain the social unit that forms human character. Moral life begins not with sexual congress but with emotional commitment—the formation and maintenance of the family.

The needs of the woman may lead her to try to select males who will invest in child care, but this preference is not strong enough to produce families unless it is powerfully reinforced by cultural expectations and social sanctions. As Lionel Tiger and Robin Fox have argued, the chief function of human kinship systems is to "protect the mother-infant bond from the relative fragility and volatility of the male-female bond."[26] The weakening of the family in many Western societies is familiar evidence that these kinship systems and their cultural and legal supports are far more fragile than one would have guessed even forty years ago.

So fragile, indeed, that one can now say that the conditions of child rearing have changed fundamentally for many youngsters. In the 1950s, the typical American child lived in a two-parent family with a stay-at-home mother, a working father, and several siblings. By the 1990s, the typical child spent at least some time (among black children, most of the time) with a single mother and had only one sibling.[27] The public believes that the consequences of this have been harmful, and the scholarly evidence bears them out. Compared to children who are raised by their biological father and mother, those raised by mothers, black or white, who have never married are more likely to be poor, to acquire less schooling, to be expelled or suspended from school, to experience emotional or behavioral problems, to display antisocial behavior, to have trouble getting along with their peers, and to start their own single-parent families. These unhappy outcomes afflict both girls and boys, but they have a more adverse effect on boys.[28]

The better-off the parent, the less likely it is that the child will have to live in a one-parent household. But one should not infer from this that the problem of single-parent children can be solved simply by raising parental incomes. Consider black children. At every income level, they are more likely to live with a single parent than are white children at those income levels.[29] And for all children, there was a sharp decline in their prospects of having a two-parent family during the very period—the 1960s and 1970s—when family incomes were rising.

This is not a peculiarly American phenomenon. David Popenoe, a sociologist, has studied families in Sweden, where he found a similar increase in single-parent households. By 1980, 18 percent of all Swedish households with children had but one parent (the figure in the United States for that year was 21.5 percent, though by 1984 it had become 26 percent).[30] There remain industrial societies in which the overwhelming majority of children grow up in families with fathers—Japan, New Zealand, and Switzerland are three of them. But as I argue in the next chapter, these three countries may be standing (for how long?) against a powerful tide that has been running in the opposite direction.

The consequences of mother-only families for the socialization of the male child seem bleak. I say "seem" because it is not easy to prove that a single-parent family, independently of other factors, produces undersocialized males. One reason is that mother-only households often suffer from so many problems, such as poverty, that isolating the effect of parenting on children is difficult. Another is that women who bear children without marrying may differ temperamentally from those who do marry. And finally, mother-child relations occupy a much more prominent place in academic studies than do father-child relations in part because "mothers are the main moral socializers of children of both sexes" in virtually every culture.[31]

The main, but not the only socializers. In one of the few studies to follow similarly situated children over many years and observe the relationship between their behavior and the role of their fathers, Sheppard Kellam and his co-workers studied several hundred poor, black first-graders living in a depressed neighborhood near the University of Chicago. Each lived in one of eighty-six different family types, depending on how many and what kinds of adults were present. Of the 1,391 families, about one-third had a mother as the only adult present; another third consisted of a mother and a father. Only a tiny fraction was headed by a father with no mother present. The remainder was made up of various combinations of mothers, grandparents, uncles, aunts, adult brothers and sisters, and various unrelated adults. By the time the children entered the third grade, those who lived with their mothers alone were the worst off in terms of their socialization.[32] After ten years, the boys who had grown up in mother-only families (which by then made up about half the total) reported more delinquencies, regardless of family income, than those who had grown up in families with multiple adults, especially a father.[33] Comparable findings have come from studies in Detroit.[34] The most common and most plausible interpretation of these studies is that the presence of a decent father helps a male child learn to control aggression; his absence impedes it.[35]

Not only does it appear that two-parent families do a better job of developing the moral senses of male children, but they also seem to have a beneficial effect on the husbands themselves. Of all of the institutions through which men may pass—schools, factories, the military—marriage has the largest effect. For every race and at every age, married males live longer than unmarried ones, having lower rates of homicide, suicide, accidents, and mental illness. Crime rates are lower for married than unmarried males and incomes are higher. Drug dealers are less likely to be married than young males who are not dealers.[36] Infant mortality rates are higher for unmarried than for married women, whether black or white, and these differences cannot be explained by differences in income or availability of medical care.[37]

Though some of these differences can be explained by female selectivity in choosing mates, I doubt that all can. Marriage not only involves screening people for their capacity for self-control, but it also provides inducements—the need to support a mate, care for a child, and maintain a home—that increase that capacity.

When the mother in a mother-only family is also a teenager, or at least a teenager living in urban America, the consequences for the child are even grimmer. The most authoritative survey of what we know about the offspring of adolescent mothers concluded that the children suffer increasingly serious cognitive deficits and display a greater degree of hyperactivity, hostility, and poorly controlled aggression than is true of children born to older mothers of the same race, and this is especially true of the boys.[38]

Gender, Temperament, and Moral Senses

These findings support the view that males and females differ in temperament, especially with respect to aggression, that boys are harder to socialize than girls, and that female choice does not guarantee the selection of dependable mates. Given these differences in temperament, socialization, and reproductive success, one should not be surprised to find evidence that men and women differ in their moral orientation.*

An awareness of these differences has led many people in the past (and some today) to argue that morality is more natural to women than to men and to justify differences in the roles and rights of the two sexes by the claim that women, being purer, finer, and more emotional than men, are properly confined to the home, where their more delicate sensibilities fit them for rearing children and sustaining a refuge from the cruelties and competition of the outside world.† The argument is not only self-serving (for males), it is also incorrect. Both males and females learn moral behavior in the family; were that not the case, human communities would be impossible. Neither sex is "more" or "less" moral than the other. But they do seem to differ.

Early childhood experiences interacting with innate temperamental differences may create a disposition to give greater emphasis to one or the other of the several moral senses. One person may be more inclined to emphasize justice, fairness, and duty, another to stress sympathy, care, and helping. If Harvard's Carol Gilligan and her colleagues are correct, the former emphasis is more characteristic of men, the latter of women.[39] For example, when people are asked to describe moral dilemmas that they have faced or that they encounter in Aesop's fables, boys overwhelmingly do so in terms of justice (honoring contracts, making a fair division, or respecting

---

*I am acutely aware of the risks I run in writing of gender differences. On no topic is it easier to produce misunderstandings or arouse resentments. To some, any talk of differences implies a claim about rights. It does not. People can be equal without being the same.

† Of course, there have been some cultures in which the seclusion of women in the home or harem was justified on the grounds that they are *less* moral than men because they are by nature lascivious, seductive, and wanton. In the extreme case, women were portrayed as witches or succubi. It is noteworthy that in medieval Europe the most common charge against witches was that they killed babies, a most unwomanly thing to do (Cohn, 1975:100). Some conjectures on the causes and consequences of these cultural differences are offered in the next chapter.

rights) while girls are more likely to do so in terms of care (helping people in need, resolving conflict). It must be stressed that these are differences in what people say about a story, not in what they will do in a real-life situation or even how they will react to a real-life dilemma. Yet they are consistent with many obvious facts of life. Women are more likely than men to dislike violence in motion pictures, less likely to enjoy sports that emphasize violence, and far less likely to commit crimes of violence. This is exactly what one would expect of people who say that they keenly experience the pain and sympathize with the plight of others.*

A clearer test of gender differences comes from the many experiments conducted to see how people will divide rewards after performing some task. Brenda Major and Kay Deaux summarize these findings this way: under every experimental condition, women take less of the reward for themselves than do men, and they do so regardless of whether the partners with whom they are sharing are male or female. This does not mean that women are less greedy than men, but rather that they seem to apply somewhat different principles to the allocation process.

When a woman has performed better than her partner in some common task, she tends to split the reward equally; when a man has performed better than his partner, he divides the reward equitably (that is, in proportion to the value of each person's contributions). Men also give more to female partners than they do to male ones, whereas women do not allow the sex of their partner to influence their allocation decisions.

---

*The Gilligan argument has not gone unopposed. For example, one review of male-female differences in empathy concluded that, while there were large differences between men and women in *self-reported* empathy, the evidence of differences in empathic *behavior* was inconclusive (Eisenberg and Lennon, 1983). A review of some fifty studies that attempt to describe the stage of moral reasoning that a person has achieved concluded that there was little evidence of a "sex bias" in the test: that is, men and women were about equally likely to be found at a given stage (Walker, 1984, 1986; for a rejoinder, see Baumrind, 1986). The difficulty with this conclusion is that these tests, based on Lawrence Kohlberg's theory of moral development, only describe the stage a person has reached based on that person's verbal reaction to some hypothetical moral dilemmas. No one has clearly shown, so far as I can tell, that how people respond to real moral issues, and especially how they behave in actual moral quandaries, can be predicted from their reaction to these fictional stories, especially since Kohlberg kept changing the way in which these reactions were to be scored. If there are no differences in empathic behavior, it is hard to explain why prisons are filled with male inmates. If there are no differences in empathic feelings, it is hard to understand why men and women spend so much time saying that they don't understand each other.

Gender

These findings hold true under one important condition: the participants expect to have further interactions with their partners. When they don't—when they perform a task with somebody they never expect to meet again—men and women allocate rewards in the same way. It is the prospect of future involvement that leads women to reduce the share they give themselves even when they are entitled to more.[40] The clear implication is that women assign a higher value to ongoing relationships than do men. Brenda Major is not quite certain how to explain this difference and suggests that it probably has a variety of causes. But it is striking how consistent this is with the Gilligan theory (Major published her work before Gilligan's appeared).

When Jean Piaget observed boys and girls at play, he noticed that boys were more concerned with rules, and girls with relationships. When a dispute arose, the boys were more likely to argue about the rules and search for fair procedures for applying them, while the girls were more inclined to manage conflict by making exceptions to the rules or ignoring them entirely. Piaget suggested that girls regarded a rule as "good as long as the game repaid it."[41] Many years later Janet Lever came to the same conclusion after observing fifth-grade children playing at school. Compared to the girls' games, the boys' games were more competitive, more complex, involved more players, often split close friends between different teams, and lasted longer.[42] The greater length reflected both the complexity of the game and the fact that disputes over what constituted fair play were resolved by boys through the application of rules or the decision to repeat the play. Girls, by contrast, were more likely to play short, simple, turn-taking games and to react to disputes by ending the game. To the girls, maintaining their relationships was more important than continuing the game.[43] Judy Dunn, watching young children at home, was struck by the fact that as early as two years of age, girls conversed more about their feelings than did boys. Similarly, the aggressiveness of males is more often expressed by direct physical confrontation, whereas the aggressive impulses of females more often takes the form of organized social ostracism.[44]

Though some students of child development suggest that individuals move through various stages of moral reasoning, with the highest stage being the one at which the individual applies universal principles of justice to moral dilemmas,[45] this claim, in my view, assigns too much importance to how a person formulates justifications for his moral inclinations and too little to the inclinations themselves. (I also am a bit suspicious of any theory that says that the highest moral stage is one in which people talk like college professors.) Ranking moral stages from low to high does not capture the reality of many moral problems, which often involve choosing which of several moral sentiments ought to govern one's action. For these reasons, the theory that men and women differ in the kinds of moral sentiments they emphasize cannot be tested by measuring what stage each gender is in; much less can the worth of a man's moral sentiments be compared to that of a woman's by noting where each stands in the presumed hierarchy of moral stages. To say that the two sexes differ is not the same thing as saying that morality defined as justice and fairness is superior to morality defined as benevolence and caring. Everyone applies various combinations of principles and feelings to the management of moral problems. Sometimes principle and feeling coincide, and so no difficulty arises; indeed, in these circumstances we act reflexively, without having engaged in moral reasoning at all. Sometimes they diverge; and then, if we are calm and self-aware, we struggle to reconcile the competing dispositions.[46]

It is difficult to say exactly how these gender differences, to the extent that they exist, emerge. Nature and nurture interact in ways that are complex and hard to disentangle. Boys are more aggressive than girls (nature at work), but over many millennia their aggressiveness has been moderated by female selection of mates (nature modified by human choices that affect reproductive success) and continues to be moderated or exacerbated by child-rearing practices (nurture) that reflect both infant temperament (nature) and parental attitudes (nurture).

Gender and Social Roles

However complex the origin of the more fundamental gender differences, they are remarkably resistant to planned change. The most impressive demonstration of that resistance—impressive both because of the quality of the research and the initial suppositions of the author—comes from the studies by Melford E. and Audrey Spiro of a kibbutz, one of the Israeli collective farms.[47] When the Spiros first studied it in 1951, the kibbutz was already thirty years old; when they returned in 1975, it had been in existence for nearly sixty years. It represented, thus, a mature example of a bold experiment: to achieve on a farm a wholly egalitarian society based on collective ownership, cooperative enterprise, a classless society, and the group rearing of children in an atmosphere that accorded no significance to differences in gender. Within a week after birth, infants were brought to a communal nursery; at one year of age, they moved into a Toddlers' House; at five years of age, they entered kindergarten; and so on through grammar school and high school, living always with other children and never with their parents, expect for brief daily visits. Although there were slight differences in dress, in general male and female children were treated in exactly the same way: they dressed together, bathed together, played together, and slept together; they were given the same toys and the same chores. Though men and women married and lived together, the family as a parent-child unit and sex-differentiated roles within the family were abolished, not only in the assignment of rights, duties, and opportunities, but even in dress. Communal facilities—the kitchen, laundry, dining room, nursery, and school—were to be staffed without regard to gender, and women, who wore pants, avoided cosmetics, and retained their maiden names, were encouraged to work the fields alongside the men.

The communal nursery was successful in discouraging clear sex-role identifications among the children. In their fantasy play, boys rarely assumed adult male roles, some boys chose to wear ribbons and dresses during their games, and boys and girls played together and not in same-sex groups.[48] But from the first some gender differences in behavior appeared despite efforts to discourage them. Just as in conventional families, boys played more strenuous games than girls.* Boys were more likely to pretend they were driving machines and girls more likely to play with dolls and baby buggies; girls engaged in more artistic games and boys in more mechanical ones. As they got older, the formal sexual equality of life continued: boys and girls lived together, took showers together, and could indulge

---

*Felton Earls (1987) observed that three-year-old boys, even when playing with girls in the same sandbox, were more likely to pretend that they were riding, flying, colliding, breaking, or plowing, while the girls were more inclined to pretend they were mothering or caretaking. Similar patterns have been observed by Jack and Jeanne Block (1980), Marjorie Honzik (1951), and Evelyn Goodenough (1957). These authors, without explaining why, ascribed these differences entirely to socialization.

their sexual curiosity without adult interference or guidance. But the signs of sexual identification continued to appear. At parties girls spontaneously sang, danced, and initiated activity; boys increasingly sat on the sidelines and watched. Girls began assisting the nurses, boys the farmers. Teachers began to remark that the girls were socially more sensitive, the boys more egotistical.[49]

As they entered high school, the behavior of the kibbutz adolescents was still different in many ways from that of conventional teenagers. In the kibbutz there was virtually no dating and no intense or morbid curiosity about sex. But evidence of shame and embarrassment had begun to appear. The girls protested against taking showers with boys, began undressing in the dark, and took to wearing nightclothes in bed, all to avoid male eyes. Teachers reported that the girls kept themselves and their living areas cleaner than did the boys, whereas the boys were more aggressive in classroom discussions. The physics class attracted boys, the psychology class girls.[50]

But the biggest changes occurred among the adults who had been born and raised on the kibbutz. The family reasserted itself: sabra women sought renewed contact with their children, though not at the expense of abandoning collective education; the children's living quarters were increasingly staffed by women; and sabra men began to do most of the major agricultural jobs and to dominate the leadership roles and discussion in the communal meetings.[51] Women returned to feminine styles in clothing and opened a beauty parlor. This is not to say that there was now sexual inequality in the kibbutz, only that there was sexual diversity—in roles, preferences, styles, and modes of thought—within a structure of legal and formal equality.

The link between Gilligan's studies of gender differences in moral dispositions and the Spiros' observations of gender differences in roles may be this: the moral role played by women in the kibbutz tended to be expressive while those played by men tended to be instrumental.* When conflict arose in the children's houses, the girls tended to handle it by supplying assistance, sharing, and cooperation, while the boys more often relied on initiating activities, applying rules, or issuing directives. Predictably, the most aggressive

---

*The distinction between instrumental and expressive roles has been made by many scholars, principally Talcott Parsons (1951:79–88).

children were boys. Both boys and girls would attempt to control the aggression, but only the girls would console the victims of it.[52]

It is hard to imagine that a free society will ever make a more determined effort to eliminate gender differences in social roles than did the Israeli kibbutzim. It is also hard to imagine that such an effort would be studied by anyone more sympathetic to its goals than Melford and Audrey Spiro. As the former put it in 1979:

> As a cultural determinist, my aim in studying personality develop-
> ment in Kiryat Yedidim [the pseudonym of the kibbutz] was to
> observe the influence of culture on human nature or, more accu-
> rately, to discover how a new culture produces a new human na-
> ture. In 1975 I found (against my own intentions) that I was
> observing the influence of human nature on culture.[53]

The effect on the author's thinking was, as he put it, a "kind of Copernican revolution." His conclusions are supported by another large-scale study of a kibbutz, this done by Lionel Tiger and Joseph Shepher.[54] These findings help explain the absence of matriarchal societies. Despite recurring claims to the contrary, some by scholars as distinguished as Lewis Henry Morgan[55] and by polemicists as skilled as Friederich Engels,[56] no credible historical evidence has been adduced to show that a society ruled by women has ever existed. Joan Bamberger, a feminist scholar, has shown that the case for matriarchy has rested on two errors: confounding myth with history (as with the myths of the Amazon women) and confusing matrilineal descent (the inheritance through the female line of property and family name) with matriarchal authority (the enduring rule of women over men).*

This argument about matriarchy is a bit misplaced, for it proceeds on the assumption that the only authority that counts is that which is wielded publicly and officially or is embodied in offices and rules. Everyday experience should remind us of the countless ways in which men and women alike wield influence without controlling offices. Peggy Reeves Sanday, an anthropologist, has ex-

---

*Bamberger (1974) goes on to argue that many of these myths, far from being celebrations of female authority, were in fact condemnations of it. The leitmotif was that of powerful women who abused their power through moral failures—for example, by incest—and as a consequence were stripped of their authority. Edward Westermarck, in his monumental history of marriage, long ago showed that male rule was quite compatible with matrilineal descent (1926:15–23).

plored in great detail the many and subtle ways in which women exercise informal power, especially in those cultures in which human survival is not threatened by invasion or deprivation. Without the prospect of war or want, a culture tends to evolve a well-understood sexual division of labor, which often leads to the creation of spheres of relatively autonomous action for females and males alike.[57]

That matriarchy has never existed says nothing, of course, about the moral worth or legal rights of men or women. But viewed in light of the evidence from the kibbutzim, it does suggest that the explanation of male domination of political structures may involve more than merely male oppression. While the greater physical strength of men has no doubt been an important factor in maintaining male authority, especially in preindustrial societies, and while cultural conventions no doubt continue to sustain many aspects of male advantage, the differing orientations of men and women of the sort suggested by Gilligan and Spiro may also help account for this pattern.

I offer this conjecture: The innately greater aggressiveness of males reflects not only a combative nature but the legacy of selection for domination. That tendency may be moderated or exaggerated by parental training. As young boys begin to take pleasure in childhood games, they discover through spontaneous interaction that some principle for controlling aggression and allocating roles must be maintained if the game, and thus its pleasures, are to continue. When each person is, in varying degrees, asserting a desire to dominate, only two principles for moderating conflict are available: the authority of the most powerful or skillful participant, or the authority of norms that allocate roles either equally (for example, taking turns) or equitably (for example, awarding positions in the game on the basis of skill or effort). Whichever principle of authority is accepted, each tends toward the creation of rule-based systems organized around roles, claims, and rights. Prolonged experience in rule-based systems, whether they rest on the authority of a dominant figure or on the legitimacy of the rules themselves, contributes to acquiring both a moral orientation that emphasizes justice or fairness and a hierarchical orientation toward the management of conflict and the organization of common undertakings. To borrow the phrase of Louis Dumont, males tend to become *homo hierarchicus.*[58]

Gender

By contrast, to the extent that young girls are innately disposed to avoid physical aggression or, as a result of natural selection, partake of a nurturant (protomaternal?) predisposition (and of course individual girls, like individual boys, will differ greatly in these inclinations), they will find that their childhood will generate fewer competing demands for domination requiring rule-based management. Their play, as Piaget, Lever, and others have observed, will be less in need of, and less receptive to, formal principles of authority; the maintenance of personal relationships will take precedence over the allocation of rights and roles. Through prolonged involvement in play where sustaining relationships is more important than managing dominance, girls tend to acquire both a moral orientation that emphasizes caring and harmony and a nonhierarchical orientation toward the organization of common undertakings. Insofar as power relationships are hierarchical (as they almost always are), women will tend to be excluded, or, if included, confined (in part by fiat and in part by choice) to less authoritative roles.

Deborah Tannen finds abundant evidence of these differences in social orientation in the everyday language of men and women, especially in the ways in which the two sexes seem to misunderstand one another (the title of her best-selling book was *You Just Don't Understand*).[59] Men speak in order to report, women to establish rapport; men give directions, women make suggestions; male discourse suggests that independence is important, female discourse that intimacy is crucial. Men are more likely to make decisions "on the merits," women to feel that consultation is as important as decisiveness. When an emotional problem arises, men are inclined to suggest a solution, women to extend sympathy, often by describing similar difficulties of their own. The complaints men and women make about each other's behavior are so well known as scarcely to bear repeating; many grow out of these linguistic—actually, personality—differences: "He is so aloof," "She is so moody"; "He doesn't listen," "She is insecure"; "He never talks to me," "She never stops talking."

Tannen's sociolinguistic analysis, taken together with Gilligan's and Major's psychological inquiries, suggests how gender may affect at least two of the moral senses described in this book. Take the sense of fairness: It is a human sentiment, common to both sexes. But fairness, as we have seen, requires a judgment about proportionality: if people ought to get what they deserve or reciprocate what they receive, then the person evaluating the situation must decide how equal or unequal are the contributions of each party. If a person greatly values intimacy, community, and mutual esteem, then that person will tend to evaluate the inputs—the work, effort, time, or manner—of each party in the group equally. Several scholars have noted that in girls' play groups there is a stress on connection and similarity, reflecting a fear of rejection.[60] From one perspective this appears to be simply an adolescent preoccupation with popularity and conformity, but seen more deeply it reveals an egalitarian ethos that is maintained by striving to see all inputs to some common endeavor as relatively equal, so that the allocation of rewards will also be roughly the same.

Boys also value popularity and certainly are in some sense conformists, but their relationships are substantially more competitive—in athletic achievements, material acquisition, and displays of masculine toughness. Like most male primates, boys participate from an early age in dominance hierarchies. This means that when contributions to joint activities are assessed, males will emphasize the differences in inputs to a greater degree than will females. It does not mean that one gender is more or less fair in its outlook than the other, only that the specific application of the norm of fairness or reciprocity will reflect a different assessment of inputs. To oversimplify, men will be more likely to value equity, women equality.

A parallel difference in emphasis can be imagined with respect to sympathy. One can respond to the plight of another by expressions of care or by offers of solutions. In the first instance, empathy is the goal ("let's share our feelings"), in the latter it is simply a motive ("I can help you fix that"). Women may be more likely to take the first view: when an acquaintance suffers a reversal, sympathy requires that one display one's feelings and thereby draw tighter the bonds of friendship. Men may be more likely to take the latter: the adversity of a friend is an occasion to supply help but not, except within narrow limits, emotion. Help is "what friends are for"; emotion, extravagantly displayed, is simply and wrongly a loss of self-control that helps neither and embarrasses both. These differences may mean, not that one sex has a greater or lesser capacity for sympathy (though they may mean that), but that people, equally affected by the plight of another, may choose to make either an expressive or an instrumental reaction to it.

Culture versus Gender

These observations about gender differences in moral sentiments are based on evidence that is fragmentary, in some cases controversial, and limited to Western sources. Despite these shortcomings, I advance them because they are consistent with my experiences. But my experiences are, of course, rather parochial. I was reminded of this when Grace Goodell, an anthropologist who has devoted years to studying the cultures of the industrialized nations of the Pacific Rim, suggested to me that in some respects the moral thinking of successful East Asian businessmen seems to resemble that of eleven-year-old Western girls.[61]

For example, East Asian businessmen often manage their commercial relationships with one another in ways that are designed to maintain those relationships more than to assert legal claims, just as Western girls manage their games in ways that keep the game going even at some cost to the rules. In the Asian business world, anyone who emphasizes contractual obligations, legal rights, or formal rules is guilty of a grave breach of etiquette. These executives are competitive, often fiercely so, but the competition is constrained by a moral sense that neither party should embarrass the other, even at some cost in money. Fairness, abstractly conceived, is less important than comity.

These dispositions may grow out of the interaction between temperamental endowments and child-rearing practices of the sort already mentioned, practices that (at least in Japan) stress emotional interdependency and control behavior by the threat of social isolation. Self-control, sincerity, and collective decision making are greatly esteemed.[62] Preschool education continues this emphasis. When teachers, parents, and child-development specialists in China, Japan, and the United States were asked to state the most important things that children ought to learn in preschool, the first choice in Japan was sympathy and a concern for others, followed by cooperation. In the United States, the most common response was self-reliance (followed by cooperation); sympathy was rarely mentioned.[63] But in the Japanese preschool, exactly the same gender differences in behavior were observed as one would see in an American preschool or an Israeli kibbutz: the boys acted like warriors, the girls like healers and peacemakers.[64] How gender differences, which seem universal, interact with culture to affect moral sentiments is a subject about which almost everything remains to be learned.

Whether the gender differences in moral sentiments that Gilligan observes in the United States will be found in East Asian (or other) cultures remains to be seen. But the problem of male socialization is, I think, the same everywhere; cultures differ not in whether they must cope with it, but how and with what success.

The Universal
Aspiration

The most remarkable change in the moral history of mankind has been the rise—and occasionally the application—of the view that all people, and not just one's own kind, are entitled to fair treatment. Americans are so familiar with the passage in the Declaration of Independence asserting that "all men are created equal" that they forget how astonishing and, in a sense, unnatural that claim is. Of course, their actions often speak louder than their words. For Americans, as for peoples everywhere, morality governs our actions toward others in much the same way that gravity governs the motions of the planets: its strength is in inverse proportion to the square of the distance between them.

Children are intuitive moralists, but the range of their moral judgments is limited by the circumstances in which they are formed. Children feel sympathy for many playmates but not for all; they often feel obliged to act fairly toward others they know but less often to those whom they do not know. A difference in age of as little as one year or in location of as little as a hundred yards can mark the boundaries of their sense of obligation: a nine-year-old boy may regard an eight-year-old as unworthy of anything save condescension, and a group playing a game in front of one house may view a group playing in front of another house with suspicion or even hostility.

Older children may be even less tolerant than younger ones. Teenage boys living in one neighborhood often view those from another as rivals in games and as challengers for territory. Teenage girls define their friendship networks by standards of dress and demeanor that, however obscure to outsiders, are well understood and

191

rigidly enforced by insiders. The minor cruelties that many adolescents practice on one another—by teasing, bullying, and social ostracism—reduce many young people to tearful despair over matters that, to adults, seem trivial.

Lest we adults think that these childlike prejudices disappear with age, we should remember the countless places where one group of adults has systematically reduced another to servitude and the numberless centuries during which men have used torture and merciless warfare to impose on others religious convictions that to someone from Mars would differ only in esoteric and irrelevant detail from the beliefs of the victims. Even people who fancy themselves too moral and cosmopolitan to practice slavery or religious persecution would do well to recall how wary they are when they encounter people who differ in race, accent, dress, or political outlook. Mankind has a moral sense, but much of the time its reach is short and its effect uncertain.

As I have attempted to show, the human proclivities and social experiences that give rise to our moral sense tend to make that sense operate in small groups more than in large ones, to say nothing of embracing mankind as a whole. Our natural sociability is reinforced by attachment to familiar others, and so we tend to value the familiar over the strange, the immediate over the distant; in common with most species, we are by nature locals, not cosmopolitans. To the extent that this is true, some observers argue that we are not, in any fundamental sense, moral at all; true morality, in their view, consists of having allegiance to and acting on the basis of principles of universal applicability. In his influential theory of moral development, Lawrence Kohlberg argued that people, as they grow up, move from lower stages of moral thinking (for example, breaking a rule is bad if you are punished for it) through higher stages (for example, you have a duty to obey rules even if you are not punished for breaking them) toward the highest stage, that of universal ethical principles (for example, the Golden Rule).[1] In his version of the highest stage, Kohlberg was following in the footsteps of Immanuel Kant, to whom moral obligation had to rest on pure reason and in particular on the degree to which the maxim of one's action could be made a universal principle.[2] In Kant's famous example, breaking a promise can never be moral, no matter how beneficial to the person who breaks it, because promise breaking, if made a universal rule, would be self-defeating: no one would ever accept a promise if it were known in advance that all promises could be broken whenever it was to the advantage of the maker.

The problem with Kant's example and with Kohlberg's stages is that they presuppose general agreement as to what constitutes the relevant universe within which a rule is to operate. It is not at all self-defeating to reformulate Kant's principle as follows: I, a white, Christian male living in a village in southern Lebanon, must always keep promises I make to others in my village, since it would be contradictory and self-defeating to will a rule that promises need not be kept, but I have no obligation to keep them to people living outside my universe, that is, to people in other villages, especially if they are Muslims, heathens, or women. They will cheat me at every opportunity and so I am free to cheat them; indeed, their readiness to cheat me shows that they are less than human and deserve no more respect than what I might give a goat. So long as my experience were consistent with this view—so long, that is, as I saw nothing self-contradictory in honoring promises to villagers and ignoring promises to strangers—I would be entitled to think of strangers as so defective in reason as to be undeserving of respect. My universe would be the village.

But mankind is not devoid of moral sense if most of its members treat villagers better than strangers and family better than nonkin. On the contrary; unless people are disposed to favor the familiar face to the strange one, their natural sociability would not become a moral sense at all. What is remarkable—indeed, what constitutes the most astonishing thing about the moral development of humanity— has been the slow, uneven, but more or less steady expansion of the idea that the moral sense ought to govern a wide range—perhaps, indeed, the whole range—of human interactions. Our universe has been enlarged.

The Rise of Universalism

However common the savagery, bloodletting, and mendacity of contemporary life, a growing fraction of mankind lives under the claim that men and women are entitled to equal respect. The spread of that claim is extraordinary; even more extraordinary is the fact that so many people sometimes obey it. We are appalled by occasional stories of torture, but at one time thoughtful people approved of its routine use.[3] We are angry at terrorists who take hostages, but once diplomacy was largely conducted by the mutual seizing of hostages, and hardly anyone save their immediate families thought their fate was of the least interest. People are inclined to treat equals equally, but where once people were thought to be equal only if they were of the same sex, age, class, and religion, today people are often thought to be equal regardless of their rank or station provided only that each has made the same contribution of time and effort to some joint endeavor. People have a natural capacity for sympathy, but where once sympathy extended to those closest to us, today it often extends to people whom we have never met and animals that are not our pets.

How can we explain the great expansion of the boundaries within which the moral sense operates? How, in particular, can we explain why we believe that moral rules ought to have universal applicability? This aspiration toward the universal is the chief feature of the moral history of mankind. It is not that modern man is kinder, fairer, or more dutiful than his primitive forebears; in fact, man for man, he may be less kind, less fair, and less dutiful. It is, instead, that whatever his moral proclivities, they now encompass a larger number of people. The Apache warrior may have been far more loyal to his family and caring of his offspring than a contemporary professor of philosophy, but where the Apache would kill without remorse a warrior from another tribe, the philosopher would feel obliged not only to spare the life of a sociologist but to go to great lengths to ensure that the latter was given equal opportunity and personal liberty.

One hint as to an answer can be found when we recognize that the greatest and most sustained expansion in the boundaries of the moral sense occurred in the West.* Slavery, for example, was common in ancient times and in all parts of the world. It existed among

---

* Throughout this chapter I use "West" to mean, not all of Europe and much less all of the western hemisphere, but, roughly, northwestern Europe (England, France, Germany, the Lowlands) and North America. By always writing "West" I risk misleading the reader, but were I always to write "most parts of northwestern Europe and North America" I would risk putting him to sleep. Much of Europe along the shores of the Mediterranean retained clan- or lineage-based family systems that supported an ethos, not of individualism, but of honor and strength. In that ethos, the respect an individual might receive from others is indistinguishable from the respect his family as a whole receives. In such a culture, great attention is paid to events that sully collective honor, such as insult, seduction, or betrayal. J. K. Campbell (1964) has given us a vivid account of such an ethos in a Greek village.

hunter-gatherers and primitive agriculturalists; among many African tribes; among the early Germans and Celts; among some Native Americans; in ancient Greece and Rome; and in China, Japan, and the Near East.[4] But it was in the West that slavery was first and most systematically challenged on principled grounds. The challenge was based on the concept of freedom, a notion that, however difficult it may be to define, we westerners consider it a self-evident good. But its value has not been self-evident in other cultures; indeed, as Orlando Patterson has noted, most non-Western peoples had no word meaning "freedom" before they came into contact with the West, and those that did, such as the Chinese, typically meant by "freedom" what we would mean by "licentiousness."[5]

Having announced the concept of freedom and decided to take it seriously, people inevitably came to see slavery as incompatible with it. However uncertain and uneven the change, and however insincere or self-serving some of its advocates, the attack on slavery gradually triumphed, not simply because slavery came to be inefficient or unprofitable but because it was wrong. Lest this conclusion be rejected because it is advanced by a white westerner, let me quote the words of a black scholar raised in a Third World nation, Professor Orlando Patterson:

> At its best, the valorization of personal liberty is the noblest achievement of Western civilization. That people are free to do as they please within limits set only by the personal freedom of others; that legally all persons are equal before the law; that philosophically the individual's separate existence is inviolable; that psychologically the ultimate human condition is to be liberated from all internal and external constraints in one's desire to realize one's self; and that spiritually the son of God made himself incarnate, then gave up his life in order to redeem mankind from spiritual thralldom and to make people free and equal before God—all add up to a value complex that not only is unparalleled in any other culture but, in its profundity and power, is superior to any other single complex of values conceived by mankind.[6]

This "valorization of personal liberty" not only undermined any principled argument in favor of slavery, it undermined any claim that one was entitled to reserve one's compassion and sense of fairness for one's own kind exclusively. One would surely feel more sympathy for a loved one than for a stranger, but one could no longer justify cruelty toward strangers on the grounds that they were fundamentally different from kinfolk: if all people were equal before the law and in the eyes of God, all had some claim to consideration and equitable treatment.

The implications of this possibility were most visibly explored in Europe during the eighteenth century as part of the movement that we call the Enlightenment. The Enlightenment meant many things —an enthusiasm for science, a desire to master nature, a belief in progress, a commitment to reform—but at its root was, as Kant put it, "man's release from his self-imposed tutelage."* By tutelage he meant having one's understanding directed by another; by self-imposed he meant a lack of courage to assert and rely on one's own reason. Tutelage came from unthinking or cowardly obedience to authority—the authority of revealed religion, ancient custom, received wisdom, or hereditary monarchs.

As far as I can tell, no other modern culture underwent an Enlightenment; or more accurately, in no other place did the enlightened ideas of a few philosophers become the common understanding of the populace at large and, in time, the general practice of reconstituted governments. Not in China, not in India, not in Japan, not in the Arab world. There were, of course, gifted philosophers and scientists in all of those places, but in none did the views that made Newton, Locke, Kant, Voltaire, Hume, and Adam Smith the most influential and celebrated men of their age take root and spread widely. The Enlightenment in the West meant many things, and some thinkers embraced one aspect but not another. For most, it meant rationalism (but David Hume criticized reason and explored the sentiments); for some it meant optimism about human nature (but Voltaire was wickedly skeptical about many human qualities); for still others it meant science (but Rousseau was hardly a friend of science). I am less interested in these differences than in what its spokesmen had in common, and this was, as the historian Henry May has suggested, a belief that man could be understood by

---

* "Aufklärung ist der Ausgang des Menschen aus seiner selbstverschuldeten Unmündigkeit" (Kant, 1784). Scholars have produced no agreed-upon definition of the Enlightenment. Paul Hazard (1963) wrote of the "era of universal criticism" and the "universal obsession" with happiness, Ernst Cassirer (1951) of a belief in intellectual progress on the basis of inductive reason and the destruction of metaphysical systems, and Henry May (1976) of the opinion that man could be understood through the use of his natural faculties without the aid of revealed religion.

the use of our natural faculties and without relying on ancient custom or revealed religion.[7] The generally shared corollaries of that belief were a commitment to skeptical reason, personal freedom, and self-expression. Elsewhere, communalism, tradition, and self-control remained the dominant ethos.

For several millennia the ruling spirit of China was harmony and conformity, whether based on the flexible moral principles of Confucian thought or the rigorous and exacting legal codes of the Ch'in and Han dynasties,[8] and the ruling doctrine was that of collective responsibility: families were accountable for the conduct of their members. Under these circumstances, it was most unlikely that claims of individual freedom would make much headway. The aspects of one's moral sense that received the strongest cultural support were duty and self-control; those that received the weakest (at least outside the immediate family) were compassion and fairness.

There appears to be no settled explanation for why the Enlightenment occurred in the West and not elsewhere, and thus why in the West, to a far greater extent than elsewhere, there has been erected a cultural commitment to individualism and universalism—that is, to the belief that all men ought to be free and each man is entitled to (roughly) equal respect. We in the West are so much the products of this view that it has never occurred to most of us to wonder why and how it has emerged. We seem to assume that the universal application of one's moral sense is natural, or at least that once arbitrary power is overthrown people will naturally seek to extend the reach of their moral judgments. But universalism is not natural, localism is: witness the frequency with which authority is challenged in the name of ethnic self-determination. Moreover, universalism and individualism are not invariably good principles; the former can be the basis of tyrannical ideologies (for example, "a proletarian revolution is necessary in order to give to all men the power to which they are entitled") and the latter can be an excuse for mindless self-indulgence ("nobody can tell me what to do or when to do it").

What needs to be explained is not why in other cultures universal standards failed to appear but why in ours they did, *and took hold.* Providing a complete and accurate explanation is a task for an army of scholars, and only the first platoons are yet visible. In what follows, I will suggest in broad outline an explanation that I believe is consistent with such facts as we have, but I would be the first to admit that we may learn facts that disprove it and that it undoubtedly overlooks other possible explanations.

Some Incomplete or Imperfect Explanations

The philosophical roots of universalism are much older than the Enlightenment. The first thinkers to argue that all men have a claim on our goodwill were the Stoics, notably Seneca, Epictetus, and Marcus Aurelius. Seneca wrote: "Nature bids me to be of use to men whether they are slave or free, freedmen or free born. Wherever there is a human being there is room for benevolence."[9] The Stoics were the first cosmopolitans. They followed Aristotle in stating that man was a social animal endowed with reason, but whereas Aristotle limited his ethical and political doctrines to man in the *polis*, the Stoics suggested that the *polis*, while necessary for man's fulfillment, by no means set the boundaries of his obligations. To them, man was a citizen of the world, at least in the sense that all men, being endowed with reason, had equal claims to respect regardless of national identities. It was, perhaps, easier to make such a claim when one lived, as did the Stoics, not in the Athenian city-state, but in the empires of Alexander the Great and Rome.[10] It was particularly important, as Patterson has stressed, that Epictetus had himself once been a Roman slave.[11] No one can imagine the freedom of others quite as clearly as someone in their midst who is denied it. Though a few Roman patricians, comfortably at home in the extended realm of the Roman Empire, may have found this cosmopolitan perspective persuasive, it was at odds with the facts of daily life for most people. A perspective as exotic as cosmopolitanism was not likely to be a very robust one, and so we are not surprised to find that, with a few exceptions, it went into a hibernation that lasted the better part of two millennia.

We are accustomed to hear assertions that the Judeo-Christian religion emphasizes the universal brotherhood of man, presumably in contrast to other religions that tolerate religious bigotry. Westerners, as a consequence, often suppose that it is our unique religious tradition that explains the emergence of universal standards of morality. If all men are equal in the sight of God, how can mere man dare to make them unequal?

But that claim is wrong in two important ways. First, it is not at all clear that Judaism or Christianity are unique in asserting a universal standard. Almost all of the great religions of the world are based on universalistic principles. The Bible enjoins us to "love thy neighbor as thyself"; the Koran (or Qur'an) reminds us that "human beings are worthy of esteem because they are human" and that the "kindness of God . . . has now bound your hearts together, so that through His goodness you may become brothers." Indeed, during many periods Islam practiced a greater tolerance toward the adherents of other faiths than did Christianity. Long after their conquest of Palestine, the Muslims allowed Jews and Christians to practice their religion so long as they paid the necessary tribute. Buddha taught compassion and self-sacrifice; "right conduct" was one of the stages of the Eightfold Path along which an individual could seek an end to suffering. Morris Ginsberg, like many others, has pointed out how much most religious doctrines have in common: "A list of virtues or duties drawn up by a Buddhist would not differ very greatly from one drawn up by a Christian, a Confucianist, a Muhammedan, or a Jew. Formally all of the ethico-religious systems are universalist in scope."[12]

Second, the Bible, especially the Old Testament but parts of the New Testament as well, recognized without criticism the existence of slavery, albeit enjoining slaveholders to treat their captives compassionately. The Koran, like the Bible, assumed the existence of slavery and prescribed regulations for its practice. Slavery was practiced throughout the Christian and Muslim worlds. In many places and for long periods it was not racial slavery—the Koran, like the Bible, does not speak of superior or inferior races—but it was slavery nonetheless, and in time it became racially based.[13]

The difficulty with all philosophical and religious explanations for universalism is that they do not explain why, or under what circumstances, that view comes to be accepted and acted upon by people who are not philosophers or theologians and in spite of the common tendency among the enthusiasts of any creed to impose their beliefs on others. Slavery was inconsistent with both Roman law and most of New Testament Christianity, but it persisted for centuries nonetheless. By the time Montesquieu launched his sarcastic and devastating attack on slavery in the early eighteenth century, it had survived for nearly two millennia despite being in clear conflict with what one scholar has called the "latent egalitarianism" of Christianity.[14] Almost every man feels a sense of duty to his neighbors. What varies is not that sentiment, but rather the answer to the question, "Who is my neighbor?"[15]

Slavery was only the most extreme form of parochialism. Feudalism—that network of mutual obligations in which a subject peasantry owed service to a class of warrior lords from whom they received protection—was an intensely parochial world of local loyalties unchallenged by any strong central government with a stake in promulgating the sort of general laws that, in time, could have formed the basis for universalistic standards of justice or equality.[16] Almost every culture—China, Japan, Egypt—seems to have been feudal for much of its history, and although we now know that there were important differences among these several feudalisms, they nonetheless serve to remind us of how long mankind has lived in a world in which only local bonds, local loyalties, and local duties had any meaning.

The Origins of the Western Family

For a belief in individualism and universalism to break down this network of assigned roles and inflexible duties, in practice as well as in theory and among the people as among the philosophers, that network, unlike its counterparts in the non-Western world, must have been uniquely vulnerable. It was. One can only guess as to the sources of that vulnerability, but an informed guess would begin with the realization that, since it is in the family that the natural sociability of the child is transformed into a moral sense, it must be in familial relations that one will find the mechanism by which this transformation acquired its distinctively Western form.

Jack Goody has put the central question this way: "How is it that after about 300 A.D., certain general features of European patterns of kinship and marriage came to take a different shape from those of ancient Rome, Greece, Israel, and Egypt, and from those societies of the Mediterranean shores of the Middle East and North Africa that succeeded them?"[17] Goody begins his search for an answer by noting the contrast Pierre Guichard observed between the family system that the Arabs brought to Spain in the eighth century and the system that they found there. The Arab or "oriental" structure was organized around the maintenance of powerful male-headed clans and lineages* that served as governments as well as kinship systems and formed the basis for the ownership and inheritance of property. To sustain and protect a clan, it was desirable that wives be found from within the clan, ideally from among the daughters of the groom's paternal uncles. In that way, property would be controlled in and by the clan. To ensure that wives would come from within the clan (that is, be endogamous), it was essential that marriages be arranged, and that, in turn, meant that the decision to marry could not be left to the couple. Accompanying this marriage system, though perhaps not essential to it, was polygyny (husbands having more than one wife), easy divorce, and the exclusion of women from the public sphere.[18]

In many parts of Europe, the structure was different. At first the differences were a matter of degree and found in some places but not others. In general, marriages were monogamous, conjugal families important, divorces difficult, and wives chosen from outside as often as from within the lineage (that is, marriages tended to be exogamous). This system was made possible in part by the absence in much of Europe of strong clans. Just why clans were less important in Europe than elsewhere is not entirely clear, but it probably has much to do with geographic and economic conditions. Where land was abundant, as along the Mediterranean plains, powerful nobles could easily exercise control over those who worked the land. Where that land was also arid, the nobles were not only prominent but essential: only the wealth they commanded and the influence they wielded could make possible the vast irrigation systems necessary to produce food. Under these circumstances, as Fernand Braudel has observed, a rigid social order operating under central direction was all but inevitable. These were hardly the circumstances in which a man and a woman could establish an independent family sustained by its own plot of land. By contrast, in the regions of northwestern Europe where arable plots of land had to be hacked out of steep hillsides or dense forests, the labor of one man and his family was all that was necessary to establish a living. Such people had less need of powerful lords for either defense or irrigation.[19] Though there were some notable exceptions, in general the plains were the property of the

---

* A *clan* is a large group that claims a common ancestor, real or mythical; a *lineage* is a smaller group in which ancestry can actually be traced to a common forebearer.

nobleman, the cleared forests of the self-sufficient peasant. Where land was under individual control there was less need for arranged marriages in order to keep wealth in the family.

But land was not the whole story, for the differences that existed between Arab and European families, and within Europe between Mediterranean and northwestern families, so marked at the time of the Arab conquest of Spain, became greater with every passing century until, by the end of the Middle Ages, something like the consensual family of today had become the norm in Christendom, sanctioned by religion and law as well as by custom and preference.

Just how that change occurred is not clearly understood and, given the absence of much in the way of a written record, may always remain somewhat puzzling. But a number of scholars now agree that the Catholic church played a key role in this development. In doing so, it had first to make up its mind what it thought about marriage and sex, and on this score the Bible was not entirely consistent. Was sexuality desirable (as in the Song of Songs) or sinful (the Psalms)? Was divorce acceptable (as in the Old Testament) or unacceptable (as in the New)?[20] Saint Augustine tried to sort all of this out. Taking his guidance from the Bible's clear endorsement of marriage, he argued that marriage must be a sacrament that had, as its central purpose, procreation. That being the case, certain things followed: divorce, adultery, and polygamy were wrong because they violated the sacred status of the conjugal union, and abortion and infanticide were wrong because they were inconsistent with the principle that sex exists for the production of children.[21] It took many centuries for these doctrines to achieve anything like their modern form, but from the beginning the central thrust of church teaching and its theological foundations were clear.

What was less clear were the reasons for the church's increasing hostility to endogamy. By the end of the seventh century, according to Frances and Joseph Geis, the church had banned not only marriages between brothers and sisters but among first cousins and even among in-laws, godparents, and godchildren.[22] Goody has argued that the church was motivated to do this by a desire to enlarge its property holdings. It achieved this by "acquiring control over the way in which it [i.e., property] passed from one generation to the next."[23] To expand its control it had to break up the control exercised by clans, lineages, and feudal lords. It did this by restricting the opportunities people had for producing heirs (hence the ban on polygamy, adultery, concubinage, and remarriage after divorce) and for acquiring nonbiological heirs (hence the ban on adopting children). With fewer legal heirs, more land would pass by default to the church.[24] Other scholars, pointing out that no direct evidence indicates that this was the church's motive, suggest other, religious reasons that might have accounted for the same policies.[25] For example, the efforts of the church to moralize behavior by subjecting its members to the discipline of the confessional required the church to deal with people as individuals, not as members of clans. And if marriage was to be a sacrament, it could be received only by an individual acting voluntarily. Whatever the motive, marriage became a church-controlled rather than a clan-controlled arrangement.

In the twelfth century, Pope Alexander III ratified the consensual theory of marriage by issuing a decretal (*Veniens ad nos*) that defined a valid marriage as one in which consent had been freely given by a man and woman of the proper age and not already married. In other writings he rejected the necessity of parental consent. Alexander's reasons for doing this in the teeth of secular opposition and the contrary views of his own teacher, Gratian, are not entirely clear, but they must have been of the utmost seriousness for he surely knew that one effect of allowing a man and a woman to decide for themselves whether to marry meant that many couples would do so clandestinely (that is, without the participation of the church). He disapproved of clandestine marriages, and he and his successors would punish the participants, but the marriage itself—at least until the time of the Council of Trent—would be recognized as valid.[26]

This extension of church control over marriage led to a great diminution in the authority of parents (to say nothing of clans and lineages) and a corresponding increase in that of the betrothed couple. By 1450, we find evidence of young Germans not only concurring in their marriages but entering into the discussion of the prospect long before the decision was a fait accompli.[27] Throughout the Middle Ages, the church increasingly emphasized its view of marriage as the voluntary "union of two hearts" acting in response to affection. The consent of the betrothed, initially advanced as an addition to parental consent, in time came to take the place of it.[28] In this, the church set itself against lay opinion, clan power, and feudal practice and, perhaps unintentionally, against the long-term prospects for male dominance of the conjugal pair. This last phrase cannot, of course, do justice to the immensely complex male-female relations in the Middle Ages, much less to the equally complex process whereby, in fits and starts and with many changes of direction, the modern emancipation of women began. But however uneven and delayed was the clarification, to say nothing of the application, of the principle, the principle had been adumbrated: namely, that if marriage was a consensual union between a man and a woman in which each was bound to the other, if the husband could no longer put aside the wife quite as easily as once was the case, then the woman had some claim for equal respect that rested on principle and not merely on convenience. Medieval customs that in various places permitted the woman to share in an inheritance, raise her children after her husband's death, and serve as his business partner hinted at the larger social changes that would become possible as the full implications of marriage law were grasped.[29]

It will be objected that my account of the rise of consensual marriages says nothing about the political position of women, and it is in the political sphere that rights are won and defended. That is true. For centuries after consensual marriages became the rule, women, other than the occasional queen, played next to no role in politics or, for that matter, in political philosophy. Only Thomas Hobbes, of all the modern theorists, seems to have argued that women are not naturally subjected to men. In the state of nature they are free, he said, but since that state is a miserable one, men (that is, the male gender) quickly enter into a contract to create marriages and government, and under the terms of those contracts, women become subjected to men.[30] My point is not that consensual marriage emancipated women but rather that, the principle of consent having been endorsed, it created an assumption that individuals have a right to accept or reject the conditions of their lives, an assumption that was very different from that which prevailed among cultures committed to clan-controlled marriages. (How important that assumption was will be seen when we consider the significance of private property.) Before the implications of this individualistic assumption were realized, there was a long, hard road to be traveled, during which time many women must have wondered whether the assumption meant anything at all. But female emancipation, like the emancipation of slaves and the principle of individual rights more generally, came first to those cultures—they were Western cultures—that first agreed to that assumption.

Accompanying the rise of consensual marriages and the breakup of clan or lineage power was church support for the child-centered family. This proposition scarcely requires documentation, as the emphasis is evident from even the most casual inspection of religious art. From the sixth century on, Christian art featured the Madonna and Child in poses of affection and nurturance.[31] There is no other contemporary religion, I think, in which a child plays so central a role or in which the child's mother is an object of veneration in her own right as well as the intermediary through which the faithful seek to invoke divine assistance. We have very little data on how medieval families treated their own children but good reason for being skeptical of the claims that childhood was invented in modern times. The religious emphasis on the family and on cultivating the virtues of little children, coupled with those fragmentary facts that shed light on Roman, Frankish, and medieval practices, casts great doubt on the proposition, advanced by some, that medieval children led emotionally impoverished lives.[32] Few today support the view that medieval parents ignored or mistreated their children; as the historian David Herlihy has put it, "The medieval family was never dead to sentiment; it is only poor in sources."[33]

The ground was prepared for the growth of individualism and universalism by the dramatic changes that occurred in family life during some thousand years, stretching from the end of the Roman Empire to the Renaissance. In this time, "monogamous marriages triumphed over polygamy and male divorce power, and gradually shifted its focus away from parental and kinship concerns to the advantage of the conjugal couple. The family they were founding, despite losses of important functions to Church, state, and society, consolidated its position as the basic cell of Western society."[34] Of course lineage considerations still played a part, often an important part, in Western marriages. A glance at the novels of Jane Austen should be enough to remind us of this; if it is not, then recall how much time people today devote to discussing whether a proposed marriage is "suitable" (by which they mean an appropriate joining of people who are sufficiently similar in intelligence, taste, prospects, and background).[35] The significant change in the West was not that these matters became unimportant but that the betrothed man and woman now had a large voice—increasingly, the decisive voice—in judging suitability.

In England and northwestern Europe (and later in North America) a distinctive family system emerged. Its features have been described in remarkably similar terms by a number of scholars, notably John Hajnal, Peter Laslett, and Lawrence Stone.[36] Not only was the family increasingly independent of clan or parental control, it was also independent in its physical location. Young couples set up house by themselves instead of moving in with one or the other of their parental families. Their households thus tended to consist of two generations (the couple and their children) rather than several. For this to be possible, the young couple needed sufficient financial resources. Because these were not quickly or easily obtained, we notice two other features of the northwestern European family: the older age at which men and women first married and the existence in many households of servants who were young people still accumulating the resources necessary to start a household of their own. Of course many never did, and never married. Some became part of a permanent serving class. Parents often made payments to facilitate a marriage, but unlike in those Mediterranean regions where these payments took the form of a bride price (men paying money to the bride's father in order to obtain—buy?—a wife), in northwestern Europe there was more likely to be a dowry (money brought *by* a bride *to* her husband to help make possible an independent household).

The key demographic facts are not in serious dispute; what is unclear is their subjective significance. Owing to the paucity of contemporary written records (we are speaking of developments that began in the fourteenth and fifteenth centuries), that significance may never be known with any precision. But as Hajnal has observed, the emotional content of a marriage cannot be the same in a society where the bride is a girl of sixteen or younger (as was the case in most of the world) and one in which she is a woman of twenty-four or older (as was characteristic of northwestern Europe),[37] especially if in the first case she was the object of an arranged marriage and in the second the participant in a consensual one. Among the easily overlooked consequences of a system of independent households made up of a husband and wife with some substantial worldly experience was the growth of the idea of privacy. Lawrence Stone has suggested that nuclear families made possible the withdrawal of family members from public rooms where many people of several generations slept, conversed, and had sex into private rooms where these things happened behind closed doors. These arrangements, he conjectures, gave further impetus to the concept of individualism.[38]

Very little of this happened in other societies. William J. Goode concluded his monumental survey of family systems across cultures this way: "For the past thousand years the Western family systems have been very different from those in China, India, Japan, and the Arab countries."[39] In the West (more accurately, northwestern Europe), unlike elsewhere, there has been no clan system (except in isolated areas), no ancestor worship, and individuals rather than families have been held responsible for crimes. Arranged marriages gave way to conjugal consent. Concubinage and polygamy were abolished in theory and sharply curtailed in practice. Many of these changes accelerated after the Protestant Reformation (during which Henry VIII claimed that he, not the pope, would determine his marital status), but they were well under way when the Roman Catholic church was the unchallenged center of European religious authority.

In the Arab, Chinese, and Indian worlds, by contrast, arranged marriages controlled by clan or lineage interests were the dominant system down almost to the present. In some places (India) exogamy was encouraged, in others (the Near East) endogamy was the rule, but everywhere outside northwestern Europe marriages were determined by political and genealogical considerations. The individual was subordinate to the family and the family to the clan.[40] As long as that practice endured, the spread of any notions of individual choice, personal freedom, and the child-centered family would occur, if at all, only in the face of powerful obstacles erected and maintained by the social structure. Philosophers and religious leaders might arise to urge reason and universalism, but their words would fall on unprepared ears.

Travel and Commerce

A complementary explanation for the emergence of the principle of equal respect and universal standards can be found in the growth in travel and the expansion of commerce. By the fifteenth century, education and travel among Europeans had increased significantly. More and more people saw strange lands, met strange people, and read of strange practices. For some, of course, those experiences only confirmed in them their sense of superiority, but for others the encounters aroused their curiosity and challenged their convictions. The Age of Discovery vastly expanded the range of European knowledge, markets, and political conflicts; that much everyone recalls. But what is sometimes forgotten is the profound implications of this exploration for morality.

The question can be simply put: Were the members of the newly encountered races to be regarded as having a human nature that made them men in the language of the Bible and classical philosophy (in which case they were entitled to full moral status, however lacking in education and culture they may be), or were they to be viewed as having a lesser nature, as being monsters or subhumans (in which case they were natural slaves)? Christopher Columbus reported that the inhabitants of the New World were not the human monstrosities many had expected; on the contrary, they were rather attractive men and women, albeit ones with dark skins. If that was the case, were not these people children of God and thus among those whom Jesus said should be baptized? Saint Augustine had thought so; "however strange he may appear to our senses in bodily form or colour or motion or utterance," such an individual "is descended from the one man who was first created."[41]

But Augustine was not a conquistador eager for cheap labor and hidden silver. And so a great debate ensued over the moral status of the people of the New World and, by implication, of non-Europeans anywhere. It was literally a debate. In 1550 Charles V suspended conquests in the New World until the question of the moral status of the Indians could be resolved by a special council of theologians who would hear a debate between Bartolomé de Las Casas, a slave-owning conquistador whose religious conversion had led him to renounce slavery,* and Juan Ginés de Sepúlveda, a scholar who, on the basis of Aristotle's *Politics*, argued that some people, and in particular the peoples of the New World, were natural slaves. The debate began in August 1550 in Valladolid, the capital of Castile, and went on for weeks. In the end, the council could not make up its mind and so the principle was left undecided.[42] The practical result of the nondecision seemed to be a victory for the views of Sepúlveda, since the conquests (now called "pacifications") resumed and Sepúlveda became a hero to Spanish colonialists.

---

* So eager was Las Casas to defend the Indians that he got a bit carried away, defending all of their practices, including cannibalism and human sacrifice. A few modern anthropologists, in their zealous commitment to cultural relativism, have made the same mistake that Las Casas made out of genuine humanism.

But in the long run Sepúlveda's views did not prevail: indeed, they were not even allowed to be published in Spain during his lifetime. And the king's regulations governing settlement were revised to bar slavery and urge kindness in the treatment of the natives. By contrast, Las Casas's writings were published and had a great impact on Catholic theology. They were taken up and enlarged upon by the late sixteenth- and early seventeenth-century followers of Thomas Aquinas. The motives of such thinkers as the Dominican Francisco de Vitoria and the Jesuit Franciso Suárez were mixed. While they may have wished to protect the Indians against exploitation, they also wanted to refute what they regarded as the heresies of the Protestant Reformation, especially the view of Martin Luther that man was by nature wicked, a slave of base passions and corrupt reason. Suárez argued that men are "by nature free," "possess the use of their reason," and have within them "an inherent justice given by Christ." Cardinal Robert Bellarmine described men as having "an inherent [sense of] justice" that enables them to apprehend the laws of God. Because of this, Sepúlveda was wrong to claim that infidels are fit subjects for enslavement: "The law of nature is written in one particular way in the minds and in the hearts even of the infidels."[43]

When we look back on the enforced baptisms that Catholic missionaries sometimes practiced, we may forget that there was growing up within the church, as a direct result of the need to confront the moral issues raised by the Age of Discovery, a distinction between viewing native peoples as heathens and viewing them as subhuman. If they were heathens (or barbarians), they needed religious instruction but could not be made slaves or denied, ultimately, the right to form a political society. If they were subhuman, they could be enslaved or, for that matter, slaughtered without justification. The debate was won, albeit only with deferred practical impact, by Suárez and the Thomists. There was, so far as I know, no equivalent debate outside Europe.

Commerce may have had an effect on moral standards comparable to that of travel, both in the sense that it potentially enlarged the reach of those standards and that for a long time only a few people drew this lesson from it. Many people believe that commerce not only requires but develops habits of impersonal valuation and fair dealing. Many European thinkers in the seventeenth and eighteenth centuries hoped that calm, commercial interests would help tame man's unruly and parochial passions.* Personal vendettas, dynastic wars, predatory sexuality, and endless duels upset the predictable routines on which large-scale commerce depends. In this view, families obsessed with honor may find it more difficult than those preoccupied with gain to prosper in commercial transactions. Commercial life requires transactions—buying, selling, lending, borrowing—that are made easier by trust and a reputation for trustworthiness. To acquire that useful reputation, fair dealing is necessary, even with people of different clans. Industry progresses with the division of labor, a process that is facilitated by (and in turn reinforces) the view that each person should be judged on merit alone; that is, on the worth of his or her contribution to the collective effort.

It is easy to overstate the contributions of commerce to the acceptance of more universal moral standards. Though impersonal valuations may be part of the commercial spirit in some places, the experience of East Asia suggests that it is hardly essential. Students of the economic development of Japan and the Little Dragons—Korea, Singapore, and the like—often report that trust, of the sort that is facilitated by familial and family-like ties, is more important than the abstract commitment to fairness that is associated with having universal rules or standards. Commerce may have encouraged universalistic principles in the West without having done so in the East.

The weakening of clan and lineage powers that has occurred in the family systems of the Near East, India, and China seems to have been caused by ideological and political factors rather than economic ones. William Goode has shown that the rise of consensual marriages to replace arranged ones and the granting of greater freedoms to wives took place in Arab countries long after great cities had come into being and industrialization had been underway, and occurred in China before the massive Communist effort at forced industrialization.[44] The clans that had once controlled marriage rules and family life were viewed, correctly, by nationalist rulers as barriers to the creation of a modern state and the extension of bureaucratic rule. The foundation of clan power was its control over marriage, inheritance, and property, which meant, in practical terms, its control over

---

* Albert Hirschman (1977) has provided an elegant summary of this view.

marriage, period. Diminishing clan power meant, of necessity, altering the marriage system.

In retrospect, we can see that the feudal system of Europe was different from that found in other regions and that these differences contained with them the seeds of the system's destruction. In the Near East, China, and India, the feudal system (or in India, the caste system) was congruent with the family system, a linkage supported in some places by those religious beliefs emphasizing reverence for ancestors. Under these conditions, the family could scarcely be expected to become the seed bed of individualism; family life, clan power, and feudal obligations combined to enforce a sense of group identity and communal obligation. In Europe, by contrast, the church challenged the feudal system for popular loyalty, economic power, and political supremacy, and by doing so began to create a family structure that was independent of feudal life. The Western family slowly became autonomous, with its autonomy protected by church-defined and church-enforced rules that weakened arranged marriages in favor of consensual ones and opposed divorce, adultery, polygyny, and concubinage.[45] To be sure, this autonomy developed unevenly, and one should not be surprised to discover that it experienced the slowest progress along the Mediterranean shores, especially in those areas once under Arab influence.

Feudalism was the enemy of the strong state; the weak feudalism of Europe was the first to give way to strong states, and those states found it easier to extend their power if they dealt with individuals rather than clans. European feudalism was weaker than that in other places in part because it was not integrated with clan loyalties (as Marc Bloch put it, "feudal ties proper were developed [in Europe] when those of kinship proved inadequate")[46] and in part because the church was a powerful rival.

Consensual marriages leading to families that were independent of clan control do not automatically produce conjugal habits or child-rearing practices that emphasize individual worth and self-determination, much less ones that inculcate universal as opposed to parochial moral understandings. Autonomous families are as capable of teaching bigotry and narrow self-interest as are clan-dominated ones. But the spread of relatively autonomous, consensual marriages prepared the ground for an extension of individualism. Individualism implies universalism, since if each person is morally equivalent then all peoples are morally equivalent. Commerce may have provided a practical reason for acting on such universalistic beliefs in order to take advantage of the division of labor and the expansion of markets, and theology provided doctrinal support—the view that all men, however primitive, have souls and natural reason—for acting as if universalism were true.

Private Property

The decline of the power of clans and lineages and the rise of consensual marriages occurred in many parts of Europe, but in one part, England, those changes were reinforced by a remarkable and still largely unexplained development in property relations. As Alan Macfarlane has shown, as far back as the thirteenth century English rural life was not peasant life; that is to say, in England, unlike in most of Europe, land was held by individuals who were free to sell or bequeath it.[47]

Peasant life, strictly understood, did not recognize individual ownership. A Polish peasant, for example, worked land that was owned, not by him or by any single man, but by the family as a whole and over time. The farm might be managed by a father or eldest son, or even by a son-in-law, but none of them owned it: they could not sell it or bequeath it.[48] The members of the family did not hold shares in the land; it was the family as a collectivity that owned it, worked it, and consumed its product. There was no market for land and precious little for market products. One can scarcely speak of peasants having property rights; they had claims as members of a kinship group to a share in the land's yield, but no claims as individuals to the land itself. The peasant village consisted of interrelated families whose members rarely visited another village, to say nothing of any sizable city. Culture was village culture; power was village power; marriages were among village members. The prevalence of arranged marriages and the relative unimportance of romantic love were reflections not simply of local custom but of psychological reality: romantic love, as the children of the Israeli kibbutzim have learned, is not likely among people who have known each other since childhood.[49] In these circumstances, the status and power of women will be especially low. They will be valued for their labor and reproductive potential, but without any chance to own land as individuals or to shape the inheritance of land among others, their capacity for independent action will be slight.[50]

For mysterious reasons, Macfarlane writes, a very different system emerged in England as early as the thirteenth century. Individualism in economic and social life existed, rooted in property rights, partible inheritances, and cash markets. Land was a commodity that could be, and was, bought and sold; fathers bequeathed their land to particular offspring, usually but not always to the eldest son;* men and women hired out for cash wages; people moved from one place to another, and many knew town as well as village life. Women, unmarried as well as married, could (and did) own property, make wills and contracts, and bring suit. Though in principle a married woman was subject to her husband's authority, in practice her concurrence was required for many of his legal actions.[51] That many women were unmarried is an indication that arranged marriages were not the exclusive custom. There were no insuperable barriers dividing poor farmers from rich ones, and so some who began poor ended up rich. The existence of individual property rights made England from a very early time a litigious society: if land could be bought and sold, inherited and bequeathed, it was inevitable that there would be countless disputes over the terms of the sale or the bequest. The courts of equity that settled these disputes inevitably decided something even more important than arguments over land; they resolved—or at least shaped—a broader set of claims about individual rights. The English common law grew out of land claims but embraced much more.

We are accustomed to thinking of individualism as having emerged as the shackles of an older communal order were thrown off and inclined to suppose that the shackles were broken at some decisive historical moment. But it is hard to imagine that anything so powerful as the peasant village, the arranged marriage, or the collective ownership of land would be easily thrown off, or even that they would be perceived as shackles. And while political institutions may be altered in a decisive revolutionary moment, the customs which shape daily life rarely experience revolutionary change. When they change, they change slowly and in response to powerful and

---

* The existence of primogeniture—the custom whereby the eldest son inherited all the land and the younger sons nothing—was itself evidence that England was not a peasant society, for this rule made it impossible for the household to maintain over time a collective or joint ownership of the land and gave rise to the existence of landless men who were obliged to seek their fortunes on the strength of their individual initiative.

lasting pressures that cut deeply into that life. Something as momentous—and as contrary to general custom—as the successful assertion of individual rights over the claims of collective obligations must have taken centuries to accomplish, for it involves the alteration of folkways possessing great inertial force. We should not be surprised, therefore, to discover that this assertion took hold most deeply in a nation, England, that had been evolving in this direction for half a millennium.*

Weakening the links between men and their clans by equipping them with the ability to buy and sell property and the right to consent to marriages slowly created the conditions under which the more terrifying requirements of custom could be challenged. At first this meant only that men and women could assert their own claims without implying that men and women everywhere had equal claims. Before men display a cosmopolitan face they acquire a human one, and they do this by challenging barbarities based on narrow superstition and tyrannies based on naked power. As the zone of autonomous action is widened, a wider scope is allowed for the expression of men's moral senses. As freedom to act and think within that wider scope is appreciated for the benefits it confers, people will rarely seek to return to an era of more limited choice. And for good reason: modern life means less disease, fewer murders, and gentler customs.[52]

In suggesting that the growth of universalism and individualism was the product, in part, of the rise of consensual marriages and the existence of private property, I have sketched out but not proved a bold thesis. That sketch ignores the many other factors that almost surely played a role, such as the rise of commercial law in European towns and the extension of the king's peace over those towns and the surrounding countryside. The laws that were valued because they best facilitated commerce turned out to be the laws that most expanded personal liberty; the predictability, regularity, and security necessary for a vibrant commerce could not easily be accomplished by laws that made particularistic distinctions among people and

---

* By the same token, the Industrial Revolution did not occur first in England because a historical window of opportunity had just been opened by some fortuitous circumstance. England had been capitalistic, albeit a capitalism without factories, for centuries before industrialization began in earnest (cf. Hartwell, 1967).

assigned them to categories or ranks with differing duties incumbent on each. Prosperity requires the division of labor and easy exchange, and these in turn require uniformity of treatment and certainty of application. The expansion of public order, necessary for commerce but also valued in its own right, reduced the risks people ran when they trusted one another. It would be foolish to expect that people would judge one another by universalistic standards if an encounter with someone not of one's own family or clan was likely to have violent consequences. All of these changes, and many more than one could no doubt enumerate, may have been an important part of the emergence of universalism, but we must not forget that these additional factors, such as the rise of commercial law and the maintenance of public order among disparate peoples, could occur far more readily in those places where the power of clans over women and property had first been broken and replaced with individual consent and private ownership.

The strength of the moral senses are revealed when circumstances permit their fuller expression and wider effect. In the new order, hardly anyone wished to return to a life in which the customs required suttee, infanticide, infibulation, cannibalism, or ritual torture. If the goal of the Enlightenment was happiness, then the historical changes leading up to it did, indeed, tend to produce greater happiness. But not complete happiness. That is an obvious impossibility so long as men have limitless and conflicting wants and resources are finite and costly. But there is a less obvious barrier to happiness, and that can be found in the limitations inherent in the life of reason.

The Ambiguous Legacy of the Enlightenment

When the philosophical movement known as the Enlightenment arrived, it took different forms in different countries, but in all it attacked both collectivism and the church, seeking to replace feudal obligation with public citizenship and revealed religion with skeptical reason. Individual man, freed from the self-incurred tutelage of which Kant wrote, was to be the measure of all things, and the modern liberal state was to be the arena in which the summation of his individual preferences would constitute public policy. What is astonishing about the Enlightenment is not that a few philosophers thought this way but that so many people believed they were right. Those people who first and most widely accepted it were the English and those Englishmen who settled North America.

The remnants of arranged marriages and patriarchal families came under intensified attack, and the attack scored impressive gains. In eighteenth-century England and France, as Peter Gay notes, the father's power over his children and the husband's over his wife markedly declined; consensual marriages, for centuries the rule, now increasingly became the practice. Monogamous marriage was praised, not as a sacrament with its attendant theological obligations, but as a contract, a partnership, with secular value and rationalistic foundations.[53] David Hume did not hesitate to push the modern view to its logical conclusion in a way that scandalized many of his contemporaries. The family and family virtues, he wrote, were based, not on revealed religion or abstract duty, nor even on an innate moral sense, but on utility. Because the "long and helpless infancy of man" requires parents for his survival, and because that in turn "requires the virtue of chastity or fidelity to the marriage bed," chastity and fidelity (and marriage generally) are virtues because they are useful.*

But what if people think that these virtues are not useful? The critics of the Enlightenment, such as Edmund Burke, and of utilitarianism, such as James Fitzjames Stephens, pointed to this possibility, but for a long time it seemed to be at worst a very remote one. In eighteenth- and nineteenth-century Europe and America, the family and communal life were so central to the customs and institutions of the day that hardly anyone could conceive of their being undermined. Ordinary folk accepted the idea that a strong family was essential to a moral life and took comfort and inspiration from the New Testament's emphasis on families in general (the "family of man") and one family in particular, that of Jesus, Mary, and Joseph. A family-based morality became the defining

* Hume, 1751:41. Hume was not, of course, a pure utilitarian. That was left for another century and for such lesser men as Mill and Bentham. Indeed, the passage quoted above hints at what Hume himself made explicit in other places: fidelity is useful to marriage, and marriage is useful to the child—but why do we care about the child? Surely not because it is "useful"; rather, because it is natural. In this regard Hume took more from Francis Hutcheson than he sometimes acknowledged.

feature of the Victorian age, and as a result mid-Victorian England "was more moral, more proper, more law-abiding than any other society in recent history."[54]

Intellectuals had a slightly different view. To many of them, the justification for the family was now reason rather than religion, and moral life was based on utility or choice rather than scripture or custom. Where the common man made the cultivation of familial morality his goal, the intellectual or artistic man made the cultivation of his talents and the expression of his sensibilities the goal. The latter assumed, of course, the continued existence of some shared moral code; after all, without that people would be rude and crime might increase. But it was only necessary to assume it; it was not necessary to work at it or even (beyond a certain conventional affirmation) to believe in it. One could take the product of a strong family life—gentlemanly conduct—for granted and get on with the task of liberating individuals from stuffy convention, myopic religion, and political error.

The newly autonomous family had two faces. One, drawing on a legacy of religious guidance and biblical purpose reinforced by the teachings of the pietistic sects, such as Methodism, emphasized the responsibility of the family to inculcate self-control and personal responsibility. This was the face most frequently seen in the nineteenth century (and still today), and it is the face most frequently exposed to criticism for the hypocrisies and pettiness that sometimes are practiced in its name. The other face, drawing on the individualistic and egalitarian principles by which the modern family was formed, emphasized the opportunity for the family to foster sympathy and self-expression. This face was less commonly seen, but it is the one that in our times is criticized for its tendency to produce self-indulgence, political radicalism, and countercultural life-styles.

The moral senses are differently cultivated in different families. The slow but distinctive evolution of the family in Europe and North America has exposed those differences more dramatically than is yet the case in the family systems of other regions. The differences go to the heart of the moral disputes of our time. Does the good life depend on rights or on virtue? Are rights inherent only in individuals, or also (and more importantly) in groups? We sometimes divide cultures into those that are "group-centered" as opposed to those that are "individual-centered." Though often simplistic and over-generalized, there is a grain of truth in this distinction.* That grain is found in the complaints of those people from China, Japan, or the Arab world who deride what they take to be the licentiousness and nihilism of Western life, and in the complaints of those people from the West who are appalled at the conformity and cruelty of some aspects of life in the Near and Far East. It is also found in the writings of Western thinkers who worry that the philosophical commitment to radical individualism is destructive not only of family life but also of those mediating institutions—small communities and face-to-face associations—that sustain a morally competent, socially connected individual against the estrangement of mass society.[55]

My view is that much wanton cruelty and unreasoning prejudice are averted by a family system that encourages a belief in individual dignity and a widely extended capacity for sympathy and by the opportunity for the widespread ownership of private property. But unlike some enthusiasts of the Enlightenment, I believe that this gain is purchased at a price, and sometimes a very high one: a lessened sense of honor and duty, and a diminished capacity for self-control.

No such worries beset some of the leading thinkers of the French version of the Enlightenment. They believed that human nature was universal. Laws and fashions may differ, but passions and sentiments are the same everywhere.[56] Hence one can scientifically deduce from this universal nature universal rules and the prescription for a generally good society.

I agree that there is a universal human nature, but disagree that one can deduce from it more than a handful of rules or solutions to any but the most elemental (albeit vitally important) human problems. The reason is that one universal truth—man's sociability, expressed and refined in the affections between child and parent—coexists with other universal truths—man's ambition, avarice, and vanity—and both tendencies are engulfed by a natural preference for one's own kind. The struggle among these sentiments is shaped by

---

* Harry Triandis (1989) has done important work in establishing the existence of individualistic and collectivistic orientations in the attitudes of people from different cultures. Collectivists see themselves as part of a group that shares a common fate, that sets important goals, and is entitled to control behavior; individualists see themselves as determining their fate, choosing their goals and allegiances, and autonomously regulating their own behavior. Both value self-reliance, but to the former it means "I am not a burden on my group" while to the latter it means "I can do my own thing."

circumstances and necessity as well as by ritual, religion, and poetry. The passions of man are in conflict; his moral sense is one of his calmer passions, but it cannot always prevail over its wilder rivals and its reach is uncertain and contingent. And even when it prevails, it provides at best a set of tests for human action, not a set of hierarchical rules for ordering that action.

These tests are limiting cases, like those in engineering that specify the maximum bearing strength of a wall; but unlike them, the moral tests cannot be discovered by precise measurement. If we exceed the bearing strength of a wall, the building collapses. But in human affairs the limiting conditions emerge more gradually and less discernibly. We may not realize that we have exceeded them until long after our happiness and that of our family and friends has been ruined, and even then we may not be aware that this calamity arose from a neglect of fundamental familial and human bonds.

Some of the philosophes who elaborated the central ideas of the French Enlightenment were much too optimistic about how deeply we could understand human nature or how confidently we could derive social principles from such knowledge as we had. In a way, they knew this, but they rarely faced up to the awareness. This vague unease about the limits of their own endeavors can be found in their attitude toward religion. To Voltaire, Christianity was an "infamy" that had to be crushed. (He was also an anti-Semite.)[57] But though the Christian religion was to Voltaire an especially oppressive form of tutelage, it was also a useful one—provided its influence was limited to the masses. "I want my attorney, my tailor, my servants, even my wife to believe in God," Voltaire wrote, because "then I shall be robbed and cuckolded less often."[58] On one occasion, he silenced his fellow philosophes from speaking further about atheism until he had sent the servants out of the room. "Do you want your throats cut tonight?" he chided.[59]

Some may explain the extremism of French views on these points by reference to "the French temperament." But I suspect that there is a simpler explanation. The Enlightenment came to most of western Europe, but in some places—France was one—it came as a revolutionary doctrine that had to be maintained in the teeth of official opposition, religious dogma, and communal customs. Embattled intellectuals are dogmatic intellectuals. But in England the Enlightenment came at the end of a long process of social and political evolution that had left scarcely any barriers to individualism standing. David Hume and Adam Smith had neither an absolute monarch to overthrow nor an orthodox creed to refute. They spoke to a generally prosperous nation of farmers who were already, to a large degree, familiar with law, philosophy, and commerce; who had long since owned land, asserted rights, and consented to marriages; and who knew something of urban life as well as of village traditions. The Enlightenment was simply the carrying forward of a philosophical tradition—skeptical reason, the scientific method, individual rights, government by consent—that had begun centuries earlier in the writings of Locke and Bacon. Hume may have been thought impious, but Smith was awarded a professorship.

Despite the differences between the commonsensical views of the Anglo-Scottish Enlightenment and the more strident and extreme claims of some of their French counterparts, thinkers in both countries were alike in attacking (with either English politeness or French bluntness) the claims of revealed religion. One may smile at Voltaire, but the best-remembered sentence in Edward Gibbon's history of the decline and fall of the Roman Empire expresses the same cynicism: "The various modes of worship which prevailed in the Roman world were all considered by the people as equally true, by the philosopher as equally false, and by the magistrate as equally useful."[60]

But it is quite possible, I would suggest, that on this matter the philosophes got things exactly wrong. They were under the illusion that it is religious fear that ensures that ordinary people will usually behave in an upright and decent manner. If these eighteenth-century thinkers had been familiar with modern China or Japan, they would not have been so confident. It is hard to find places where people are less frequently told that the prospect of divine wrath awaits their every misdeed or ones where, at least in the ordinary affairs of everyday life, misdeeds are less common. It was not the fear of eternal damnation that kept Voltaire safe from his servant's knives or his wife's adultery, but the instincts and habits of a lifetime, founded in nature, developed in the family, and reinforced by quite secular fears of earthly punishment and social ostracism. Habituation, as Aristotle said, is the source of most of the moral virtues. Religion is for many a source of solace and for a few a means of redemption, but if everyday morality had depended on religious conviction, the human race would have destroyed itself eons ago.

But for the elites it may be a different matter. Intellectuals are, almost by definition, people who question custom, alter habits, and challenge common sense. What they question they tend to destroy, for themselves if not for others. If they decide—as some did in the seventeenth and eighteenth centuries—that religion is myth, it is they, and not the people who have no interest in reading their clever essays and whose lives are governed by habit and not doctrine, who must find something with which to replace God. Friedrich Nietzsche's bold statement that God is dead had greater significance for people who read Nietzsche than it did for the common man. Believing, as they do, in systems of thought rather than habits of life, it is intellectuals who must find a foundation for any system by which they hope to live. The history of mankind is littered with the rubble of these systems, mute testimony to the enlightened ignorance that governed their construction: nihilism, Marxism, hedonism, artistic self-indulgence. Systems collapse faster, and with greater collateral damage, than habits; habits have lasted for centuries, surviving even the most oppressive regimes erected on the most "enlightened" principles.

For several generations after the Enlightenment had begun, most men, intellectual as well as practical, lived lives of ordinary virtue without giving much thought to why they did. Even Voltaire believed that man's nature was fundamentally moral; man had, he wrote, "certain inalienable feelings" that constitute "the eternal bonds and first laws of human society."[61] Indeed, elites and masses pursued many of the same reformist activities: intellectuals and workers alike urged temperance, fostered uplift, and stressed duty. But the former were living on borrowed moral capital, a debt they scarcely were aware of in the eighteenth century, began to worry about in the nineteenth, and found they could not repay in the twentieth.[62]

Today it is customary to refer to intellectuals and artists as being part—indeed, as having created—an "adversary culture,"[63] by which is meant a culture opposed to the habits and preferences of the working and middle classes. In its extreme form, it represents the effort to carry to its ultimate conclusion the individualistic tendencies of the Western family while rejecting all of its other tendencies. In doing so, adherents of the adversary culture would be surprised to learn that they are taking advantage of opportunities created by the Catholic church and English farmers starting in the twelfth century.

PART THREE
Character

The Moral Sense
and Human Character

To say that there exists a moral sense (or, more accurately, several moral senses) is to say that there are aspects of our moral life that are universal, a statement that serious thinkers from Aristotle to Adam Smith had no trouble in accepting. In this view, cultural diversity, though vast, exotic, and bewildering, is not the whole story. In modern times, historians, philosophers, and anthropologists have sought for scientific evidence by which the existence of such universals could be proved; a few claim to have found it, but most feel that they have not, an outcome that has left many scholars skeptical about whether anything of universal significance can be said about our moral life.* The box score has been something like this: Relativists 10, Universalists 1.

I am reckless enough to think that many conducting this search have looked in the wrong places for the wrong things because they have sought for universal rules rather than universal dispositions. It would be astonishing if many of the rules by which men lived were everywhere the same, since almost all rules reflect the indeterminate intersection of sentiment and circumstance. Rules (or customs) are the adjustment of moral sensibilities to the realities of economic circumstances, social structures, and family systems, and one should not be surprised to find that the great variety of these conditions have produced an equally great variety in the rules by which they are

* A useful account of this search by a scholar who contributed greatly to it is Clyde Kluckhohn's 1955 essay on ethical relativity.

regulated. There is a universal urge to avoid a violent death, but the rules by which men seek to serve this urge require in some places that we drive on the right-hand side of the road, in others on the left-hand side, and in still others that we give the right of way to cows. Infanticide, as we saw in the first chapter in this book, has been tolerated if not justified at some time and in some places, depending on the ability of parents to feed another child or cope with a deformed one. Even so, some universal rules have been discovered: those against incest, for example, or against homicide in the absence of defined excusing conditions.

Are There Moral Universals?

To find what is universal about human nature, we must look behind the rules and the circumstances that shape them to discover what fundamental dispositions, if any, animate them and to decide whether those dispositions are universal. If such universal dispositions exist, we would expect them to be so obvious that travelers would either take them for granted or overlook them in preference to whatever is novel or exotic.

Those fundamental dispositions are, indeed, both obvious and other-regarding: they are the affection a parent, especially a mother, bears for its child and the desire to please that the child brings to this encounter. Our moral senses are forged in the crucible of this loving relationship and expanded by the enlarged relationships of families and peers. Out of the universal attachment between child and parent the former begins to develop a sense of empathy and fairness, to learn self-control, and to acquire a conscience that makes him behave dutifully at least with respect to some matters. Those dispositions are extended to other people (and often to other species) to the extent that these others are thought to share in the traits we find in our families. That last step is the most problematic and as a consequence is far from common; as we saw in the preceding chapter, many cultures, especially those organized around clans and lineages rather than independent nuclear families based on consensual marriages and private property, rarely extend the moral sense, except in the most abstract or conditional way, to other peoples. The moral sense for most people remains particularistic; for some, it aspires to be universal.

Because our moral senses are at origin parochial and easily

blunted by even trivial differences between what we think of as familiar and what we define as strange, it is not hard to explain why there is so much misery in the world and thus easy to understand why so many people deny the existence of a moral sense at all. How can there be a moral sense if everywhere we find cruelty and combat, sometimes on a monstrous scale? One rather paradoxical answer is that man's attacks against his fellow man reveal his moral sense because they express his social nature. Contrary to Freud, it is not simply their innate aggressiveness that leads men to engage in battles against their rivals, and contrary to Hobbes, it is not only to control their innate wildness that men create governments. Men are less likely to fight alone against one other person than to fight in groups against other groups. It is the desire to earn or retain the respect and goodwill of their fellows that keeps soldiers fighting even against fearsome odds,[1] leads men to accept even the most distorted or implausible judgments of their peers,[2] induces people to believe that an authority figure has the right to order them to administer shocks to a "student,"[3] and persuades many of us to devalue the beliefs and claims of outsiders.[4]

We all, I believe, understand this when we think of families sticking together against interlopers, friends banding together against strangers, and soldiers standing fast against enemies. But the affiliative drive is so powerful that it embraces people unrelated and even unknown to us. Patriotic nationalism and athletic team loyalties are obvious examples of this, but the most important case—most important because it both precedes nationalism and professional sports and animates so much of history right down to the present—is ethnic identity.

What makes Serbs, Croats, Slovaks, Ghegs, Tosks, Armenians, Kurds, Bantus, Masai, Kikuyus, Ibos, Germans, and countless—literally countless—other peoples argue, fight, and die for "ethnic self-determination"? Why do they seek to be ruled by "one's own kind" when what constitutes "one's own kind" is so uncertain and changeable, being variously defined as people whom you think are like you in language, customs, place of origin, and perhaps other, inexpressible, things as well? Donald Horowitz, who has puzzled over this phenomenon as persistently as anyone I know, has observed that we lack any good explanation and that the inclusiveness of the ethnic group with which someone feels associated often changes over time.[5] For some reason, the need for affiliation is so powerful that it reaches as far as one can find a historically plausible and emotionally satisfying principle of similarity.

We may bemoan what we sometimes think of as the "senseless" violence attendant on ethnic conflict. But imagine a world in which people attached no significance to any larger social entity than themselves and their immediate families. Can we suppose that in such a world there would be any enlarged sense of duty, any willingness to sacrifice oneself for the benefit of others, or even much willingness to cooperate on risky or uncertain tasks for material gain?

Edward C. Banfield has portrayed a world something like this in his account of the peasants living in the southern Italian village of Montegrano (a pseudonym), where the unwillingness of people to cooperate in any joint endeavor kept them in a condition of the most extreme poverty and backwardness. Their reluctance to cooperate was not the product of ignorance (many of the peasants were quite well informed about local affairs), a lack of resources (other peoples just as poorly endowed have created bustling economies), or political oppression (the Montegranese were free to organize, vote, and complain, but few did). The lack of cooperative effort, Banfield argued, was chiefly the result of a culture that made people almost entirely preoccupied with their families' short-run material interest and led them to assume that everybody else would do likewise.[6] Under these circumstances, there was no prospect of collective effort on behalf of distant or intangible goals. Whatever its source, this ethos of "amoral familism" prevented people from identifying and affiliating with any group larger than the nuclear family.

If the Montegranese had acquired larger patterns of identifications and affiliations such that common endeavors without immediate material benefit became possible, they would also, I suspect, have acquired a set of relationships binding them together against people who were dissimilar on a larger scale than the family: people in other villages, northern Italians, non-Catholics, or whatever. Affiliation requires boundaries; a "we" must be defined on some basis if there are to be any obligations to the "we"; and once there is a we, there will be a "they." Truly parochial people may not engage in "senseless violence," but then they may not engage in "senseless cooperation" either.

But note that even in Montegrano, adults cared for their children. They were not "amoral individualists," even though child care was costly and burdensome; indeed, being poor, it was especially burdensome. Despite the burdens, the birth of a child was a joyous event and its illnesses a cause for great concern. As the children grew up, they were greatly indulged and inconsistently disciplined, so much so, indeed, that the somewhat selfish and irresponsible behavior of adults was taught to the children.

I have said that our moral senses are natural. I mean that in two related senses of the word: they are to some important degree innate, and they appear spontaneously amid the routine intimacies of family life. Since these senses, though having a common origin in our natural sociability, are several, gender and culture will profoundly influence which of them—sympathy or duty, fairness or self-control—are most valued. And since these senses are to a degree indeterminate, culture will affect how they are converted into maxims, customs, and rules. In some places and at some times men cherish honor above all else; at other times and in other places, they value equity. Often they restrict these sentiments to kith and kin; sometimes they extend them to humankind as a whole. Some cultures emphasize the virtues of duty and self-control, others those of sympathy and fairness.

The existence of so much immoral behavior is not evidence of the weakness of the moral senses. The problem of wrong action arises from the conflict among the several moral senses, the struggle between morality and self-interest, and the corrosive effect of those forces that blunt the moral senses. We must often choose between duty and sympathy or between fairness and fidelity. Should I fight for a cause that my friends do not endorse, or stand foursquare with my buddy whatever the cause? Does my duty require me to obey an authoritative command or should my sympathy for persons hurt by that command make me pause? Does fairness require me to report a fellow student who is cheating on an exam, or does the duty of friendship require me to protect my friend? The way we make those choices will, for most of us, be powerfully shaped by particular circumstances and our rough guess as to the consequences of a given act. Sociability has two faces. Our desire to love and be loved, to please others and to be pleased by them, is a powerful source of sympathy, fairness, and conscience, and, at the same time, a principle by which we exclude others and seek to make ourselves attractive in the eyes of friends and family by justifying our actions by specious arguments.

I write these lines not long after terrible riots wracked the city that I love, Los Angeles. What struck me most forcibly about the behavior of those who looted and burned was not that they did it—looting and burning go on in many places whenever social controls are sufficiently weakened—but that invariably the participants felt obliged to justify it even when they faced no chance of punishment and thus had no reason to evade it. If there is any truly universal moral standard, it is that every society, without exception, feels obliged to have—and thus to appeal to—moral standards. Though we act out of narrow self-interest much of the time, something in us makes it all but impossible to justify our acts as mere self-interest whenever those acts are seen by others as violating a moral principle. This need to justify suggests to me that Adam Smith was not conjuring up some literary ghost when he wrote of the impartial spectator, "the man within the breast." We want our actions to be seen by others—and by ourselves—as arising out of appropriate motives. And we judge the actions of others even when those actions have no effect on us.

Morality and Commitment

Though these moral senses make partially competing claims upon us, they have in common—in their origin and their maintenance—the notion of commitment. Marriage differs from sexual congress because the former involves a commitment. Raising children in a family differs from raising them in a foster home or an orphanage in that the parents do so out of a commitment to the welfare of the child whereas surrogate parents, however fond they may become of the child, are in part motivated by financial advantage. The child instinctively wishes to please its parents but in time must learn that it is not enough to please them when they are watching; he is expected to please them when they are not, which will occur only if he is committed to them. When a child forms friendships, he takes on commitments to peers and expects commitments in return; they test one another's commitments with games and teasings that challenge each other's self-control, sense of fair play, and obligation to honor the group and its members. Employees are hired not simply in the expectation that every day their productivity will exceed their costs but out of a desire to bring them into a commitment; since the boss cannot closely supervise more than a few workers all of the time, he wants the workers to make a commitment that when he is not

The Moral Sense and Human Character

watching they will, up to a point, make his interests their interests. By the same token, employees do not view their employers simply as entities that pay wages, but also as people who have assumed obligations. Our towns and teams, our nations and peoples, are objects of loyalties that transcend the costs and benefits of daily transactions; they are part of a network of commitments that we have and that we share with others.

Commitments are both useful and honorable. We are fair both because we wish others to make commitments to us and because we condemn unfairness as a violation of a general social contract—a commitment—to treat others as deserving of respect. We develop self-control both because we wish our commitments to be taken seriously and because we view a lack of self-control as a sign that people are excessively self-indulgent. We are faithful both because we wish others to accept our word and because we consider dishonesty and infidelity to be signs of wickedness. We avoid inflicting unjustified harm on others both because we wish no like harm to befall us and because we are aggrieved by the sight of innocent people suffering. We act as if we were sympathetic to the plight of others both because we wish our favors to be reciprocated and because we regard people who never display sympathy as wrongly indifferent to man's social nature and our mutual dependence.

The economist Robert Frank has pointed out how many human actions that are otherwise puzzling (to an economist!) can be explained once we understand the practical value of commitments visibly made and "irrationally" obeyed. Why do we stick with a spouse even after a more attractive mate has become available, raise children through the years when the rewards seem nonexistent, keep bargains when it would be easy to evade them, and insist on fair division when an unfair one would work to our advantage? And why have we done these things for centuries, suggesting that they have some evolutionary advantage?

It is in part because a person who makes and keeps commitments provides other people with a prediction of his future behavior: by his present behavior he is saying, "you can count on me." Someone who can be counted on is likely to attract more opportunities for profitable transactions than is someone who, by his past waffling on commitments, seems a poor risk. Most economists understand the monetary value of investing in a good reputation. But it is not enough merely to keep commitments. A clever person could keep his promises only when breaking them would easily be discovered. People thinking of offering to someone a good deal know this, and so must wonder whether his reputation for keeping commitments is deserved or faked. One important way that they decide this matter is by observing the emotions he displays when confronting a moral choice. Emotions communicate commitments more persuasively than arguments. One can contrive an argument, but it is much less easy (at least for most of us) routinely to fake love, guilt, indignation, or enthusiasm. In the long run, and up to a point, these emotions will confer advantages on people who express them; people displaying them will get more offers of marriage, partnerships, and employment than people who seem calculating.[7]

The persuasive power of emotional display may help explain why over the millennia the capacity for genuine emotion has survived as a fundamental part of human nature. But the evolutionary advantages of expressing genuine emotions are not the reason why we express them on any particular occasion. These emotions for us are not strategic weapons by which we elicit better deals, they are, by definition, real feelings. They are moral sentiments.*

For all their differences, many of the dominant ideologies and intellectual tendencies of the nineteenth and twentieth centuries have had in common the replacement of the idea of commitment with the idea of choice. Analytic philosophy replaced the idea of commitments arising out of moral intuitions with the idea of choosing among "values" that, in principle, were little different from the flavors of ice cream. Freudian psychoanalysis, as popularly expressed, offered us the prospect of understanding and thereby choosing to modify or even terminate the "repression" that supposedly lay at the root of our cruel superego.

Marxism, like most other secular ideologies, assumed that man could create a wholly new social circumstance for himself. He could choose not to be self-interested, he could choose cooperation without compensation, and he could choose equality over equity. When this Marxist theory did not prove to be self-executing, Marxist practice required that he choose to dull his sympathies in order to accept the horrors of forced collectivization, the Gulag labor camps, and

---

* Frank's analysis (1988) is extraordinarily insightful, limited only by its relentless effort to stay within the framework of economics and to concentrate on the material advantages of emotionality and commitment.

psychiatric hospitals used to "cure" people who refused to accept the vision of the New Soviet Man.

Utilitarianism reminded us of the truism that men choose pleasure over pain, but its founder, Jeremy Bentham, added the dubious corollary that the pleasures they choose are equal in value if they are equal in their intensity, duration, certainty, and propinquity. His wary disciple, John Stuart Mill, struggled to correct this by discussing the pleasures that were better than others, but of course saying one pleasure is better than another implies the existence of some standard other than pleasure by which to judge things.[8] This is obvious to anyone who has sought pleasure in the reckless satisfaction of the bodily appetites only to discover that differences in the quality of pleasures affect our chances of finding true happiness. Among the higher pleasures are the satisfactions that come from honor, sympathy, and self-respect.

The more passionate exponents of the Enlightenment taught us that patriotism was a parochial and unworthy sentiment; sophisticated people should ignore national boundaries and ethnic identities. We should freely choose to be universal men and women, owing our allegiance only to humanity, and then only when humanity lived up to our expectations. And above all, we have been taught cultural relativism: since men choose their values, we cannot judge other men, we can only try to understand them. In the most extreme form of this relativism, other cultures not only cannot be judged but cannot even be compared or fully comprehended,[9] an odd and often hypocritical view for those of its proponents who cannot bring themselves to criticize witchcraft or animal torture in other societies but who do not hesitate to denounce the Ku Klux Klan (surely, a "unique culture") in their own.

Not even the family has been immune to the ideology of choice. In the 1960s and 1970s (but less so today) books were written advocating "alternative" families and "open" marriages. A couple could choose to have a trial marriage, a regular marriage but without an obligation to sexual fidelity, or a revocable marriage with an easy exit provided by no-fault divorce. A woman could choose to have a child out of wedlock and to raise it alone. Marriage was but one of several "options" by which men and women could manage their intimate needs, an option that ought to be carefully negotiated in order to preserve the rights of each contracting party. The family, in this view, was no longer the cornerstone of human life, it was one of several

"relationships" from which individuals could choose so as to maximize their personal goals. This line of argument could be sustained
only by people who believed that human nature was infinitely plastic
(we can be socialized to accept anything) and human wisdom infinitely profound (we can design whatever sexual or child-rearing bond
we want).[10]

Choice is a magnificent standard, up to a point. Men have made
it clear that they want freedom and will die for it. But the freedom
they want is not unconstrained choice; it is rather the opportunity to
express themselves, enrich themselves, and govern themselves in a
world that has already been organized and defined by a set of intuitively understood commitments. Ordinary people understand this
very well, as when they insist that individual freedom is meaningful
only in an orderly society.

Political liberty, which is one of the greatest gifts a people can
acquire for themselves, is threatened when social order is threatened.
It is dismaying to see how ready many people are to turn to strong
leaders in hopes that they will end, by adopting strong measures, the
disorder that has been the product of failed or fragile commitments.
Drug abuse, street crime, and political corruption are the expression
of unfettered choices. To end them, rulers, with the warm support of
the people, will often adopt measures that threaten true political
freedom. The kind of culture that can maintain reasonable human
commitments takes centuries to create but only a few generations to
destroy. And once destroyed, those who suddenly realize what they
have lost will also realize that political action cannot, except at a very
great price, restore it.

The idea of autonomous individuals choosing everything—their
beliefs and values, their history and traditions, their social forms and
family structures—is a vainglorious idea, one that could be invented
only by thinkers who felt compelled to construct society out of
theories. When Thomas Hobbes asked what could make government
legitimate, he decided that the answer to that question required him
first to explain what could make social order possible. Given his
radically individualistic conception of human nature, the only con-
ceivable answer to that question was that people had somehow
agreed to establish a social order by a series of individual choices. But
of course no such answer is possible, for men are not born into a state
of nature, they are born into a social compact that has long preceded
them and without which their survival would have been impossible.

It can be put in the form of a thought experiment. Imagine people stripped of every shred of their social experiences and set loose in some Arcadian paradise, free to invent "culture." What would emerge? If they are young boys, the answer may be something akin to William Golding's *Lord of the Flies*,[11] but if they are men and women, the answer is: something with strange customs, odd dress, and unfamiliar gods, but invariably with familiar systems of infant care, familial obligation, kinship distinctions, and tribal loyalties.

The results of such a thought experiment cast doubt, in my mind, on the philosophical value of imagining a man who is presocial, driven by a single motive, or unaware of the main and necessary features of social life. John Rawls may ask us to imagine ourselves in an "original position" behind a "veil of ignorance,"[12] but no human being is ever in such a position and, to the extent that he is human, cannot possibly be ignorant. Hobbes may ask us to believe that man is driven by the fear of violent death, but were that our overriding concern we would not give birth to children or lavish so much care on them. Why should women risk death in childbirth or men and women expend so much effort on caring for something so perishable and whose protection increases their vulnerability to the predation of others? Rousseau may imagine an equally implausible alternative, man born with no inclination to civil society and corrupted by that society when it is invented and imposed upon him, but no such man can exist and, were he to exist, cannot learn goodness by reading *Robinson Crusoe*.[13]

Moral and political philosophy must begin with a statement about human nature. We may disagree about what is natural, but we cannot escape the fact that we have a nature—that is, a set of traits and predispositions that set limits to what we may do and suggest guides to what we must do. That nature is mixed: we fear violent death but sometimes deliberately risk it; we want to improve our own happiness but sometimes work for the happiness of others; we value our individuality but are tormented by the prospect of being alone. It is a nature that cannot be described by any single disposition, be it maximizing our utility or enhancing our reproductive fitness. Efforts to found a moral philosophy on some single trait (the desire for happiness or the fear of punishment) or political philosophy on some single good (avoiding death, securing property, maximizing freedom) will inevitably produce judgments about what is right that at some critical juncture are at odds with the sober second thoughts of people

The Moral Sense

who deliberate about what constitutes praiseworthy conduct and who decide, out of that deliberation, to honor the hero who risked violent death, to sympathize with the mother who sacrificed one child to save another, and to reproach the man who asserted his rightful claim to property at the expense of a fairer distribution of that property.

Aristotle gave such an account, but his views became unfashionable among those who sought to base moral or political philosophy on a single principle (e.g., utility, liberty, or self-preservation), who worried about Aristotle's apparently easy acceptance of the Athenian status quo, or who believed in the priority of the right over the good. But if one acknowledges that there is no single moral principle but several partially consistent ones, and that neither happiness nor virtue can be prescribed by rule, one is better prepared for a more complete understanding of man's moral capacities, an understanding stated by Aristotle in phrases that in most respects precisely anticipate the findings of modern science. Though Aristotle's account is often dismissed as teleological (much as those of later scientists were dismissed as functionalist), his view does not involve any "mysterious non-empirical entities"[14] or any suspiciously conservative functionalism.

There is certainly nothing mysterious or conservative about Aristotle's assertion that men and women unite out of a "natural striving to leave behind another that is like oneself" because a "parent would seem to have a natural friendship for a child, and a child for a parent," or that "the household is the partnership constituted by nature for [the needs of] daily life." These are as close to self-evident propositions as one could utter; only slightly less obvious, but still scarcely mysterious, are the arguments that "in the household first we have the sources and springs of friendship, of political organization, and of justice" and that "there is in everyone by nature an impulse toward this sort of partnership [that is, to the city]."*

These natural moral sentiments are an incomplete and partial

---

* *Politics*: 1252a30; 1985:155a17; 1984b:1252b11; 1984a:1242b1; 1984b:1253a29. Many contemporary writers might grant all of the above and still object that Aristotle's claim that women were by nature subordinate to men disqualifies his view from serious, respectable consideration. Though I will not pursue the matter here, I do not read Aristotle as making such an argument; in this I am supported, I think, by Arlene Saxonhouse (1985), Stephen Salkever (1990), and Larry Arnhart (1990). But I realize that I am opposed by, among others, Susan Okin (1979) and, to a degree, by Jean Bethke Elshtain (1981). I do not think that resolving this dispute is central to the argument I am making.

guide to action. They are incomplete in that they cannot resolve a choice we must make between two loved persons or between the desire to favor a loved one and the obligation to honor a commitment. They are partial in that these sentiments extend chiefly to family and kin, leaving nonkin at risk for being thought nonhuman. Resolving conflicts and extending our sentiments across the high but necessary walls of tribe, village, and racial grouping, an extension made more desirable by the interdependence of cosmopolitan living, requires moral reasoning to take up the incomplete task of natural development.

The incomplete and partial guidance provided by our moral senses can lead the unwary philosopher to one or both of two errors: to suppose that if a sentiment does not settle everything it cannot settle anything, or to infer that if people differ in their practical choices they must do so on the basis of different sentiments. The first error leads to logical positivism, the second to cultural relativism, the two together to modern nihilism. A proper understanding of human nature can rarely provide us with rules for action, but it can supply what Aristotle intended: a grasp of what is good in human life and a rough ranking of those goods.[15]

Can We Rationally Justify a Moral Sentiment?

Students of philosophy will recall the moment at which they first acquired reasoned doubts about the possibility of saying anything meaningful about the good life. It was when they read, or heard about, David Hume, the eighteenth-century Scottish philosopher who set himself the task, taken up also by Adam Smith, to find a basis for morality that was independent of revealed religion.

In this *Treatise of Human Nature*, Hume wrote that in every book of moral thought that he had so far encountered, the author would at some point make an imperceptible but vastly important change. At one point he would be asserting that something *is*; in the next breath he would assert that these things *ought to be*.[16] For example, the phrase, "men make and keep promises" suddenly becomes, "men ought to keep promises." I learned from Hume, as did legions of my fellow students, that this transition is impossible; one cannot infer an "ought" statement from an "is" statement; in modern parlance, one cannot infer values from facts. It is logically untenable.

But the rest of Hume's book is a discussion of morality in which he uses language that seems to contradict his own admonition. For example, he says that justice is a convention invented by man to make him more secure in his possession of property.[17] Without rules governing the ownership and transmission of property, social life would be impossible. But why do men form society? Because of their natural impulses, especially sexual attraction and the children that result from sexual union. Fine, this makes rules governing the *existing* distribution of property—the rules of justice, if you will—useful. But why should men care about the *future* transmission of their property? Because, Hume answers, of "the natural affection, which they bear their children." And what does that affection imply? A "duty, the care of children."[18]

Here Hume derives an "ought" statement from an "is" statement scarcely eight pages after asserting that this cannot be done. Lest his readers think this was a careless slip of the pen, he repeats his conclusion in many other places. Benevolence—that is, being "humane, merciful, grateful, friendly, generous"—"universally express[es] the highest merit." These sentiments are "natural," and even though they are fainter than self-love, "it is impossible for such a creature as man to be totally indifferent to the well or ill-being of his fellow-creatures, and not readily, of himself, to pronounce, where nothing gives him any particular bias, that what promotes their happiness is good, what tends to their misery is evil."[19] Moral sentiments are "so rooted in our constitution and temper, that without confounding the human mind by disease or madness, 'tis impossible to extirpate and destroy them."[20]

It is clear that Hume's famous separation of "is" from "ought" was meant as a challenge only to those systems of moral thought that attempted to rely purely on reason to prove a moral obligation, and only to "vulgar systems" at that.[21] Morality, he said, rests on sentiment, and of course generations of students have understood this. But morality does not rest on *mere* sentiment, because there is nothing "mere" about certain sentiments. There are many ways of knowing; the teachings of the heart deserve to be taken as seriously as the lessons of the mind.

The heart's teachings are subtle and often contradictory, as difficult to master as logic and science. But they are not the same as whim or caprice; the most important of them are quite compelling. This fact is often obscured by professional philosophers and thus overlooked by their students. As every such student will recall, a course or book on moral philosophy is in large measure an argument intended to show that each school of philosophy (except perhaps the teacher's or the author's) is fatally flawed. These flaws are typically revealed by demonstrating that a given theory, if rigorously applied, leads to an inference that we find repugnant. How do we know that Plato, or Mill, or Kant was wrong? Because Plato wanted children taken from their parents; because Mill's utilitarianism, strictly applied, would justify punishing an innocent man; because Kant's commitment to truth telling would require him to tell a homicidal maniac where an innocent child was hiding. But why are we sure that most people find these outcomes repugnant? And what is the "scientific" or "logical" status of "repugnance"?

The answer, of course, is our sentiments or, as philosophers would put it, our intuitions. Russell Hardin stated the matter exactly when he observed that "remarkably much of the debate in moral theory turns on assertions of what we intuit to be true or right or good."[22] But having relied on our intuitions to demolish a theory, we then discard them as serious philosophical principles. How odd.

Judith Jarvis Thomson is a philosopher who is prepared to defend certain intuitions (or as I prefer, sentiments).[23] Suppose your heart tells you that it is wrong to torture babies to death for fun. Can anyone deny the truth of this statement and thus deny its moral force?* There is no benefit that offsets the hurt of a tortured baby; no one thinks that torturing babies will produce better crops, for example. But even if somebody does believe in this result, we can think of no reason why the torturer should do it for fun, as evidenced by his laughing during the torture. And even if we were able to persuade ourselves to overlook baby torturing accompanied by laughter in a particular case, we cannot imagine how one might justify a rule that allowed laughter-inducing baby killings in some set of cases. The principle of amusing baby tortures violates so profoundly the natural affection that people have for infants and thus contravenes so powerfully the affections that bind us together that acknowledg-

---

* Lest readers think that my question is put purely for rhetorical effect, I invite their attention to a book by one of America's leading philosophical figures, Richard Rorty, who asserts that there is no universally valid answer to the question, "Why not be cruel?" (1989:xv; for a spirited rejoinder, see Elshtain, 1992). Now, a lot depends on how you define a "universally valid answer," but if he means to suggest that there is no point at which a disinterested person could stop his pondering and be comfortable in the settled conviction that, at least in *this* case, cruelty is wrong, I think he is very much mistaken.

ing the principle would make it all but impossible for people to live together in an orderly society.

When we think about it, we realize that the aversion we feel to baby torturing for fun not only springs from deeply held sentiments whose truth we find self-evident, it also has important practical value. We don't think a society can be run on the basis of a principle that condones such a practice and we can't think of a society that has ever been run on the basis of such a rule. Indeed, if we were of an evolutionary turn of mind, we might suspect that any society that did endorse such a principle would have left so few viable offspring that either it would have disappeared in a few generations or, to save itself, abandoned the practice.

Character

If the moral senses can conflict with one another and with what prudent action requires under particular circumstances, then living a good life requires striking a delicate balance among those senses and between them and prudent self-interest. Common sense, to say nothing of modern philosophy, shows that there is no single rule or principle by which that balance can be struck. But common sense also gives us a language to use in describing people who have struck that balance well.

When we describe people we admire, we do not often use the word "moral"—partly, I suppose, because that word strikes contemporary ears as suggesting that the person is priggish, severe, or stuffy. But we also do not use that word, I conjecture, because we do not judge people (unless we do not know them well) by any single trait; we judge them as having a set of traits, a character. Now by character we mean two things: a distinctive combination of personal qualities by which someone is known (that is, a personality), and moral strength or integrity. We judge people whole, assessing their strengths and weaknesses and reckoning up the totals into a kind of human balance sheet. People with the best balance sheets—that is, the most admirable characters—are usually not people who are perfect or have every single virtue to the highest degree; since the virtues—that is, the moral senses—are partially in conflict, that would be impossible. People with the best balance sheets are those who are the best balanced. In common parlance they are "nice persons" or "good guys," or in polite (and vanishing) discourse, "ladies" and "gentlemen."

A nice person or gentleman takes into account the feelings of others and sympathizes with the joys and sorrows of those with whom he deals to the extent that those joys and sorrows are justifiable and proportional to the circumstances. But even when not expressing sympathy, the nice person does not inflict unjustified harm on innocent parties. The good guy is fair in dealings with others and does not attempt to be a judge in his own case. He or she has prudent self-control; that is, he is not in the grip of extravagant passions that compel others to deal with him only on his terms, but that self-control does not prevent him from taking strong actions or expressing justified anger when important matters are at stake. The nice person tries to take the long view when the more distant goal is clearly superior to the immediate one (being human, he will not always succeed in doing so). When this is difficult he looks for ways to force himself to do the right thing. Among these are habits: routine ways of acting, each rather unimportant in itself, but, taken together, producing action on behalf of quite important sensibilities. For example: the habit of courtesy (which over the long run alerts us to the feelings of others), the habit of punctuality (which disposes us to be dutiful in the exercise of our responsibilities and confirms to others that we have a sense of duty), and the habit of practice (by which we master skills and proclaim to others that we are capable of excellence).

When, as inevitably happens, we confront circumstances that require us to choose among our moral senses or confuse us as to whether there is a moral dimension to the problem, the good guy, the nice person, engages in an inner dialogue about what is required of him. For the moral senses to speak to us clearly and affect our actions importantly, we must be capable of disinterested reflection. We must, that is, be capable of seeing ourselves as others see us and, even more importantly, as we wish the noblest others to see us. Countless emotions—greed, passion, anger, self-love—are constantly at work to suppress disinterested reflection, so much so that some among us may think such reflection is impossible. Man, in this view, is entirely a creature of his desires, and goodness is nothing but what makes him happy at the moment. But in fact all but the most cynical of us recognize and attach value to the fruits of disinterested reflection—namely, an expressed justification for an action that will persuade an objective observer. Insofar as we grant the necessity for and the power of justification, we grant the possibility of disinterested reflection.

Now, in some cultures the qualities of a good person might be slightly different from what I have just listed. In many places a man must also earn respect by displaying dignity and honor and a woman must be thought virtuous by having a reputation for chastity and reticence. That the lists are different in different places is important, but not as important as some imagine, for it does not imply that a good character is purely a matter of local custom. If you doubt this, go to the most distant and exotic land and seek to employ an excellent carpenter, boatwright, gardener, or tailor. You will discover, I think, general agreement in those places as to who is and who is not excellent at these crafts, and their qualities of excellence will not be limited to technical skill but also embrace dependability, fair dealing, and an interest in your wishes.

We make somewhat different judgments about people whose achievements have elevated them to greatness in art, war, commerce, or politics. We are willing, up to a point, to overlook deficiencies in sympathy, duty, or fairness in the case of those whose talents and self-mastery have enabled them to scale great heights and thereby win great praise, and we are saddened or angered by people who have wasted a great talent through a lack of self-mastery. Indeed, we are especially critical of the moral weaknesses of someone who conspicuously fails to realize his great promise because of these weaknesses. We will forgive some things if great things result, but they had better be truly great. The special honors we reserve for the great reflect our respect for excellence and our gratitude for service. But we recognize these to be singular, not everyday, accomplishments, and we would have a very different view if everyone justified some moral lapse by pointing to his artistic or political skills.

Today, at least in the West, we defer less to greatness as an excuse for a lack of sympathy, fairness, or self-control than once was the case. This has occurred, not just because the popular press so relentlessly exposes the clay feet of even the most magnificent idols, but because modern civilization under the dual influence of Christianity and the Enlightenment has made ordinary life—the life of production and the family—the center of our moral universe and the reference point for how we judge one another. In earlier times, greatness was thought more important than it is today. Aristotle devoted many pages to a discussion of the virtues of honor, bravery, magnificence, and liberality. A magnificent man was one who spent his fortune wisely; people without a fortune to spend had less opportunity for expressing this aspect of virtue. Charles Taylor, for many years the professor of moral philosophy at Oxford, has observed that this "affirmation of the ordinary life" has become "one of the most powerful ideas of modern [Western] civilization."[24] Much has been gained by this affirmation, but something has been lost as well.

A good character, however defined, is not life lived according to a rule (there rarely is a rule by which good qualities ought to be combined or hard choices resolved), it is a life lived in balance. The balance among the moral senses is, to me, more an aesthetic than a philosophical matter. It is aesthetic in two senses: it is a balance that is struck without deliberation or reasoned justifications, and in the character thereby formed there is no clear distinction between form and content. In this view as in many others I am much influenced by the late British philosopher Michael Oakeshott. He wrote once of the "poetic character of all human activity," by which he meant that (unlike academic philosophy) moral action does not ordinarily spring from the deliberate effort to translate into reality some idealized conception of what ought to be. Moral ideals arise out of habitual human behavior; they are what philosophers (and we) find to be implicit in our predispositions.

Morality bears to much contemporary philosophy something of the same relationship that poetry bears to contemporary literary criticism. Some teachers of philosophy treat morality as if it were the product of intellectual analysis that gives rise to rules, which can then be translated into behavior. This, as Oakeshott has warned, is as mistaken as supposing that poetry is an expression in words of an idea worked out in advance. "A poem is not a translation into words of a state of mind. What the poet says and what he wants to say are not two things, the one succeeding and embodying the other, they are the same thing; he does not know what he wants to say until he has said it."[25] Much the same is true of everyday moral conduct. The "capital of moral ideals," he continued, "has always been accumulated by a morality of habitual behaviour, and appears in the form of abstract ideas only because [or when] it has been transformed by reflective thought into a currency of ideas."[26] Just as it is interesting to study poetry formally to learn about meter, rhyme, and metaphor, it can be stimulating to study moral arguments formally in order to learn about utilitarian, deontological, and intuitionist theories of ethics. But no one should make the mistake of thinking that explaining utilitarianism teaches morality, any more than explaining meter teaches poetry.

Aristotle understood this perfectly. We become virtuous—and thus truly happy—by the practice of virtue. We acquire virtues, he wrote, just as we acquire crafts. We learn how to build by building and how to become a harpist by playing the harp; "so also, then, we become just by doing just actions, temperate by doing temperate actions, brave by doing brave actions." A good character arises from the repetition of many small acts, and begins early in youth.[27] That habituation operates on a human nature innately prepared to respond to training: "The virtues arise in us neither by nature nor against nature, but we are by nature able to acquire them, and reach our complete perfection through habit."[28]

We may be inclined to dismiss Aristotle's view as too simple; after all, what did he know, several centuries before Christ, of the temptations of modern life—tobacco, addictive drugs, lush gambling casinos, violent and sexually explicit motion pictures, and the anomie and opportunity of the big city? In fact Aristotle was keenly aware that we are powerfully tempted to do that which is not in our long-term interests and that we give way to those temptations even knowing their likely bad consequences.*

Culture, Politics, and the Moral Senses

It is not hard to point to features of any culture, especially that of contemporary America, that affect the chances that our moral senses will become moral habits and our habits will constitute what most people would regard as a worthy character.

We all live in a world shaped by the ambiguous legacy of the Enlightenment. That epochal development enlarged the scope of

---

* Much of the *Eudemian Ethics* was devoted to this problem, as was much of Book 7 of the *Nichomachean Ethics*, in which he tried to explain the difference between being a temperate person and being a continent one. The former does the right thing easily or habitually, the latter does it only after having overcome contrary inclinations. To Aristotle, the former was a better person, but I would say, and he might agree, that the latter is far more common. A heavy smoker is incontinent, and so are all of us who, having made an appointment to see the dentist to have our teeth examined (and maybe drilled), cancel out at the last minute.

human freedom, prepared our minds for the scientific method, made man the measure of all things, and placed individuality and individual consent front and center on the political stage. By encouraging these views it strengthened the sense of sympathy and fairness. If man is the measure of all things and men generally must consent to whatever regime is to rule them, then each man is entitled to equal rights and to respect proportional to his merit. Kant was hardly breaking new ground when he argued that man must be treated as an end and not merely as a means to someone else's (God's? the king's?) end. It took a few generations for the principle to be worked out in practice, but when it was, the result was what the legal scholar Mary Ann Glendon has called "rights talk"—the widespread tendency to define the relation of the self to others and to society as a whole in terms of rights and to judge whether one has been treated properly by whether one has had one's rights fairly defended.[29] The worthy desire to replace a world in which people were born, lived, and died in a fixed social slot with a world in which people faced a career open to talents and a political system in which they participated gave rise, as most worthy desires do, to a tendency to carry matters to an extreme. Even some of the leading spokesmen of the Enlightenment would have been astonished to read the words of a contemporary legal scholar, Ronald Dworkin, who wrote that "if someone has a right to do something, then it is wrong for the government to deny it to him even though it would be in the general interest to do so."[30] Indeed, even today many European philosophers would have trouble with Dworkin's claim for the absolute priority of rights.

However extreme its modern formulation, the Enlightenment encouraged sympathy ("we are all brothers under the skin") and fairness ("I am entitled to the same rewards for a given effort as you"). Here was a great gain for humanity, providing, as it did, a basis for rejecting slavery, ending absolutist rule, encouraging free inquiry, and defending property. But it was a gain that came at a price. The price was not just the multiplication of lawsuits, it was more importantly the challenges to self-control and duty posed by radicalized individualism. If rights are all that is important, what will become of responsibilities? If the individual man is the measure of all things, what will become of the family that produces and defines man? If being sympathetic with the plight of distant or less fortunate people is the best test of a decent man, what will become of his duties to those nearest to and most like him? The relationships of parent to child, friend to friend, or comrade to comrade cannot be defined in terms of rights. They must be defined in terms of commitments.

Ample evidence indicates that even within the rights framework of modern discourse there lurks an unresolved problem. Enmity is the inevitable companion of sympathy. We express our concern for the oppressed or the victimized by hating the oppressor or the victimizer. Good Samaritans rush to the aid of a rapist's victim instinctively, enraged by the rapist's actions. The Enlightenment and its disciples did not tell us how to handle rage. Indeed, some variants of the Enlightenment—in particular, the various political ideologies that sought to mobilize opposition to oppression, real and imagined—depended crucially on rage as the animating motives of their adherents.

I am struck in reading accounts of the lives of some of the most dedicated ideologues by how little the content of the ideology mattered and how much anger at "society," "the ruling classes," "the government," "meddling bureaucrats," or "inferior races" mattered. Anger is the necessary handmaiden of sympathy and fairness, and we are wrong to try to make everyone sweet and reasonable. But anger, like those moral senses that it exists to defend, must be checked by other senses. Those others are self-control and duty. By the same token, self-satisfaction and narrow loyalties, which are emotions growing out of self-control and duty, must be checked by other sentiments, and these are sympathy and fairness.

In its worst forms, radical individualism is mere self-indulgence; in its best forms it is a life governed by conscience and a cosmopolitan awareness. In its worst forms, extreme communalism is parochial prejudice; in its best forms, it is a life governed by honor and intimate commitments.

Liberal, democratic politics, the politics of a free society, are an impressive—indeed, virtually the only—safeguard against the various tyrannies that political theorists and their enraged acolytes can invent. The fundamental aim of the totalitarian state is the destruction of civil society; only the openness, spontaneity, and confusing hubbub of pluralist, democratic politics can guard against that destruction.[31] Civil society—the nexus of families, groups, neighborhoods, and associations—was neither foreseen nor planned by anyone. Man could no more invent the family system than he could plan an economy. We do not know enough and cannot learn enough to do either. Human nature is knowable only in broad outline; human wants and the best means for satisfying them are not knowable at all by any single mind or single agency. Democratic politics matches, better than any alternative, the diversity and spontaneity of the human spirit.

But democratic politics carries its own risks. It tends to magnify some of the moral senses and mute others. It certainly magnifies sympathy, at least as that sentiment is politically defined. Participatory politics encourages officials to seek out "unmet needs" and meet them, or at least pretend to. The more participatory the system, the more voices are heard and the more unmet needs are identified; those who deny that these are real needs or that they are unmet risk being branded as unsympathetic ("insensitive") to the plight of their fellow man (or to that of any of several other species).

By magnifying sympathy, democratic politics tends to redefine fairness, attack self-control, and mute fidelity. It certainly values fairness, but in the electoral competition to meet needs, all needs and all claimants tend to acquire equal worth. Our disposition to judge rewards as fair when they are proportionate to worth or effort is confronted by the political verdict that rewards are fair when they are equal. The endless struggle over social welfare policies and affirmative action rules are, at root, arguments over fairness: Is it fair for someone to receive as much from welfare as from work? Is it fair to grant entry into jobs and universities on the basis of criteria other than merit, narrowly defined? Democratic politics does not ignore these questions (indeed, it often seems convulsed by them), but it does tend to provide a privileged platform for those who speak on behalf of the radically egalitarian answer.

Self-control is minimized by democratic politics. For the government to pay attention to impulse control is tantamount to its assuming a tutelary role in private lives, and of course the democratic revolution was in large part a rebellion against governmental tutelage. This was especially the case of American democracy, with its radical assault on paternalism, royal patronage, and established religion, and its novel belief that society could be held together by the natural affinities of free men.[32] Under the United States Constitution, the federal government was to have no role in teaching or morally uplifting the people; as interpreted, that document made the government's chief task the expansion of human freedom and the allocation of tax revenues. Politically engaged Americans believe deeply in this, and so resist any but the mildest legal restraints on public speech and behavior. But politically unengaged Americans believe that civil speech and decent behavior are desperately important to the quality of life in their communities and worry that a government concerned solely with rights and redistribution is a government indifferent to those excesses of personal self-indulgence that seem so threatening on the streets of our big cities. And in at least one sense the latter are right; by its omissions if not by its actions, governing is about character formation.

Duty is taken for granted by democratic politics. Duty is supposed to make us vote and to be ready to serve in the military should the need arise. We are disturbed by the decline in voting but unsure what to do about it, and we have embraced the idea of an all-volunteer military in part because some people think that compulsory service is a violation of our right to be left alone. But many more people, though proud of what a volunteer armed force has accomplished, are uneasy with the view that defending the nation ought to be entirely a matter of personal choice. Many Americans are attracted by the idea of requiring of all of our young people some period of community or national service. Whatever the legislative fate of that notion, it is a powerful indicator of how strongly many people feel that duty is an impulse that ought to be encouraged.

Some of these feelings of duty have animated the revival of a communitarian outlook in intellectual discourse that is attempting to carve out a place for the idea of responsibility in a nation suffused with rights.[33] Some of this talk is a bit vague as to specifics, some of it is ambiguous about the relationship between self-interest and group interest, and some of it seems to want only to graft neighborhood associations onto existing bureaucratic structures so that the taxing and redistributing can continue but now with more legitimacy and consent. But the best of these writings give philosophical voice to the yearnings of ordinary folk who wish to preserve their liberties while reclaiming their vision of a decent community, one in which the moral senses will become as evident in public as they now are in private life.

Those aspects of modern life that have stimulated these arguments about community are well known. The contemporary legal system views people as autonomous individuals endowed with rights and entering into real or implied contracts. The liberalization of laws pertaining to marriage and divorce arose out of just such a view.

Marriage, once a sacrament, has become in the eyes of the law a contract that is easily negotiated, renegotiated, or rescinded. Within a few years, no-fault divorce on demand became possible, after millennia in which such an idea would have been unthinkable.[34] It is now easier to renounce a marriage than a mortgage; at least the former occurs much more frequently than the latter. Half of all divorced fathers rarely see their children, and most pay no child support. We can no longer agree even on what constitutes a family. Husbands and wives? Heterosexual lovers? Homosexual lovers? Any two people sharing living quarters? It is not necessary to accept some traditional view of ruling husbands and subservient wives in order to realize how misdirected much of this discussion is. A family is not an association of independent people; it is a human commitment designed to make possible the rearing of moral and healthy children. Governments care—or ought to care—about families for this reason, and scarcely for any other.

We are also convulsed by a debate over whether our schools should teach morality. Much of that debate is as misguided as the debate over families, because it is based on a misunderstanding of the sources of morality. Some conservatives argue that the schools should impress upon their pupils moral maxims; some liberals argue that, at most, the schools should clarify the "value" choices the pupils might want to make. But if the argument of this book is correct, children do not learn morality by learning maxims or clarifying values. They enhance their natural sentiments by being regularly induced by families, friends, and institutions to behave in accord with the most obvious standards of right conduct—fair dealing, reasonable self-control, and personal honesty. A moral life is perfected by practice more than by precept; children are not taught so much as habituated. In this sense the schools inevitably teach morality, whether they intend to or not, by such behavior as they reward or punish. A school reinforces the better moral nature of a pupil to the extent it insists on the habitual performance of duties, including the duty to deal fairly with others, to discharge one's own responsibilities, and to defer the satisfaction of immediate and base motives in favor of more distant and nobler ones.

Many of us worry about the effects of the mass media, and especially of prolonged television viewing, on the character of our young people. But often we state the issue too narrowly, as when we complain that violent scenes on television produce violent behavior among its viewers. The former may cause the latter under some circumstances; the evidence I have seen suggests that the causal connection is weak, uncertain, and explains rather little of the total level of violence in society.[35] The real problem with prolonged television viewing is the same as the problem with any form of human isolation: it cuts the person off from those social relationships on which our moral nature in large part depends. As the psychiatrist George Ainslie writes, "the mass media [in heavy doses] impoverish a society in the same way as drugs and other addictions, by draining away more attention than they return."[36] Passive, individual entertainment, whether in a drugged stupor, in a video arcade, or before an endlessly running TV screen, leads to self-absorption, and self-absorption in extreme doses is the enemy of moral competence, especially that form of competence that depends on our controlling our impulses.

In all three areas—families, schools, and entertainment—we have come face to face with a fatally flawed assumption of many Enlightenment thinkers, namely, that autonomous individuals can freely choose, or will, their moral life. Believing that individuals are everything, rights are trumps, and morality is relative to time and place, such thinkers have been led to design laws, practices, and institutions that leave nothing between the state and the individual save choices, contracts, and entitlements. Fourth-grade children being told how to use condoms is only one of the more perverse of the results.

The Light of Human Nature

We want to live in a community of reasonable order and general decency. What does this desire imply? Scholars have not always been as helpful as they might in answering that question. Sociologists and anthropologists have stressed that order is the product of cultural learning, without pausing to ask what it is we are naturally disposed to learn. Economists have rejoiced by saying that we are disposed to learn whatever advances our interests without pausing to ask what constitutes our interests. And despite their differences in approach, they have both supported an environmental determinism and cultural relativism that has certain dangers.

If man is infinitely malleable, he is as much at risk from the various despotisms of this world as he would be if he were entirely shaped by some biochemical process. The anthropologist Robin Fox has put the matter well: "If, indeed, everything is learned, then surely men can be taught to live in any kind of society. Man is at the mercy of all the tyrants . . . who think they know what is best for him. And how can he plead that they are being inhuman if he doesn't know what being human is in the first place?"[37] Despots are quite prepared to use whatever technology will enable them to dominate mankind; if science tells them that biology is nothing and environment everything, then they will put aside their eugenic surgery and selective breeding programs and take up instead the weapons of propaganda, mass advertising, and educational indoctrination. The Nazis left nothing to chance; they used all methods.

Recent Russian history should have put to rest the view that everything is learned and that man is infinitely malleable. During seventy-five years of cruel tyranny when every effort was made to destroy civil society, the Russian people kept civil society alive if not well. The elemental building blocks of that society were not isolated individuals easily trained to embrace any doctrine or adopt any habits; they were families, friends, and intimate groupings in which sentiments of sympathy, reciprocity, and fairness survived and struggled to shape behavior.

Mankind's moral sense is not a strong beacon light, radiating outward to illuminate in sharp outline all that it touches. It is, rather, a small candle flame, casting vague and multiple shadows, flickering and sputtering in the strong winds of power and passion, greed and ideology. But brought close to the heart and cupped in one's hands, it dispels the darkness and warms the soul.

Notes

Preface

1. For a penetrating critique of this view, see Richards, 1987.
2. Sidgwick, 1956:30.
3. Cf. ibid., 35, with Aristotle, *Nichomachean Ethics*, book X, chap. 9; see also Burnyeat, 1980:81.
4. Wilson and Herrnstein, 1985.

The Moral Sense

1. Marx, *The German Ideology* (1845–46) and *Economic and Philosophical Manuscripts* (1844):85, 154–55.
2. Ayer, 1946:103, 108.
3. Not only does God not exist, but, Sartre added, "there is no human nature" and so man "cannot find anything to depend upon either within or outside himself." Sartre, 1948:28, 33.
4. Rorty, 1989:189.
5. Freud, 1923: ch. 3; 1930:107–8.
6. Sumner, 1906:521.
7. Benedict, 1934. On cannibalism, see 131.
8. "Values clarification" was proposed by Raths, Harmin, and Simon, 1966. Cf. Damon, 1988:133–41.
9. Lockwood, 1978.
10. Lickona, 1991.
11. Rorty, 1989:189.
12. Ibid.
13. Wilson, 1983, ch. 12.
14. Farrington and Langan, 1992.
15. Wilson, 1983, ch. 12.

16. Wolfgang, Figlio, and Sellin, 1972; Tracy, Wolfgang, and Figlio, 1990; Wilson and Herrnstein, 1985:21; Farrington, 1979, 1981.
17. Farrington, personal communication, January 1992.
18. Elster, 1989a.
19. Hobbes, 1652:1.13; 2.17–18.
20. Hirschman, 1977.
21. A. Smith, 1776.
22. Durkheim, 1893, 1897, 1912.
23. Benoit-Smullyan, 1949:511–12 and notes 42–44.
24. A. Smith, 1759:1.
25. Cf. Westermarck, 1932:196–99.
26. Hoebel, 1954; cf. also Westermarck, 1906:II, 742–43.
27. Shepher, 1983; Fox, 1983.
28. Fox, 1989:191–92.
29. Shorter, 1975; de Mause, 1974; Stone, 1977.
30. Locke, 1706.
31. de Mause, 1974.
32. Shorter, 1975:203–4.
33. Konner, 1982, 301–4; see also LeVine, 1970.
34. Westermarck, 1906:I, 529–31.
35. Brazelton, 1972; Marvick, 1974; Trumbach, 1978.
36. Macfarlane, 1979; Anderson, 1980.
37. Sussman, 1977; Wrightson, 1982.
38. Ozment, 1983:220, n. 83; cf. also 118–19.
39. Langer, 1974; see also Noonan, 1965:85–7, and Herlihy, 1985:23–27.
40. Noonan, 1965:86.
41. Langer, 1974:358–59.
42. Dickemann, 1984:433; Scrimshaw, 1984:449–52.
43. Divale and Harris, 1976; cf. also Scrimshaw, 1984.
44. Daly and Wilson, 1984:488–95; Daly and Wilson, 1988: ch. 3; Scrimshaw, 1984:444–60.
45. Daly and Wilson, 1987:207; see also Konner, 1990:173–76.
46. Dickemann, 1979:456; Konner, 1990:173–76.
47. Daly and Wilson, 1988:75–76; Daly and Wilson, 1987:208–9; Scrimshaw, 1984:440, 448–49; Eibl-Eibesfeldt, 1989:194; Trevathan, 1987: 231–32; Westermarck, 1906: I:404.
48. Scheper-Hughes, 1987:203–4.
49. Murdock, 1965:144–50.
50. Taylor, 1989: ch. 1.

Sympathy

1. A. Smith, 1759:1.1.1.1.
2. Ibid., 3.

3. Ibid., 1.
4. Campbell, 1964:70.
5. A. Smith, 1759:3.2.1.
6. Ibid., 6.1.2.
7. Ibid., 2.2.28.
8. Eisenberg and Miller, 1987; Coke, Batson, and McDavis, 1978; Batson et al., 1988; Hoffman, 1981.
9. Batson, 1990.
10. Piliavin et al., 1981.
11. Ibid., 115–18.
12. Piliavin and Piliavin, 1972.
13. Piliavin, Rodin, and Piliavin, 1969; Piliavin and Piliavin, 1972.
14. Clark and Word, 1974.
15. Latané and Darley, 1968, 1970.
16. Cf. Alexander, 1987.
17. Latané and Nida, 1981.
18. Oliner and Oliner, 1988.
19. Ibid., 189–99.
20. Ibid., 190.
21. Ibid., 174.
22. Ibid., 184, 297–98.
23. London, 1970.
24. Rosenhan, 1970.
25. Mill, 1861:50–51.
26. Darwin, 1859.
27. Hamilton, 1964.
28. Holldobler and Wilson, 1990: ch. 4; Trivers, 1985:177–79.
29. Haldane, 1955.
30. Smith and Sherwen, 1983:95.
31. Hoopes, 1982:97–98.
32. Trivers, 1971; Alexander, 1987.
33. Cf. Sidgwick, 1907:386–87.
34. Latané and Darley, 1970.
35. Schachter, 1959.
36. Cosmides and Tooby, 1987.
37. Eisenberg and Mussen, 1989:151; Piliavin and Charng, 1990:31.
38. Hartshorne and May, 1928–30.
39. Burton, 1963, 1976; Rushton, 1980: ch. 4; Eisenberg and Mussen, 1989:16–22.
40. Baumrind, 1971; Koestner et al., 1990.
41. Hoffman, 1984.
42. Zahn-Waxler, Radke-Yarrow, and King, 1979.
43. Underwood and Moore, 1982.

44. Kohlberg, 1981; Eisenberg, 1986.
45. Whiting and Whiting, 1975; S. Kagan, Knight, and Martinez-Romero, 1982; Madsen, 1967, 1971.
46. Summarized in Eisenberg and Mussen, 1989:44–46.
47. Whiting and Whiting, 1975:82, 95, 106–7, 113, 175–76.
48. Berghe, 1987.
49. Feldman, 1968.
50. Hornstein, Fisch, and Holmes, 1968.
51. Piliavin, Rodin, and Piliavin, 1969; Hornstein, 1978.
52. Hornstein et al., 1971.
53. Krebs, 1970, 1975; Stotland, 1969.
54. Tafjel et al., 1971.
55. Bornstein, 1979; Newman and McCauley, 1977.
56. Milgram, 1970.
57. Bickman et al., 1973; Piliavin et al., 1981:226.
58. Eibl-Eibesfeldt, 1989:291; Hornstein, 1976.
59. Cf. Hardin, 1982.
60. A. Smith, 1759:3.3.4.
61. Milgram, 1974.
62. Lerner, 1970, 1974, 1980; Piliavin et al., 1981:114–15.
63. Lerner, 1980.
64. Browning, 1992.

Fairness

1. Damon, 1988:32–33; Bronson, 1981.
2. Dunn, 1988:177.
3. Frank, 1988:168.
4. Damon, 1988:36.
5. Dunn, 1988.
6. Eibl-Eibesfeldt, 1989:341.
7. Damon, 1988:169.
8. Ibid., 172.
9. Dunn, 1988:182.
10. Damon, 1988:36–39.
11. Ibid., 39–43.
12. Aristotle, *Nichomachean Ethics* Book V, 1131b17.
13. Adams and Rosenbaum, 1962; Adams, 1963; Adams and Jacobson, 1964.
14. Lawler and O'Gara, 1967.
15. Walster, Walster, and Berschied, 1978:128.
16. Schmitt and Maxwell, 1972.
17. Guth, Schmittberger, and Schwarze, 1982; cf. also Kahneman, Knetsch, and Thaler, 1986a, 1986b; Frank, 1988:163–84.

18. Kahneman, Knetsch, and Thaler, 1986b.
19. Gorman and Kehr, 1992.
20. Okun, 1981:89.
21. Olmstead and Rhode, 1985.
22. Austin and Walster, 1974.
23. Piaget, 1965:315–18; Hook and Cook, 1979; Walster et al., 1978:211.
24. Walster et al., 1978:212; Staub, 1978:180.
25. Gergen, 1969.
26. Greenberg and Shapiro, 1971.
27. Gouldner, 1960:171; Westermarck, 1906, 2:154; Singer, 1981:136.
28. Singer, 1981:48.
29. Axelrod, 1984; Axelrod and Hamilton, 1981; Trivers, 1983.
30. Tyler, Casper, and Fisher, 1989; Casper, Tyler, and Fisher, 1988.
31. Lind and Tyler, 1988:205; Tyler, 1990.
32. McEwen and Maiman, 1984.
33. Wilson and Wilson, 1985: ch. 8.
34. Darwin, 1871: ch. 3.
35. Grace Goodell, personal communication.
36. Rawls, 1971:14–15.
37. Lee, 1974, 1979, 1984; Wiessner, 1982; Shostak, 1981.
38. Konner, 1982:9, 199, 204, 274.
39. Lee, 1974, 1979; Cashdan, 1980.
40. Volkman, 1982:43–47.
41. Rousseau, 1758:192, 195, 196.
42. Ibid., 205.
43. Ibid., 201, 201–2, 221.
44. Marx and Engels, 1848:21.
45. *Politics*, 1263all–15, 29, 41; 1263b4.
46. *Politics*, 1295b5–23.
47. Bakeman and Brownlee, 1982, as quoted in Eibl-Eibesfeldt, 1989:345.
48. Rawls, 1971:488.

Self-Control

1. Aristotle, *Nichomachean Ethics*, 1107b, 1117b23–1119b20, and book VII.
2. Cf. Hardie, 1980:122–28.
3. Ainslie, 1975, 1992.
4. Elias, 1939:80.
5. Ibid., 187.
6. Kagan, 1984:30.
7. Ibid., 29.
8. Rutter and Garmezy, 1983:839–42.
9. Wallander and Hubert, 1985.

10. Weiss and Hechtman, 1986; Rutter and Garmezy, 1983:847.
11. West and Farrington, 1977.
12. For example, Satterfield et al., 1982; Gittelman et al., 1985.
13. Farrington, Loeber, and Van Kammen, 1990; Wilson and Herrnstein, 1985:201–2, 204–5; White et al., 1992. The White et al. review distinguished between cognitive impulsivity and behavioral impulsivity and found that the latter was more strongly related to delinquency.
14. Moffitt, 1990.
15. Weiss and Hechtman, 1986.
16. Block, Block, and Keyes, 1988.
17. Shedler and Block, 1990.
18. Cantwell, 1974; Morrison and Stewart, 1973.
19. Eaves, Eysenck, and Martin, 1989:259–73; Torgersen, 1981.
20. Schalling et al., 1988.
21. Garfinkel, 1986; Rapoport et al., 1980.
22. Wallander and Hubert, 1985:138–39.
23. Gawin and Ellinwood, 1988; Koob and Bloom, 1988; Ritz et al., 1987.
24. Fishbein, Lozovsky, and Jaffe, 1989; Virkkunen et al., 1989; Stanley and Stanley, 1990.
25. Roy et al., 1988; Roy, DeJong, and Linnoila, 1989.
26. Cloninger et al., 1982; Bohman et al., 1982.
27. Rutter and Garmezy, 1983:848.
28. Barkley, 1981; Barkley and Cunningham, 1980.
29. Jacobvitz and Sroufe, 1987.
30. Rutter and Garmezy, 1983:849.
31. Weiss et al., 1979; Weiss and Hechtman, 1985:105–6, 319–21.
32. Werner and Smith, 1977.
33. Block and Block, 1980.
34. Cloninger, 1987:575.
35. Aristotle, *Nichomachean Ethics*, 1117b23–1119b20, 1148a13–1152a35.
36. Wilson and Herrnstein, 1985: ch. 5; Hirschi and Gottfredson, 1983.
37. Wilson and Abrahamse, 1993.
38. Schelling, 1980.
39. Carpenter et al., 1988; Feldman et al., 1979.
40. Herrnstein and Prelec, 1991a, 1991b.
41. Wilson and Herrnstein, 1985:360–63; Kaprio et al., 1987; Cadoret et al., 1979; Bohman, 1978.
42. Noble, 1991; Noble et al., 1991.
43. Wilson and Herrnstein, 1985: ch. 3; Farrington et al., 1990.

Duty

1. Frank, 1988, chs. 4 and 5, esp. pp. 99–102.
2. Huston et al., 1981; Huston et al., 1976.

3. Oliner and Oliner, 1988:209–20; cf. also Tec, 1986.
4. Freud, 1923:32.
5. Ibid., ch. 3.
6. Freud, 1930:68, 91.
7. Freud, 1923:50, 53, 56–57.
8. Konner, 1991:112–14; this book, ch. 7.
9. Fisher and Greenberg, 1977: ch. 4. See also Ainslie, 1992:214–15; Aronfreed, 1968:308–9.
10. On the relationship between guilt and shame, see Aronfreed, 1968:249–54.
11. Eysenck, 1977, ch. 5. But cf. Ainslie, 1992:25–27, 43–45.
12. Cleckley, 1976:367–76.
13. Hare, 1970:76–77.
14. Ibid., 82–83.
15. Hare, 1978.
16. Gough, 1948; Hare and Schalling, 1978:104.
17. Schalling, 1978:96–99.
18. Zuckerman, 1978.
19. A. Smith, 1759:3.2.32.
20. Oliner and Oliner, 1988:214, 217, 219–20; Tec, 1986:160–64.
21. Flacks, 1967; Braungart, 1972.
22. Klineberg et al., 1979:276.
23. Stockdale, 1984:8.
24. Koestler, 1941.
25. Stockdale, 1984:10.
26. Stockdale and Stockdale, 1990:247–52.
27. Ibid., 188–89.
28. Stockdale, 1984:30.
29. Bettelheim, 1960:169.
30. Pawelczynska, 1979:44–45.
31. Ibid., 121, 130, 141, xxix.
32. Personal communication from KCET.
33. Marwell and Ames, 1981.

The Social Animal

1. Geertz, 1973:49.
2. Ibid., 40.
3. Eibl-Eibesfeldt, 1989:200; Field, 1990:27–39; Hay and Rheingold, 1983.
4. Eibl-Eibesfeldt, 1989:30–31.
5. Meltzoff and Moore, 1977; Meltzoff, 1988.
6. Meltzoff and Moore, 1983.
7. Jacobson, 1979.
8. Meltzoff, 1985.

9. Field, 1990:61.
10. Eibl-Eibesfeldt, 1989:53; Radke-Yarrow et al., 1983:479; Sagi and Hoffman, 1976; Field, 1990:31.
11. Malatesta and Izard, 1984.
12. Radke-Yarrow et al., 1983:480.
13. Garcia and Koelling, 1966a, 1966b; Konner, 1982:26–30; Garcia et al., 1974; Garcia, 1981, 1990; Rozin and Schull, 1988.
14. Seligman and Hager, 1972:8–9.
15. Rachman, 1990:156–58.
16. Shepher, 1983.
17. Bowlby, 1982:216–20.
18. Rajecki, Lamb, and Obsmacher, 1978:425. The literature does not permit a strong generalization, but many clinical cases find heightened attachment among abused children.
19. Cosmides and Tooby, 1987:281; Herrnstein, 1977; Caporeal, 1987; Caporeal et al., 1989.
20. McKenna, 1987:161; Super, 1981; Sternglanz, Gray, and Murakami, 1977; Lorenz, 1943; Eibl-Eibesfeldt, 1989.
21. Bustad, 1991; Serpell, 1986; Katcher and Beck, 1991.
22. Watson, 1928; quotation at p. 81; West, 1914:59–60.
23. Kagan, 1981:122–26; Kagan, 1984; ch. 4; Dunn, 1987.
24. Konner, 1982:160.
25. E.g., Pinker, 1991; Pinker and Bloom, 1990.
26. MacLean, 1985:412.
27. Royce and Powell, 1983; Eysenck and Eysenck, 1985.
28. Eaves, Eysenck, and Martin, 1989:10–14.
29. Eaves, Eysenck, and Martin, 1989; Loehlin, Willerman, and Horn, 1988; Cloninger, 1987; Bouchard et al., 1990.
30. Plomin and Dunn, 1986; Loehlin, Willerman, and Horn, 1988; Rose et al., 1988; Eaves, Eysenck, and Martin, 1989.
31. Rushton et al., 1986; Matthews et al., 1981.
32. Bouchard et al., 1990.
33. Segal, 1984.
34. Reviewed in Piliavin and Charng, 1990:44–50; Matthews et al., 1981.
35. Freedman and Freedman, 1979; Trevathan, 1987:137–38.
36. Brown et al., 1979; Coursey, Buchsbaum, and Murphy, 1980; Brown and Linnoila, 1990; Schalling, Edman, Asberg, and Oreland, 1988.
37. Knorring, Oreland, and Winblad, 1984.
38. Coursey, Buchsbaum, and Murphy, 1982.
39. Rosenberg and Kagan, 1987, 1988.
40. Thomas and Chess, 1976, 1984; Thomas, Chess, and Birch, 1968.
41. Eysenck, 1977; Hare and Schalling, 1978.
42. Raine, Venables, and Williams, 1990.

43. Kagan, 1989.
44. Zahn-Waxler and Radke-Yarrow, 1982; Dunn and Munn, 1985.
45. Hay and Rheingold, 1978:119.

Families

1. Shweder, Turiel, and Much, 1981:289.
2. Ibid.; Turiel, 1983.
3. Freud, 1930. Cf. also Turiel, 1983:166–73.
4. Skinner, 1971:107–9. Cf. also Turiel, 1983:173–74.
5. Dunn and Plomin, 1990:16.
6. Ibid., 157; Patterson, 1982.
7. Dunn and Plomin, 1990.
8. Bowlby, 1982; Ainsworth et al., 1978.
9. Main and Cassidy, 1988; Main, Kaplan, and Cassidy, 1986.
10. Main, 1983; Bretherton, 1985:20–22; Sroufe, 1983:48, 1985:1.
11. Egeland et al., 1990:892–93.
12. Main and George, 1985; Renken et al., 1989.
13. Main, 1990; Bretherton, 1985:24–28.
14. Harlow and Harlow, 1969.
15. Rutter, 1979.
16. Meaney et al., 1988; Diamond, 1988.
17. Schanberg and Field, 1987.
18. Karen, 1990.
19. Baumrind, 1967, 1971, 1978; Baumrind and Black, 1967. Cf. also Damon, 1988: ch. 4.
20. Clark, 1983; Dornbusch et al., 1987.
21. Wilson and Herrnstein, 1985: ch. 8; West and Farrington, 1973; McCord, McCord, and Howard, 1961.
22. Cf. Baumrind, 1973:6, 1989:351; Coriat, 1926; Naumburg, 1928; Lewin et al., 1939.
23. Baumrind, 1973:32–33, 39; Pikas, 1961; Middleton and Snell, 1963.
24. Bandura, 1977; Bandura and Walters, 1963.
25. For a government report that supports this fear, see Surgeon General's Scientific Advisory Committee on Television and Social Behavior, 1972; other studies are cited in Wilson and Herrnstein, 1985: ch. 13.
26. Evidence that popular fears are exaggerated is summarized in Wilson and Herrnstein, 1985: ch. 13.
27. Boyd and Richerson, 1985:41; Bandura, 1977:12.
28. Konner, 1982:301–10, 1991:89, 103–5.
29. Lamb et al., 1985:183.
30. Fuller et al., 1986; Conroy et al., 1980; Benedict, 1946: ch. 12.
31. Kagan, Kearsley, and Zelazo, 1978.
32. De Vos, 1973:49–50, 479–81.

33. R. Smith, 1983.
34. Zinsmeister, 1990.
35. Bronfenbrenner, 1979:273.
36. For a summary, see Wilson and Herrnstein, 1985: chs. 8, 9.
37. Wolfgang, Figlio, and Sellin, 1972.
38. Popenoe, 1988:4–7; Symons, 1979:109.
39. Symons, 1979: ch. 4., esp. 112–13.
40. Fuchs, 1988:111.
41. Cf. Belsky and Steinberg, 1978.
42. Belsky, 1988:257; cf. also Belsky, 1990.
43. Field, 1990:90–93; Phillips et al., 1987.
44. Fox, 1975:93.
45. Chesterton, 1950.

Gender

1. Rossi, 1987:68; Durden-Smith and DeSimone, 1983; Hoyenga and Hoyenga, 1979.
2. Eibl-Eibesfeldt, 1989:271–72.
3. Breslau, Klein, and Allen, 1988.
4. Rossi, 1987:68.
5. Earls, 1987.
6. Hoffman, 1981:364.
7. Maccoby and Jacklin, 1974, 1980; Hyde, 1986.
8. Symons, 1979:144–46; Edgerton, 1992:204; Chagnon, 1968.
9. Wilson and Herrnstein, 1985: ch. 4.
10. Olweus, 1979, 1984a, 1984b.
11. Symons, 1979:214; Lawson and Samson, 1988.
12. Symons, 1979:213–15.
13. Murdock and White, 1969.
14. Trivers, 1985:311.
15. Ibid., 239.
16. Lynn, 1974; Rypma, 1976; Berman, 1980; Katz and Konner, 1981; Lancaster and Lancaster, 1983.
17. West and Konner, 1976; Katz and Konner, 1981.
18. Edgerton, 1971:273–76, 289–91.
19. Wilson, 1991: ch. 3.
20. Helper, 1855; Courtwright, 1991.
21. Farrington and Langan, 1992.
22. Burford, 1992.
23. Tiger, 1970.
24. Symons, 1979:23.
25. Aristotle, *Politics*, 1252a29, 1252b13.
26. Tiger and Fox, 1971:71; see also Tiger and Shepher, 1975:279.

27. Sawhill, 1992.
28. Ibid., and Dawson, 1991.
29. Farley and Allen, 1987.
30. Popenoe, 1988:174.
31. Hoffman, 1981:372.
32. Kellam, Ensminger, and Turner, 1977.
33. Ensminger, Kellam, and Rubin, 1983.
34. Hoffman, 1971.
35. Hoffman, 1981:365.
36. Kraus and Lilienfeld, 1959; Gove, 1973; Rand, 1987; Reuter, 1990.
37. Eberstadt, 1991.
38. Brooks-Gunn and Furstenberg, 1986.
39. Gilligan, 1982; Lyons, 1983; Gilligan and Wiggins, 1987; Gilligan, Ward, and Taylor, 1988; Johnston, 1985.
40. Major and Deaux, 1982; Major and Adams, 1983.
41. Piaget, 1932:83.
42. Lever, 1976, 1978.
43. Gilligan, 1982:10.
44. Cairns and Cairns, 1985.
45. Kohlberg, 1981.
46. Cf. Kagan, 1984:124.
47. Spiro and Spiro, 1975, 1979.
48. Spiro and Spiro, 1975:240–44.
49. Ibid., 280–82.
50. Spiro and Spiro, 1975:329–36.
51. Ibid., 350–51, 469–71; Spiro and Spiro, 1979:15–25.
52. Spiro and Spiro, 1979:92–94.
53. Ibid., 106.
54. Tiger and Shepher, 1975, esp. 262–63. See also Spiro and Spiro, 1975.
55. Morgan, 1877.
56. Engels, 1884.
57. Sanday, 1981, esp. ch. 6.
58. Dumont, 1970.
59. Tannen, 1990; Maltz and Borker, 1982; Goodwin and Goodwin, 1987.
60. Tannen, 1990: 217–18; Goodwin and Goodwin, 1987.
61. Grace Goodell, private communication.
62. Wagatsuma and De Vos, 1984:148–51, 230–33.
63. Tobin, Wu, and Davidson, 1989:190.
64. Ibid., 34.

The Universal Aspiration

1. Kohlberg, 1981.
2. Kant, 1785.

3. Langbein, 1977:3.
4. O. Patterson, 1982: vii, 350–64; O. Patterson, 1991:11–12.
5. O. Patterson, 1991: x.
6. Ibid., 402–3.
7. May, 1976:xiii.
8. Edgerton, 1985:16–21.
9. Quoted in Copleston, 1985:1.431.
10. Westermarck, 1908:2.177–78.
11. O. Patterson, 1991:277.
12. Ginsberg, 1947:307–8. Cf. also Westermarck, 1908:2.176–77.
13. Lewis, 1990:4–5, 85.
14. Davis, 1966:294; Gay, 1977:408.
15. Green, 1906:240 and, generally, 237–53.
16. Cf. Bloch, 1961: esp. 441–47.
17. Goody, 1983:4–5.
18. Guichard, 1977:19.
19. Braudel, 1972:1.75–77.
20. Cf. Geis and Geis, 1987:37–38.
21. Noonan, 1965:126–31; Herlihy, 1985:11.
22. Geis, 1987:83.
23. Goody, 1983:221.
24. Ibid., 68–73, 93–96, 101–2, 123–25.
25. Geis, 1989:83–98; Herlihy, 1985:11–13, 61–62.
26. Donahue, 1976.
27. Beer, 1991:97–104.
28. Duby, 1978:16–17, 21, 36, 59; Goody, 1987:193.
29. Geis and Geis, 1989:102–3, 110, 149–53; Wemple, 1981.
30. Pateman, 1991.
31. Cf. Goody, 1987:153–54.
32. Geis, 1989:297.
33. Herlihy, 1985:158; cf. also 112–30.
34. Geis, 1989:306.
35. Cf. Fox, 1973: ch. 5.
36. Hajnal, 1965, 1983; Laslett, 1977; Stone, 1982.
37. Hajnal, 1965:132.
38. Stone, 1982:74.
39. Goode, 1963:22.
40. Berger, 1962; Kagitcibasi, 1982.
41. Quoted in Boorstin, 1983:627.
42. Hanke, 1949: ch. 8; cf. also Hanke, 1959; Boorstin, 1983:626–35.
43. Quoted in Q. Skinner, 1978:2, 165, 167–69.
44. Goode, 1963.
45. Ibid., 322–25.

46. Bloch, 1961:443.
47. Macfarlane, 1978. In 1776 Adam Smith predicted that the evidence would support this view (3.3.4–5).
48. Thomas and Znaniecki, 1927:1.158–59, 194–95.
49. Ibid., 125–26.
50. Macfarlane, 1978:27. Cf. also Riesenfeld, 1962, who stresses the importance of the rise, beginning at the time of Henry II, of a corps of professional judges who produced a detailed land law.
51. Macfarlane, 1978:131–34; Pollock and Maitland, 1959:1.482; 2.404, 406–7. But cf. Pateman, 1988:90–91. I think Pateman, relying on Blackstone, overstates the legal subjection of married English women in the late medieval period.
52. Edgerton, 1992: chs. 5, 8.
53. Gay, 1969:31–33.
54. Himmelfarb, 1987:21.
55. Nisbet, 1953: ch. 10.
56. Cf. Berlin, 1991:70.
57. Gay, 1988:239–49, 351–54.
58. Quoted in Gay, 1977:527.
59. Ibid., 526.
60. Gibbon, 1776:1.22.
61. Quoted in Cassirer, 1951:245.
62. Wilson, 1991: ch. 3.
63. Trilling, 1965: preface and ch. 1.

The Moral Sense and Human Character

1. Shils and Janowitz, 1948.
2. Asch, 1952.
3. Milgram, 1974.
4. Lerner, 1980.
5. Horowitz, 1975.
6. Banfield, 1958.
7. Frank, 1988: chs. 4, 5, and p. 237.
8. Bentham, 1780:151; Mill, 1861:8–10.
9. Edgerton, 1992, is a devastating critique of this view.
10. An influential example of the choice-based attack on marriage is Bernard, 1982. Cf. Whitehead, 1992; Macklin, 1980.
11. Golding, 1962.
12. Rawls, 1971.
13. Rousseau, 1762:184ff; cf. also Bloom, 1978; Melzer, 1990: ch. 3.
14. Nussbaum, 1978:60.
15. Salkever, 1990.
16. Hume, *Treatise*, 469–70.

17. Ibid., 478, 480–83.
18. Ibid., 486.
19. Hume, *Enquiry*, 8, 65.
20. *Treatise*, 474.
21. Ibid., 470.
22. Hardin, 1988:180.
23. Thomson, 1989.
24. Taylor, 1989:14.
25. Oakeshott, 1962:72.
26. Ibid., 73.
27. *Nichomachean Ethics*, 1103a32–1103b2, 1104a21; cf. also Burnyeat, 1980; Hardie, 1980:104–7.
28. *Nichomachean Ethics*, 1103a23–26.
29. Glendon, 1991.
30. Dworkin, 1977:269.
31. Arendt, 1951.
32. Wood, 1991: esp. 215.
33. Glendon, 1991; Bellah et al., 1985; Etzioni, 1991; Galston, 1988.
34. Glendon, 1989; Glendon, 1991:121–30.
35. Wilson and Herrnstein, 1985: ch. 13.
36. Ainslie, 1992:300, 366.
37. Fox, 1975:17–18.

References

Adams, J. Stacy. 1963. Toward an understanding of inequity. *Journal of Abnormal and Social Psychology* 67:422–36.

Adams, J. Stacy, and P. R. Jacobsen. 1964. Effects of wage inequities on work quality. *Journal of Abnormal and Social Psychology* 69:19–25.

Adams, J. Stacy, and W. B. Rosenbaum. 1962. The relationship of worker productivity to cognitive dissonance about wage inequities. *Journal of Applied Psychology* 46:161–64.

Ainslie, George. 1975. Specious reward: A behavioral theory of impulsiveness and impulse control. *Psychological Bulletin* 82:463–96.

———. 1992. *Picoeconomics.* New York: Cambridge University Press.

Ainsworth, Mary, et al. 1978. *Patterns of Attachment.* Hillsdale, N.J.: Erlbaum.

Alexander, Richard D. 1987. *The Biology of Moral Systems.* New York: De Gruyter.

Anderson, Michael. 1980. *Approaches to the History of the Western Family, 1500–1914.* London: Macmillan.

Arendt, Hannah. 1951. *The Origins of Totalitarianism.* New York: Harcourt Brace & World.

Aristotle. *Eudemian Ethics.* Trans. J. Solomon. In Jonathan Barnes, ed., *The Complete Works of Aristotle,* 2:1922–81. Princeton, N.J.: Princeton University Press, 1984.

———. *Politics.* Trans. Carnes Lord. Chicago: University of Chicago Press, 1984.

———. *Nichomachean Ethics.* Trans. Terence Irwin. Indianapolis: Hackett, 1985.

Arnhart, Larry. 1990. A sociobiological defense of Aristotle's sexual politics. Paper delivered to the annual meeting of the American Political Science Association, San Francisco, Calif.

267

References

Aronfreed, Justin. 1968. *Conscience and Conduct.* New York: Academic Press.

Asch, Solomon E. 1956. *Social Psychology.* Englewood Cliffs, N.J.: Prentice-Hall.

Austin, W., and Elaine Walster. 1974. Reactions to confirmations and disconfirmations of expectancies of equity and inequity. *Journal of Personality and Social Psychology* 30:208–16.

Axelrod, Robert. 1984. *The Evolution of Cooperation.* New York: Basic Books.

Axelrod, Robert, and W. D. Hamilton. 1981. The evolution of cooperation. *Science* 211:1390–96.

Ayer, Alfred Jules. [1936] 1946. *Language, Truth and Logic.* New York: Dover.

Bakeman, R., and J. R. Brownlee. 1982. Social rules governing object conflicts in toddlers and preschoolers. In K. H. Rubin and H. S. Ross, eds., *Peer Relations and Social Skills in Childhood,* 99–111. New York: Springer.

Bamberger, Joan. 1974. The myth of matriarchy: Why men rule in primitive society. In Michelle Zimbalist Rosaldo and Louise Lamphere, eds., *Woman, Culture, and Society,* 263–80. Stanford, Calif.: Stanford University Press.

Bandura, Albert. 1977. *Social Learning Theory.* Englewood Cliffs, N.J.: Prentice-Hall.

Bandura, Albert, and R. Walters. 1963. *Social Learning and Personality Development.* New York: Holt, Rinehart & Winston.

Banfield, Edward C. 1958. *The Moral Basis of a Backward Society.* With the assistance of Laura Fasano Banfield. Glencoe, Ill.: Free Press.

Barkley, R. A. 1981. *Hyperactive Children: A Handbook for Diagnosis and Treatment.* New York: Guilford Press.

Barkley, R. A., and C. E. Cunningham. 1980. The parent-child interactions of hyperactive children and their modification by stimulant drugs. In R. M. Knight and D. J. Bakker, eds., *Treatment of Hyperactive and Learning Disabled Children,* 219–36. Baltimore: University Park Press.

Batson, C. Daniel. 1990. How social an animal? The human capacity for caring. *American Psychologist* 45:336–46.

Batson, C. Daniel, Bruce D. Duncan, Paula Ackerman, Terese Buckley, and Kimberly Birch. 1981. Is empathic emotion a source of altruistic motivation? *Journal of Personality and Social Psychology* 40:290–302.

Batson, C. Daniel, Janine L. Dyck, J. Randall Brandt, Judy G. Batson, Anne L. Powell, M. Rosalie McMaster, and Cari Giffitt. 1988. Five studies testing two new egoistic alternatives to the empathy-altruism hypothesis. *Journal of Personality and Social Psychology* 55:52–77.

Baumrind, Diana. 1967. Child care practices anteceding three patterns of preschool behavior. *Genetic Psychology Monographs* 75:43–88.

———. 1971. Current patterns of parental authority. *Developmental Psychology Monographs* 4:1–103.

———. 1973. The development of instrumental competence through socialization. *Minnesota Symposium in Child Psychology* 7:3–46.

———. 1978. Parental disciplinary patterns and social competence in children. *Youth and Society* 9:239–76.

———. 1986. Sex differences in moral reasoning: Response to Walker's (1984) conclusion that there are none. *Child Development* 57:511–21.

———. 1989. Rearing competent children. In William Damon, ed., *Child Development Today and Tomorrow*, 349–78. San Francisco: Jossey-Bass.

Baumrind, Diana, and A. E. Black. 1967. Socialization practices associated with dimensions of competence in preschool boys and girls. *Child Development* 38:291–327.

Becker, Gary S., and K. M. Murphy. 1988. A theory of rational addiction. *Journal of Political Economy* 96:675–700.

Beer, Mathias. 1991. *Eltern und Kinder des Späten Mittelalters in ihren Briefen*. Nürnberg: Schriftreihe des Stadtarchivs Nürnberg.

Bellah, Robert N., et al. 1985. *Habits of the Heart: Individualism and Commitment in American Life*. Berkeley and Los Angeles: University of California Press.

Belsky, Jay. 1988. The "effects" of infant day care reconsidered. *Early Childhood Research Quarterly* 3:235–72.

———. 1990. Developmental risks associated with infant day care: Attachment insecurity, noncompliance, and aggression? In S. Chehraz, ed., *Psychosocial Issues in Day Care*. Washington, D.C.: American Psychiatric Press.

Belsky, Jay, and David Eggebeen. 1991. Early and extensive maternal employment and young children's socioemotional development: Children of the National Longitudinal Survey of Youth. *Journal of Marriage and the Family* 53:1083–1110.

Belsky, Jay, and Michael Rovine. 1987. Temperament and attachment security in the strange situation: An empirical rapprochement. *Child Development* 58:787–95.

Belsky, Jay, and L. D. Steinberg. 1978. The effects of day care: A critical review. *Child Development* 49:929–49.

Benedict, Ruth. 1934. *Patterns of Culture*. Boston: Houghton Mifflin.

———. 1946. *The Chrysanthemum and the Sword: Patterns of Japanese Culture*. Boston: Houghton Mifflin.

Benoit-Smullyan, Emile. 1948. The sociologism of Emile Durkheim and his school. In Harry Elmer Barnes, ed., *An Introduction to the History of Sociology*. Chicago: University of Chicago Press.

References

Bentham, Jeremy. [1780] 1948. *An Introduction to the Principles of Morals and Legislation.* Ed. Wilfrid Harrison. Oxford: Basil Blackwell.

Berger, Morroe. 1962. *The Arab World Today.* New York: Doubleday.

Berghe, Pierre L. van den. 1987. *The Ethnic Phenomenon.* New York: Praeger.

Berlin, Isaiah. 1991. *The Crooked Timber of Humanity.* New York: Knopf.

Berman, Phyllis. 1980. Are women more responsive than men to the young? A review of developmental and situational factors. *Psychological Bulletin* 88:668–95.

Bernard, Jessie. 1982. *The Future of Marriage.* Rev. ed. New Haven: Yale University Press.

Bettelheim, Bruno. 1960. *The Informed Heart.* Glencoe, Ill.: Free Press.

Bickman, Leonard, et al. 1973. Dormitory density and helping behavior. *Environment and Behavior* 5:465–90.

Bloch, Marc. 1961. *Feudal Society.* Trans. L. A. Manyon. Chicago: University of Chicago Press.

Block, Jack H., and Jeanne H. Block. 1980. The role of ego-control and ego-resiliency in the organization of behavior. *Minnesota Symposia on Child Psychology* 13:39–101.

Block, Jack H., Jeanne H. Block, and Susan Keyes. 1988. Longitudinally foretelling drug usage in adolescence: Early childhood personality and environmental precursors. *Child Development* 59:336–55.

Bloom, Allan. 1978. The education of democratic man: *Emile. Daedalus* 107:135–53.

Bohman, Michael. 1978. Some genetic aspects of alcoholism and criminality: A population of adoptees. *Archives of General Psychiatry* 35:269–78.

Bohman, Michael, C. Robert Cloninger, S. Sigvardsson, and A.-L. von Knorring. 1982. Predisposition to petty criminality in Swedish adoptees: Genetic and environmental heterogeneity. *Archives of General Psychiatry* 39:1233–41.

Bohman, Michael, and Soren Sigvardsson. 1990. Outcome in adoption: Lessons from longitudinal studies. In David M. Brodzinsky and Marshall D. Schecter, eds., *The Psychology of Adoption,* 93–106. New York: Oxford University Press.

Bonar, James. 1930. *Moral Sense.* New York: Macmillan.

Boorstin, Daniel J. 1983. *The Discoverers.* New York: Random House.

Bornstein, Marc H. 1979. The pace of life revisited. *International Journal of Psychology* 14:83–90.

———. 1989. *Maternal Responsiveness: Characteristics and Consequences.* San Francisco: Jossey-Bass.

Bouchard, Thomas J., David T. Lykken, Matthew McGue, Nancy L. Segal, and Auke Tellegen. 1990. Sources of human psychological differences: The Minnesota study of twins reared apart. *Science* 250:223–28.

References

Bowlby, John. 1982. *Attachment and Loss*. 2d ed. New York: Basic Books.

Boyd, Robert, and Peter J. Richerson. 1985. *Culture and the Evolutionary Process*. Chicago: University of Chicago Press.

Braudel, Fernand. 1972. *The Mediterranean and the Mediterranean World in the Age of Philip II*. Trans. Sian Reynolds. New York: Harper & Row.

Braungart, Richard G. 1972. Family status, socialization, and student politics. *American Journal of Sociology* 77:108–30.

Braungart, Richard G., and Margaret M. Braungart. 1990. The life-course development of left- and right-wing youth activist leaders from the 1960s. *Political Psychology* 11:243–82.

Brazelton, T. B. 1972. Implications of human development among the Mayan Indians of Mexico. *Human Development* 15:90–111.

Breslau, Naomi, Nancy Klein, and Lida Allen. 1988. Very low birthweight: Behavioral sequelae at nine years of age. *Journal of the American Academy of Child and Adolescent Psychiatry* 27:605–12.

Bretherton, Inge. 1985. Attachment theory: Retrospect and prospect. *Monographs of the Society for Research in Child Development* 50:3–35.

Bridge, T. Peter, et al. 1985. Platelet monoamine oxidase activity: Demographic characteristics contribute to enzyme activity variability. *Journal of Gerontology* 40:23–28.

Bridgeman, Diane L. 1983. Benevolent babies: Emergence of the social self. In Diane L. Bridgeman, ed., *The Nature of Prosocial Development*. New York: Academic Press.

Bronfenbrenner, Urie. 1979. *The Ecology of Human Development*. Cambridge, Mass.: Harvard University Press.

Bronson, W. 1981. *Toddlers' Behavior with Agemates: Issues of Interaction, Cognition, and Affect*. Norwood, N.J.: Ablex.

Brooks-Gunn, Jeanne, and Frank F. Furstenberg, Jr. 1986. The children of adolescent mothers: Physical, academic, and psychological outcomes. *Developmental Review* 6:224–51.

Brown, Gerald L., et al. 1979. Aggression in humans correlates with cerebrospinal fluid amine metabolites. *Psychiatry Research* 1:131–39.

Brown, Gerald L., and Markku Linnoila. 1990. CSF serotonin metabolite (5-HIAA) studies in depression, impulsivity, and violence. *Journal of Clinical Psychiatry* 51:31–43.

Brown, Peter. 1988. *The Body and Society*. New York: Columbia University Press.

Browning, Christopher R. 1992. *Ordinary Men*. New York: HarperCollins.

Burford, Bill. 1992. *Among the Thugs*. New York: Norton.

Burnyeat, M. F. 1980. Aristotle on learning to be good. In Amelie Oksenberg Rorty, ed., *Essays on Aristotle's Ethics*. Berkeley and Los Angeles: University of California Press.

References

Burton, R. V. 1963. The generality of honesty reconsidered. *Psychological Bulletin* 70:481–99.

———. 1976. Honesty and dishonesty. In Thomas Lickona, ed., *Moral Development and Behavior*, 173–97. New York: Holt, Rinehart & Winston.

Bustad, Leo K. 1991. Man and beast interface. In Michael H. Robinson and Lionel Tiger, eds., *Man and Beast Revisited*. Washington, D.C.: Smithsonian Institution Press.

Cadoret, Remi. 1990. Biologic perspectives of adoptee adjustment. In David M. Brodzinsky and Marshall D. Schecter, eds., *The Psychology of Adoption*, 93–106. New York: Oxford University Press.

Cadoret, Remi, C. A. Cain, and W. M. Grove. 1979. Development of alcoholism in adoptees reared apart from alcoholic biologic relatives. *Archives of General Psychiatry* 37:561–63.

Cairns, R. B., and B. D. Cairns. 1985. The developmental–interactional view of social behavior: Four issues of adolescent aggression. In D. Olweus, J. Block, and M. Radke-Yarrow, eds., *The Development of Antisocial and Prosocial Behavior*, 315–42. New York: Academic Press.

Campbell, J. K. 1964. *Honour, Family and Patronage*. Oxford: Clarendon Press.

Cantwell, D. P. 1974. Genetic studies of hyperactive children: Psychiatric illness in biologic and adopting parents. In R. Fieve, D. Rosenthal, and H. Brill, eds., *Genetic Research in Psychiatry*, 273–80. Baltimore, Md.: Johns Hopkins University Press.

Caporeal, Linnda R. 1987. Homo sapiens, homo faber, homo socians: Technology and the social animal. In Werner Callebaut and Rik Pinxter, eds., *Evolutionary Epistemology*. Boston: Reidel.

Caporeal, Linnda R., et al. 1989. Selfishness examined: Cooperation in the absence of egoistic incentives. *Behavioral and Brain Sciences* 12:683–739.

Carlson, Mary, Felton Earls, and Richard D. Todd. 1988. The importance of regressive changes in the development of the nervous system: Toward a neurobiological theory of child development. *Psychiatric Developments* 1:1–22.

Carpenter, Cheryl, et al. 1988. *Kids, Drugs, and Crime*. Lexington, Mass.: D.C. Heath.

Cashdan, Elizabeth. 1980. Egalitarianism among hunters and gatherers. *American Anthropologist* 82:116–20.

Casper, Jay D., Tom R. Tyler, and B. Fisher. 1988. Procedural justice among felony defendants. *Law & Society Review* 22:483–507.

Cassirer, Ernst. 1951. *The Philosophy of the Enlightenment*. Trans. Fritz C. A. Koelln and James P. Pettegrove. Princeton, N.J.: Princeton University Press.

Chagnon, Napoleon A. 1968. *Yqnomamö: The Fierce People*. New York: Holt, Rinehart & Winston.

Chesterton, G. K. 1950. *Heretics*. New York: Devon Adair.

Chodorow, Nancy. 1978. *The Reproduction of Mothering*. Berkeley and Los Angeles: University of California Press.

Clark, Reginald M. 1983. *Family Life and School Achievement: Why Poor Black Children Succeed or Fail*. Chicago: University of Chicago Press.

Clark, R. D., and L. E. Word. 1974. Where is the apathetic bystander? Situational characteristics of the emergency. *Journal of Personality and Social Psychology* 29:279–87.

Cleckley, Hervey. 1976. *The Mask of Sanity*. 5th ed. St. Louis, Mo.: C. V. Mosby.

Cloninger, C. Robert. 1987. A systematic method for clinical description and classification of personality variants. *Archives of General Psychiatry* 44:573–88.

Cloninger, C. Robert, S. Sigvardsson, Michael Bohman, and A.-L. von Knorring. 1982. Predisposition to petty criminality in Swedish adoptees: Cross-fostering analysis of gene-environment interaction. *Archives of General Psychiatry* 39:1242–47.

Cohn, Norman. 1975. *Europe's Inner Demons*. New York: Basic Books.

Coke, J. S., C. D. Batson, and K. McDavis. 1978. Empathic mediation of helping: A two-stage model. *Journal of Personality and Social Psychology* 36:752–66.

Conroy, Mary, et al. 1980. Maternal strategies for regulating children's behavior: Japanese and American families. *Journal of Cross-Cultural Psychology* 11:153–72.

Copleston, Frederick. 1985. *A History of Philosophy*. Vol. 1, *Greece and Rome*. New York: Doubleday/Image.

Coriat, I. H. 1926. The psychoanalytic approach to education. *Progressive Educator* 3:19–25.

Cosmides, Leda, and John Tooby. 1987. From evolution to behavior: Evolutionary psychology as the missing link. In J. Dupre, ed., *The Latest on the Best*. Cambridge, Mass.: MIT Press.

Coursey, Robert D., Monte S. Buchsbaum, and Dennis L. Murphy. 1980. Psychological characteristics of subjects identified by platelet MAO activity and evoked potentials as biologically at risk for psychopathology. *Journal of Abnormal Psychology* 89:151–64.

———. 1982. 2-year follow-up of subjects and their families defined as at risk for psychopathology on the basis of platelet MAO activities. *Neuropsychobiology* 8:51–6.

Courtwright, David T. 1991. Disease, death, and disorder on the American frontier. *Journal of the History of Medicine and Allied Sciences* 46:457–92.

Crockenberg, Susan. 1986. Are temperamental differences in babies associated with predictable differences in care giving? In Jacqueline V. Lerner and Richard M. Lerner, eds., *Temperament and Social Interaction in Infants and Children*, 53–73. San Francisco: Jossey-Bass.

Daly, Martin, and Margo Wilson. 1984. A sociobiological analysis of human infanticide. In Glenn Hausfater and Sarah Blaffer Hrdy, eds., *Infanticide: Comparative and Evolutionary Perspectives*, 487–502. New York: De Gruyter.

———. 1987. Children as homicide victims. In Richard J. Gelles and Jane B. Lancaster, eds., *Child Abuse and Neglect: Biosocial Dimensions*, 201–14. New York: De Gruyter.

———. 1988. *Homicide*. New York: De Gruyter.

Damon, William. 1988. *The Moral Child*. New York: Free Press.

Darwin, Charles. [1859] 1962. *The Origin of Species*. New York: Collier Books.

———. [1871] 1981. *The Descent of Man, and Selection in Relation to Sex*. Princeton, N.J.: Princeton University Press.

Davis, David Brion. 1966. *The Problem of Slavery in Western Culture*. Ithaca, N.Y.: Cornell University Press.

———. 1984. *Slavery and Human Progress*. New York: Oxford University Press.

Dawson, Deborah A. 1991. *Family Structure and Children's Health: United States, 1988*. Vital and Health Statistics, ser. 10, no. 178. Hyattsville, Md.: National Center for Health Statistics.

De Mause, Lloyd, ed. 1974. *The History of Childhood*. New York: Psychohistory Press.

De Vos, George A. 1973. *Socialization for Achievement: Essays on the Cultural Psychology of the Japanese*. Berkeley and Los Angeles: University of California Press.

Diamond, Marian. 1988. *Enriching Heredity*. New York: Free Press.

Dickemann, Mildred. 1979. Female infanticide, reproductive strategies, and social stratification: A preliminary model. In N. Chagnon and W. Irons, eds., *Evolutionary Biology and Human Social Behavior*, 321–67. North Scituate, Mass.: Duxbury Press.

———. 1984. Concepts and classification in the study of human infanticide. In Glenn Hausfater and Sarah Blaffer Hrdy, eds., *Infanticide: Comparative and Evolutionary Perspectives*, 427–38. New York: De Gruyter.

Divale, W. T., and M. Harris. 1976. Population, warfare, and the male supremacist complex. *American Anthropologist* 78:521–38.

Donahue, Charles. 1976. The policy of Alexander the Third's consent theory of marriage. In Stephan Kuttner, ed., *Proceedings of the*

References

Fourth International Congress of Medieval Canon Law. Vol. 5 in *Monumenta Iuris Canonici.* Citta del Vaticano: Biblioteca Apostolica Vaticana.

Dornbusch, S. M., et al. 1987. The relation of parenting style to adolescent school performance. *Child Development* 58:1244–57.

Duby, G. 1978. *Medieval Marriage: Two Models from Twelfth-Century France.* Baltimore: Johns Hopkins University Press.

Dumont, Louis. 1970. *Homo Hierarchicus: An Essay on the Caste System.* Trans. Mark Sainsbury. Chicago: University of Chicago Press.

Dunn, Judy. 1987. The beginnings of moral understanding: Development in the second year. In Jerome Kagan and Sharon Lamb, eds., *The Emergence of Morality in Young Children,* 91–112. Chicago: University of Chicago Press.

———. 1988. *The Beginnings of Social Understanding.* Oxford: Blackwell.

Dunn, Judy, and Penny Munn. 1985. Becoming a family member. *Child Development* 56:480–92.

Dunn, Judy, and Robert Plomin. 1990. *Separate Lives: Why Siblings Are So Different.* New York: Basic Books.

Durden-Smith, J., and D. DeSimone. 1983. *Sex and the Brain.* New York: Arbor House.

Durkheim, Emile. [1893] 1960. *The Division of Labor.* Trans. George Simpson. Glencoe, Ill.: Free Press.

———. [1897] 1951. *Suicide.* Trans. J. A. Spaulding and George Simpson. Glencoe, Ill.: Free Press.

———. [1912] 1961. *The Elementary Forms of the Religious Life.* Trans. J. W. Swain. New York: Collier.

Dworkin, Ronald. 1977. *Taking Rights Seriously.* Cambridge, Mass.: Harvard University Press.

Earhardt, Anke A., and Susan W. Baker. 1974. Fetal androgens, human central nervous system differentiation, and behavior sex differences. In R. C. Friedman, R. M. Richart, and R. L. Vande Wiele, eds., *Sex Differences in Behavior,* 33–51. New York: Wiley.

Earls, Felton. 1987. Sex differences in psychiatric disorders: Origins and developmental influences. *Psychiatric Developments* 1:1–23.

Eaves, L. J., H. J. Eysenck, and N. G. Martin. 1989. *Genes, Culture and Personality.* London: Academic Press.

Eberstadt, Nicholas. 1991. America's infant mortality puzzle. *Public Interest* 105:37–38.

Edgerton, Robert B. 1971. *The Individual in Cultural Adaptation.* Berkeley and Los Angeles: University of California Press.

———. 1985. *Rules, Exceptions, and Social Order.* Berkeley and Los Angeles: University of California Press.

References

————. 1992. *Sick Societies: Challenging the Myth of Primitive Harmony.* New York: Free Press.

Egeland, Byron, et al. 1990. Preschool behavior problems: Stability and factors accounting for change. *Journal of Child Psychology and Psychiatry* 6:891–909.

Eibl-Eibesfeldt, Irenaus. 1989. *Human Ethology.* New York: De Gruyter.

Eisenberg, Nancy. 1986. *Altruistic Emotion, Cognition, and Behavior.* Hillsdale, N.J.: Erlbaum.

Eisenberg, Nancy, and Randy Lennon. 1983. Sex differences in empathy and related capacities. *Psychological Bulletin* 94:100–31

Eisenberg, Nancy, and Paul A. Miller, 1987. The relation of empathy to prosocial and related behaviors. *Psychological Bulletin* 101:91–119.

Eisenberg, Nancy, and Paul A. Mussen. 1989. *The Roots of Prosocial Behavior in Children.* Cambridge: Cambridge University Press.

Elder, Glen H. 1974. *Children of the Great Depression.* Chicago: University of Chicago Press.

Elder, Glen H., and R. C. Rockwell. 1978. Economic depression and postwar opportunity: A study of life patterns in hell. In R. A. Simmonds, ed., *Research in Community and Mental Health.* Greenwich, Conn.: JAI Press.

Elias, Norbert. [1939] 1978. *The Civilizing Process: The Development of Manners.* Trans. Edmund Jephcott. New York: Urizen.

Elshtain, Jean Bethke. 1981. *Public Man, Private Woman.* Princeton, N.J.: Princeton University Press.

————. 1992. Don't be cruel: Reflections on Rortyian liberalism. In Daniel W. Conway and John E. Seery, eds., *The Politics of Irony,* 199–218. New York: St. Martin's Press.

Elster, Jon. 1989a. *The Cement of Society.* Cambridge: Cambridge University Press.

————. 1989b. *Nuts and Bolts for the Social Sciences.* Cambridge: Cambridge University Press.

Engels, Friedrich. [1884] 1978. *The Origin of the Family, Private Property, and the State.* Reprinted in Robert C. Tucker, ed., *The Marx-Engels Reader,* 734–59. 2d ed. New York: Norton.

Ensminger, Margaret E., Sheppard G. Kellam, and B. R. Rubin. 1983. School and family origins of delinquency: Comparisons by sex. In K. T. Van Dusen and S. A. Mednick, eds., *Prospective Studies of Crime and Delinquency.* Boston: Kluwer-Nijhoff.

Etzioni, Amitai. 1991. *A Responsive Society.* San Francisco: Jossey-Bass.

Eysenck, Hans J. 1977. *Crime and Personality.* London: Routledge & Kegan Paul.

————. 1990. Biological dimensions of personality. In Lawrence C. Pervin, ed., *Handbook of Personality: Theory and Research,* 244–76. New York: Guilford Press.

References

Eysenck, Hans J., and M. W. Eysenck. 1985. *Personality and Individual Differences*. New York: Plenum Press.

Farley, Reynolds, and Walter R. Allen. 1987. *The Color Line and the Quality of Life in America*. New York: Russell Sage Foundation.

Farrington, David P. 1979. Longitudinal research on crime and delinquency. In Norval Morris and Michael Tonry, eds., *Crime and Justice: An Annual Review of Research*, vol. 1. Chicago: University of Chicago Press.

————. 1981. The prevalence of convictions. *British Journal of Criminology* 21:173–75.

Farrington, David P., and Patrick A. Langan. 1992. Changes in crime and punishment in England and America in the 1980s. *Justice Quarterly* 9:5–46.

Farrington, David P., Rolf Loeber, Delbert S. Elliott, et al. 1990. Advancing knowledge about the onset of delinquency and crime. *Advances in Clinical and Child Psychology* 13:283–342.

Farrington, David P., Rolf Loeber, and W. B. Van Kammen. 1990. Long-term criminal outcomes of hyperactivity-impulsivity-attention deficit and conduct problems in childhood. In Lee N. Robins and Michael Rutter, eds., *Straight and Devious Pathways from Childhood to Adulthood*, 62–81. Cambridge: Cambridge University Press.

Feldman, Harvey W., Michael H. Agar, and George M. Beschner. 1979. *Angel Dust: An Ethnographic Study of PCP Users*. Lexington, Mass.: D.C. Heath.

Feldman, Roy E. 1968. Response to compatriot and foreigner who seek assistance. *Journal of Personality and Social Psychology* 10:202–14.

Field, Tiffany. 1990. *Infancy*. Cambridge, Mass.: Harvard University Press.

Field, Tiffany, R. Woodson, R. Greenberg, and D. Cohen. 1982. Discrimination and imitation of facial expressions by neonates. *Science* 218:179–81.

Fish, Margaret, and Jay Belsky. 1991. Temperament and attachment revisited. *American Journal of Orthopsychiatry* 61:418–27.

Fishbein, Diana H., David Lozovsky, and Jerome H. Jaffe. 1989. Impulsivity, aggression, and neuroendocrine responses to serotonergic stimulation in substance abusers. *Biological Psychiatry* 25:1049–66.

Fisher, Seymour, and Roger P. Greenberg. 1977. *The Scientific Credibility of Freud's Theories and Therapy*. New York: Basic Books.

Flacks, Richard. 1967. The liberated generation: An exploration of the roots of student protest. *Journal of Social Issues* 23:52–75.

Fox, Robin. 1975. *Encounter with Anthropology*. New York: Dell.

————. 1983. *The Red Lamp of Incest*. New York: Dutton.

————. 1989. *The Search for Society: Quest for a Biosocial Science and Morality*. New Brunswick, N.J.: Rutgers University Press.

Frank, Robert H. 1988. *Passions within Reason*. New York: Norton.

278

References

Freedman, D. G., and N. Freedman. 1979. Ethnic differences in babies. *Human Nature* 2:36–44.

Freud, Sigmund. [1923] 1961. *The Ego and the Id*. Trans. Joan Riviere. New York: Norton.

———. [1930] 1961. *Civilization and Its Discontents*. Trans. James Strachey. New York: Norton.

Fuchs, Victor R. 1988. *Women's Quest for Economic Equality*. Cambridge, Mass.: Harvard University Press.

Fuller, Bruce, et al. 1986. Contrasting achievement rules: Socialization of Japanese children at home and in school. *Research in Sociology of Education and Socialization* 6:165–201.

Funder, D. C., Jeanne H. Block, and Jack Block. 1983. Delay of gratification: some longitudinal personality correlates. *Journal of Personality and Social Psychology* 44:1198–1213.

Galston, William A. 1988. Liberal virtues. *American Political Science Review* 82:1277–90.

Garcia, John. 1981. Tilting at the paper mills of academe. *American Psychologist* 36:149–58.

———. 1990. Learning without memory. *Journal of Cognitive Neuroscience* 2:287–305.

Garcia, John, Walter G. Hankins, and Kenneth W. Rusiniak. 1974. Behavioral regulation of the milieu interne in man and rat. *Science* 185:824–31.

Garcia, John, and Robert A. Koelling. 1966a. Relation of cue to consequence in avoidance learning. *Psychonomic Science* 4:123–24.

———. 1966b. Learning with prolonged delay of reinforcement. *Psychonomic Science* 5:121–22.

Garfinkel, Barry D. 1986. Recent developments in attention deficit disorder. *Psychiatric Annals* 16:11–15.

Gawin, Frank H., and H. Ellinwood. 1988. Cocaine and other stimulants: Actions, abuse, and treatment. *New England Journal of Medicine* 318:1173–82.

Gay, Peter. 1977. *The Enlightenment: The Science of Freedom*. New York: Norton.

———. 1988. *Voltaire's Politics: The Poet as Realist*. New Haven, Conn.: Yale University Press.

Geertz, Clifford. 1973. *The Interpretation of Cultures*. New York: Basic Books.

Geis, Frances, and Joseph Geis. 1989. *Marriage and the Family in the Middle Ages*. New York: Harper & Row.

Gergen, Kenneth J. 1969. *The Psychology of Behavior Exchange*. Reading, Mass.: Addison-Wesley.

Gibbon, Edward. [1776–88] 1946. *The Decline and Fall of the Roman Empire*. 3 vols. New York: Heritage Press.

References

Gilligan, Carol. 1982. *In a Different Voice*. Cambridge, Mass.: Harvard University Press.

Gilligan, Carol, Janie Victoria Ward, and Jill McLean Taylor. 1988. *Mapping the Moral Domain*. Cambridge, Mass.: Harvard University Press.

Gilligan, Carol, and Grant Wiggins. 1987. The origins of morality in early childhood relationships. In Jerome Kagan and Sharon Lamb, eds., *The Emergence of Morality in Young Children*, 277–305. Chicago: University of Chicago Press.

Ginsberg, Morris. 1947. *Reason and Unreason in Society*. London: Longmans, Green.

———. 1956a. *Reason and Experience in Ethics*. Auguste Comte Memorial Lecture No. 2. London: Oxford University Press.

———. 1956b. *On the Diversity of Morals*. Vol. 1 of *Essays in Sociology and Social Philosophy*. Melbourne: Heinemann.

Gittelman, R., S. Mannuzza, R. Shenker, and N. Bonagura. 1985. Hyperactive boys almost grown up. *Archives of General Psychiatry* 42:937–47.

Glass, Brent D. "Poor men with rude machinery": The formative years of the Gold Hill mining district. *North Carolina Historical Review* 61:1–35.

Glendon, Mary Ann. 1989. *The Transformation of Family Law*. Chicago: University of Chicago Press.

———. 1991. *Rights Talk: The Impoverishment of Political Discourse*. New York: Free Press.

Golding, William. 1962. *Lord of the Flies*. New York: Coward-McCann.

Goldsmith, H. H., and Jennifer A. Alansky. 1987. Maternal and infant temperamental predictors of attachment: A meta-analytic review. *Journal of Consulting and Clinical Psychology* 55:805–16.

Goldstein, Avram, and H. Kalant. 1990. Drug policy: Striking the right balance. *Science* 249:1513–21.

Goode, William J. 1963. *World Revolution and Family Patterns*. New York: Free Press.

Goodenough, Evelyn W. 1957. Interest in persons as an aspect of sex difference in the early years. *Genetic Psychology Monographs* 55:287–323.

Goodwin, Marjorie Harness, and Charles Goodwin. 1987. Children's arguing. In Susan U. Phelps, Susan Steele, and Christine Tanz, eds., *Language, Gender, and Sex in Comparative Perspective*. Cambridge: Cambridge University Press.

Goody, Jack. 1983. *The Development of the Family and Marriage in Europe*. Cambridge: Cambridge University Press.

Gorman, Raymond F., and James B. Kehr. 1992. Fairness as a constraint on profit seeking: Comment. *American Economic Review* 82:355–58.

Gough, Harrison G. 1948. A sociological theory of psychopathy. *American Journal of Sociology* 53:359–66.

References

Gouldner, Alvin. 1960. The norm of reciprocity. *American Sociological Review* 25:161–78.

Gove, Walter R. 1973. Sex, marital status, and mortality. *American Journal of Sociology* 79:45–67.

Green, Thomas Hill. [1883] 1906. *Prolegomena to Ethics*, 5th ed., ed. A. C. Bradley. Oxford: Clarendon Press.

Greenberg, M. S., and S. P. Shapiro. 1971. Indebtedness: an adverse aspect of asking for and receiving help. *Sociometry* 34:290–301.

Guichard, Pierre. 1977. *Structures Sociales "Orientales" et "Occidentales" dans l'Espagne Musulmane.* Paris: Mouton.

Guth, Werner, Rolf Schmittberger, and Bernd Schwarze. 1982. An experimental analysis of ultimatum bargaining. *Journal of Economic Behavior and Organization* 3:367–88.

Hajnal, J. 1965. European marriage patterns in perspective. In David Victor Glass, ed., *Essays in Historical Demography.* London: Arnold.

———. 1983. Two kinds of pre-industrial household formation system. In Richard Wall, ed., *Family Forms in Historic Europe.* Cambridge: Cambridge University Press.

Haldane, J. B. S. 1955. Population genetics. *New Biology* 18:34–51.

Hamilton, James B., Ruth S. Hamilton, and Gordon E. Mestler, 1969. Duration of life and causes of death in domestic cats: Influence of sex, gonadectomy, and inbreeding. *Journal of Gerontology* 24:427–37.

Hamilton, James B., and Gordon E. Mestler, 1969. Mortality and survival: Comparison of eunuchs with intact men and women in a mentally retarded population. *Journal of Gerontology* 24:395–411.

Hamilton, W. D. 1964. The genetical evolution of social behaviour. *Journal of Theoretical Biology* 7:1–52.

Hanke, Lewis. 1949. *The Spanish Struggle for Justice in the Conquest of America.* Boston: Little, Brown.

———. 1959. *Aristotle and the American Indians.* Chicago: Regnery.

Hardie, W. F. R. 1980. *Aristotle's Ethical Theory.* 2d ed. Oxford: Oxford University Press.

Hardin, Garrett. 1982. Discriminating altruisms. *Zygon* 17:163–86.

Hare, Robert D. 1970. *Psychopathy.* New York: Wiley.

———. 1978. Electrodermal and cardiovascular correlates of psychopathy. In Robert D. Hare and Daisy Schalling, eds., *Psychopathic Behavior.* New York: Wiley.

Hare, Robert D., and Daisy Schalling. 1978. *Psychopathic Behavior.* New York: Wiley.

Harlow, H. F., and M. K. Harlow. 1969. Effects of various infant–mother relationships on rhesus monkey behaviors. In B. M. Foss, ed., *Determinants of Infant Behaviour*, vol. 4. London: Methuen.

Hartshorne, Hugh, and Mark A. May. 1928–1930. *Studies in the Nature of Character.* 3 vols. New York: Macmillan.

References

Hartwell, R. M., ed., 1967. *Causes of the Industrial Revolution in England.* London: Methuen.

Hay, Dale F., and Harriet L. Rheingold. 1983. The early appearance of some valued social behaviors. In Diane L. Bridgeman, ed., *The Nature of Prosocial Development*, 73–94. New York: Academic Press.

Hayek, Friedrich A. von. 1984. *The Essence of Hayek.* Ed. Chiaki Nishiyama and Kurt R. Leube. Stanford, Calif.: Hoover Institution Press.

Hazard, Paul. 1963. *European Thought in the Eighteenth Century.* Trans. J. Lewis May. Cleveland: World/Meridian.

Heine, Bernd. 1985. The mountain people: Some notes on the Ik of northeastern Uganda. *Africa* 55:3–16.

Helper, Hinton R. 1855. *The Land of Gold: Reality versus Fiction.* Baltimore: Henry Taylor.

Herlihy, David. 1985. *Medieval Households.* Cambridge, Mass.: Harvard University Press.

Herrnstein, Richard J. 1977. The evolution of behaviorism. *American Psychologist* 32:593–603.

Herrnstein, Richard J., and Drazen Prelec. 1991. Melioration: A theory of distributed choice. *Journal of Economic Perspectives* 5:137–56.

———. 1992. A theory of addiction. In G. F. Lowenstein and Jon Elster, eds., *Choice over Time:* 331–60. New York: Russell Sage.

Herzog, E., and C. E. Suida. 1973. Children in fatherless families. In B. M. Caldwell and H. N. Riccuti, eds., *Review of Child Development Research* 3:141–232. Chicago: University of Chicago Press.

Himmelfarb, Gertrude. 1987. *Marriage and Morals among the Victorians.* New York: Random House/Vintage.

Hinshaw, Stephen P. 1987. On the distinction between attentional deficits/hyperactivity and conduct problems/aggression in child psychopathology. *Psychological Bulletin* 101:443–63.

Hirschi, Travis. 1969. *Cause of Delinquency.* Berkeley and Los Angeles: University of California Press.

Hirschi, Travis, and Michael Gottfredson. 1983. Age and the explanation of crime. *American Journal of Sociology* 89:552–84.

Hirschman, Albert O. 1977. *The Passions and the Interests.* Princeton, N.J.: Princeton University Press.

Hobbes, Thomas. [1651] 1957. *Leviathan.* Ed. Michael Oakeshott. Oxford: Oxford University Press.

Hoebel, E. A. 1954. *The Law of Primitive Man.* Cambridge, Mass.: Harvard University Press.

Hoffman, Elizabeth, and Matthew L. Spitzer. 1982. The Coase theorem: Some experimental tests. *Journal of Law and Economics* 25:73–98.

———. 1985. Entitlements, rights, and fairness: An experimental examination of subjects' concepts of distributive justice. *Journal of Legal Studies* 14:259–97.

References

Hoffman, Martin L. 1971. Father absence and conscience development. *Developmental Psychology* 4:400–406.

———. 1981a. Is altruism a part of human nature? *Journal of Personality and Social Psychology* 40:121–37.

———. 1981b. The role of the father in moral internalization. In Michael E. Lamb, ed., *The Role of the Father in Child Development*, 359–78. 2nd ed. New York: Wiley.

———. 1984. Empathy, its limitations, and its role in a comprehensive moral theory. In William M. Kurtines and Jacob L. Gewirtz, eds., *Morality, Moral Behavior, and Moral Development*. New York: Wiley.

Holldobler, Bert, and Edward O. Wilson. 1990. *The Ants*. Cambridge, Mass.: Harvard University Press.

Holmberg, Allan R. 1950. *Nomads of the Long Bow*. Publications of the Institute of Social Anthropology, No. 10. Washington, D.C.: Smithsonian Institution.

Honzik, Marjorie P. 1951. Sex differences in the occurrence of materials in the play constructions of pre-adolescents. *Child Development* 22:15–35.

Hook, J. G., and Thomas D. Cook. 1979. Equity theory and the cognitive ability of children. *Psychological Bulletin* 86:429–45.

Hoopes, Janet L. 1982. *Prediction in Child Development: A Longitudinal Study of Adoptive and Nonadoptive Families*. New York: Child Welfare League of America.

Hornstein, Harvey A. 1976. *Cruelty and Kindness: A New Look at Aggression and Altruism*. Englewood Cliffs, N.J.: Prentice-Hall.

———. 1978. Promotive tension and prosocial behavior: A Lewinian analysis. In Lauren Wispe, ed., *Altruism, Sympathy, and Helping*, 177–207. New York: Academic Press.

Hornstein, Harvey A., Elisha Fisch, and Michael Holmes. 1968. Influence of a model's feeling about his behavior and his relevance as a comparison other on observers' helping behavior. *Journal of Personality and Social Psychology* 10:222–26.

Hornstein, Harvey A., H. N. Masor, K. Sole, and M. Heilman. 1971. Effects of sentiment and completion of a helping act on observer helping. *Journal of Personality and Social Psychology* 17:107–12.

Horowitz, Donald. 1975. Ethnic identity. In Nathan Glazer and Daniel P. Moynihan, eds., *Ethnicity: Theory and Practice*, 111–40. Cambridge, Mass.: Harvard University Press.

Horowitz, Maryanne Cline. 1976. Aristotle and woman. *Journal of the History of Biology* 9:183–213.

Hoyenga, Katherine B., and Hoyenga, K. T. 1979. *The Question of Sex Differences: Psychological, Cultural, and Biological Issues*. Boston: Little, Brown.

Hume, David. [1740] 1978. *A Treatise of Human Nature*. Ed. L. A. Selby-

References

Bigge. 2d ed. revised by P. H. Nidditch. Oxford: Clarendon Press.

———. [1751] 1966. *An Enquiry Concerning the Principles of Morals.* La-Salle, Ill.: Open Court.

Huston, Ted L., Gilbert Geis, and Richard Wright. 1976. The angry Samaritans. *Psychology Today,* June, 61–85.

Huston, Ted L., et al. 1981. Bystander intervention into crime: A study based on naturally occurring episodes. *Social Psychology Quarterly* 44: 14–23.

Hutcheson, Francis. [1742] 1969. *An Essay on the Nature and Conduct of the Passions and Affections, with Illustrations on the Moral Sense.* 3d ed. Gainesville, Fla.: Scholars' Facsimiles and Reprints.

Hyde, Janet Shibley. 1986. Gender differences in aggression. In Janet Shibley Hyde and Marcia C. Lin, eds., *The Psychology of Gender,* 51–66. Baltimore: Johns Hopkins University Press.

Imperato-McGinley, Julianne, et al. 1979. Androgens and the evolution of male-gender identity among pseudohermaphrodites with 5α-reductase deficiency. *New England Journal of Medicine* 300:1233–37.

Jacobson, Sandra W. 1979. Matching behavior in the young infant. *Child Development* 50:425–30.

Jacobvitz, Deborah, and L. Alan Sroufe. 1987. The early caregiver-child relationship and attention-deficit disorder with hyperactivity in kindergarten: A prospective study. *Child Development* 58:1488–95.

Johansson, Sheila Ryan. 1984. Deferred infanticide: Excess female mortality during childhood. In Glenn Hausfater and Sarah Blaffer Hrdy, eds., *Infanticide: Comparative and Evolutionary Perspectives,* 463–85. New York: De Gruyter.

Johnston, K. 1985. Two moral orientations, two problem-solving strategies: Adolescents' solutions to dilemmas in fables. Ed.D. dissertation, Harvard Graduate School of Education.

Kagan, Jerome. 1981. *The Second Year: The Emergence of Self-Awareness.* Cambridge, Mass.: Harvard University Press.

———. 1984. *The Nature of the Child.* New York: Basic Books.

———. 1989. Temperamental contributions to social behavior. *American Psychologist* 44:668–74.

Kagan, Jerome, R. B. Kearsley, and P. R. Zelazo. 1978. *Infancy: Its Place in Human Development.* Cambridge, Mass.: Harvard University Press.

Kagan, Jerome, and Sharon Lamb. 1987. *The Emergence of Morality in Young Children.* Chicago: University of Chicago Press.

Kagan, Spencer, G. P. Knight, and S. Martinez-Romero. 1982. Culture and the development of conflict resolution style. *Journal of Cross-Cultural Psychology* 13:43–58.

Kagitcibasi, Cigdem. 1982. *Sex Role, Family, and Community in Turkey.* Indianapolis: University of Indiana Press.

Kahneman, Daniel, Jack L. Knetsch, and Richard Thaler. 1986a. Fairness and the assumptions of economics. *Journal of Business* 59: Supp. 285–300.

———. 1986b. Fairness as a constraint on profit seeking: Entitlements in the market. *American Economic Review* 76:728–41.

Kant, Immanuel. [1784] 1950. *What is Enlightenment?* Trans. Lewis White Beck. Chicago: University of Chicago Press.

———.[1785] 1950. *Foundations of the Metaphysics of Morals.* Trans. Lewis White Beck. Chicago: University of Chicago Press.

Kaprio, Jaakko, Markku Koskenuvo, Heimo Langinvaino, et al. 1987. Genetic influences on use and abuse of alcohol: A study of 5638 adult Finnish twin brothers. *Alcoholism: Clinical and Experimental Research* 11:349–56.

Karen, Robert. 1990. Becoming attached. *Atlantic Monthly,* February: 35–70.

Katcher, Aaron Honori, and Alan M. Beck. 1991. Animal companions: More companion than animal. In Michael H. Robinson and Lionel Tiger, eds., *Man and Beast Revisited.* Washington, D.C.: Smithsonian Institution Press.

Katz, Mary Maxwell, and Melvin J. Konner. 1981. The role of the father: An anthropological perspective. In Michael E. Lamb, ed., *The Role of the Father in Child Development,* 155–86. New York: Wiley.

Kayden, Xandra. 1990. *Surviving Power.* New York: Free Press.

Kellam, Sheppard G., R. G. Adams, and Margaret E. Ensminger. 1982. The long-term evolution of the family structure of teenage and older mothers. *Journal of Marriage and the Family* 44:539–54.

Kellam, Sheppard G., Margaret E. Ensminger, and R. Jay Turner. 1977. Family structure and the mental health of children. *Archives of General Psychiatry* 34:1012–22.

Klineberg, Otto, et al. 1979. *Students, Values, and Politics.* New York: Free Press.

Kluckhohn, Clyde. 1955. Ethical relativity: Sic et non. *Journal of Philosophy* 52:663–77.

Knorring, Lars von, Lars Oreland, and Bengt Winblad. 1984. Personality traits related to monoamine oxidase activity in platelets. *Psychiatric Research* 12:11–26.

Koestler, Arthur. 1941. *Darkness at Noon.* Trans. Daphne Hardy. New York: Modern Library.

Koestner, Richard, Carl Franz, and Joel Weinberger. 1990. The family origins of empathic concern: A 26-year longitudinal study. *Journal of Personality and Social Psychology* 58:709–17.

Kohlberg, Lawrence. 1981. *The Philosophy of Moral Development: Moral Stages and the Idea of Justice.* New York: Harper & Row.

References

Konner, Melvin. 1982. *The Tangled Wing: Biological Constraints on the Human Spirit.* New York: Holt, Rinehart, Winston.

———. 1990. *Why the Reckless Survive.* New York: Viking Press.

———. 1991. *Childhood.* Boston: Little, Brown.

Koob, George F., and Floyd E. Bloom. 1988. Cellular and molecular mechanisms of drug dependence. *Science* 242:715–23.

Kraemer, Gary W. 1992. A psychobiological theory of attachment. *Behavioral and Brain Sciences* 15:493–541.

Kraus, Arthur S., and Abraham M. Lilienfeld. 1959. Some epidemiologic aspects of high mortality rates in the young widowed group. *Journal of Chronic Diseases* 10:207–17.

Krebs, Dennis. 1970. Altruism—an examination of the concept and a review of the literature. *Psychological Bulletin* 73:258–302.

———. 1975. Empathy and altruism. *Journal of Personality and Social Psychology* 32:1134–46.

Krebs, Dennis, and Phillip Whitten. 1972. Guilt-edged giving: the shame of it all. *Psychology Today*, January, 50–78.

Lamb, Michael E., et al. 1985. *Infant-Mother Attachment.* Hillsdale, N.J.: Erlbaum.

Langan, Patrick A. 1991. America's soaring prison population. *Science* 251:1568–73.

Langbein, John H. 1977. *Torture and the Law of Proof.* Chicago: University of Chicago Press.

Langer, William L. 1974. Infanticide: A historical survey. *History of Childhood Quarterly* 1:353–66.

Laslett, Peter. 1977. *Family Life and Illicit Love in Earlier Generations.* Cambridge: Cambridge University Press.

Latané, Bibb, and John M. Darley. 1968. Group inhibition of bystander intervention. *Journal of Personality and Social Psychology* 10:215–21.

———. 1970. *The Unresponsive Bystander: Why Doesn't He Help?* New York: Appleton-Century-Crofts.

Latané, Bibb, and Steve Nida. 1981. Ten years of research on group size and helping. *Psychological Bulletin* 89:308–24.

Lawler, E. E., and P. W. O'Gara. 1967. The effects of inequity produced by underpayment on work output, work quality, and attitudes toward work. *Journal of Applied Psychology* 351:403–10.

Lawson, Annette, and Colin Samson. 1988. Age, gender, and adultery. *British Journal of Sociology* 39:409–40.

Lee, Richard L. 1974. Eating Christmas in the Kalahari. In J. Spradley and D. McCurdy, eds., *Conformity and Conflict: Readings in Cultural Anthropology*, 14–21. 2d ed. Boston: Little, Brown.

———. 1979. *The !Kung San: Men, Women and Work in a Foraging Society.* Cambridge: Harvard University Press.

References

————. 1984. *The Dobe !Kung.* New York: Holt, Rinehart & Winston.

Lerner, Melvin J. 1970. The desire for justice and reactions to victims. In J. Macaulay and L. Berkowitz, eds., *Altruism and Helping Behavior*, 241–50. New York: Academic Press.

————. 1974. Social psychology of justice and interpersonal attraction. In T. Huston, ed., *Foundations of Interpersonal Attraction.* New York: Academic Press.

————. 1980. *The Belief in a Just World.* New York: Plenum.

Lever, Janet. 1976. Sex differences in the games children play. *Social Problems* 23:478–87.

————. 1978. Sex differences in the complexity of children's play and games. *American Sociological Review* 43:471–83.

LeVine, Robert. 1970. Cross-cultural study in child psychology. In P. H. Mussen, ed., *Carmichael's Manual of Child Psychology.* New York: Wiley.

Lewin, Kurt, R. Lippitt, and R. K. White. 1939. Patterns of aggressive behavior in experimentally created social climates. *Journal of Social Psychology* 10:271–99.

Lickona, Thomas. 1991. *Educating for Character.* New York: Bantam.

Lilienfeld, Scott O., and Irwin D. Waldman. 1990. The relation between childhood attention-deficit hyperactivity disorder and adult antisocial behavior reexamined: The problem of heterogeneity. *Clinical Psychology Review* 10:699–725.

Lind, E. Allan, and Tom R. Tyler. 1988. *The Social Psychology of Procedural Justice.* New York: Plenum.

Locke, John. [1706] 1979. *An Essay Concerning Human Understanding.* Ed. Peter H. Nidditch. Oxford: Clarendon Press.

Lockwood, Alan L. 1978. Effects of values clarification and moral development curricula on school-age subjects: A critical review of recent research. *Review of Educational Research* 48:325–64.

Loehlin, John C., Lee Willerman, and Joseph M. Horn. 1988. Human behavior genetics. *Annual Review of Psychology* 39:101–33.

London, Perry. 1970. The rescuers: Motivational hypotheses about Christians who saved Jews from the Nazis. In J. Macaulay and L. Berkowitz, eds., *Altruism and Helping Behavior*, 241–50. New York: Academic Press.

Lorber, Judith, 1981. On *The Reproduction of Mothering*: A methodological debate. *Journal of Women in Culture and Society* 6:482–86.

Lorenz, Konrad. 1943. Die angeborenen Formen möglicher Erfahrung. *Zeitschrift für Tierpsychologie* 5:235–409.

Lynn, D. C. 1974. *The Father: His Role in Child Development.* Belmont, Calif.: Wadsworth.

Lyons, Nona Plessner. 1983. Two perspectives: On self, relationships, and morality. *Harvard Education Review* 2:125–45.

McCartney, Kathleen, and Saul Rosenthal. 1991. Maternal employment

References

should be studied within social ecologies. *Journal of Marriage and the Family* 53:1103–6.

Maccoby, Elinor Emmons, and Carol Nagy Jacklin. 1974. *The Psychology of Sex Differences*. Stanford, Calif.: Stanford University Press.

———. 1980. Sex differences in aggression: A rejoinder. *Child Development* 51:964–80.

McCord, William, Joan McCord, and A. Howard. 1961. Familial correlates of aggression in non-delinquent male children. *Journal of Abnormal Social Psychology* 62:79–93.

MacDonald, Michael. 1982. *Mystical Bedlam: Madness, Anxiety, and Healing in Seventeenth-Century England*. Cambridge: Cambridge University Press.

McEwen, Craig A., and Richard J. Maiman. 1984. Mediation in small claims court: achieving compliance through consent. *Law & Society Review* 18:11–49.

Macfarlane, Alan. 1978. *The Origins of English Individualism*. New York: Cambridge University Press.

———. 1979. Review. *History and Theory* 18:103–26.

McKenna, James J. 1987. Parental supplements and surrogates among primates: Cross-species and cross-cultural comparisons. In Jane B. Lancaster, Jeanne Altmann, Alice S. Rossi, and Lonnie R. Sherrod, eds., *Parenting Across the Life Span: Biosocial Dimensions*, 143–84. New York: De Gruyter.

Macklin, Eleanor D. 1980. Nontraditional family forms: A decade of research. *Journal of Marriage and the Family* 42:905–22.

MacLean, Paul D. 1985. Brain evolution relating to family, play, and the separation call. *Archives of General Psychiatry* 42:405–17.

———. 1990. *The Triune Brain in Evolution*. New York: Plenum.

McMillen, Marilyn M. 1979. Differential mortality by sex in fetal and neonatal deaths. *Science* 204:89–91.

Madsen, M. C. 1967. Cooperative and competitive motivation of children in three Mexican sub-cultures. *Psychological Reports* 20:1307–20.

———. 1971. Developmental and cross-cultural differences in the cooperative and competitive behavior of young children. *Journal of Cross-Cultural Psychology* 2:365–71.

Magnus, Elisabeth M. 1980. Sources of maternal stress in the postpartum period. In Jacquelynne E. Parsons, ed., *The Psychobiology of Sex Differences and Sex Roles*, 177–208. New York: McGraw-Hill.

Main, Mary. 1983. Exploration, play, and cognitive functioning related to infant-mother attachment. *Infant Behavior and Development* 6:167–74.

———. 1990. Cross-cultural studies of attachment organization. *Human Development* 33:48–61.

Main, Mary, and Jude Cassidy. 1988. Categories of response to reunion with the parent at age 6: Predictable from infant attachment classifications and stable over a 1-month period. *Developmental Psychology* 24: 415–26.

Main, Mary, and Carol George. 1985. Responses of abused and disadvantaged toddlers to distress in agemates: A study in the day care setting. *Developmental Psychology* 21:407–12.

Main, Mary, Nancy Kaplan, and Jude Cassidy. 1985. Security in infancy, childhood, and adulthood: a move to the level of representation. *Monographs of the Society for Research in Child Development* 50:66–104.

Major, Brenda, and Jeffrey B. Adams. 1983. Role of gender, interpersonal orientation, and self-presentation in distributive-justice behavior. *Journal of Personality and Social Psychology* 45:598–608.

Major, Brenda, and Kay Deaux. 1982. Individual differences in justice behavior. In Jerald Greenberg and Ronald L. Cohen, eds., *Equity and Justice in Social Behavior*, 43–76. New York: Academic Press.

Malatesta, Carol Zander, and Carroll E. Izard. 1984. The ontogenesis of human social signals: From biological imperative to symbol utilization. In Nathan A. Fox and Richard J. Davidson, eds., *The Psychobiology of Affective Development*. Hillsdale, N.J.: Erlbaum.

Maltz, Daniel N., and Ruth A. Borker. 1982. A cultural approach to male-female miscommunication. In John J. Gumperz, ed., *Language and Social Identity*, 196–216. Cambridge: Cambridge University Press.

Mansbridge, Jane J. 1990. *Beyond Self-Interest*. Chicago: University of Chicago Press.

Marshall, J., and C. Ritchie. 1984. *Where Are the Ju/Wasi of Nyae? Changes in a Bushman Society*. Capetown, South Africa: Centre for African Studies of the University of Capetown.

Marvick, E. 1974. Nature versus nurture: Patterns and trends in seventeenth-century French child-rearing. In Lloyd De Mause, ed., *The History of Childhood*. New York: Psychohistory Press.

Marwell, Gerald, and Ruth E. Ames. 1981. Economists free ride, does anyone else? *Journal of Public Economics* 15:295–310.

Marx, Karl, and Friedrich Engels. [1848] 1959. *Communist Manifesto*. In Lewis S. Feuer, ed., *Marx and Engels: Basic Writings on Politics and Philosophy*, 1–41. New York: Doubleday/Anchor Books.

Matthews, Karen A., C. Daniel Batson, Joseph Horn, and Ray H. Rosenman. 1981. "Principles in his nature which interest him in the fortune of others . . .": The heritability of empathic concern for others. *Journal of Personality* 49:237–47.

Mauss, Marcel. [1925] 1967. *The Gift*. Trans. Ian Cunnison. New York: Norton.

May, Henry F. 1976. *The Enlightenment in America*. New York: Oxford University Press.

References

Meaney, Michael J., et al. 1988. Effect of neonatal handling on age-related impairments associated with the hippocampus. *Science* 239:766–68.

Melzer, Arthur M. 1990. *The Natural Goodness of Man: On the System of Rousseau's Thought.* Chicago: University of Chicago Press.

Meltzoff, Arthur N. 1985. The roots of social and cognitive development: Models of man's original nature. In Tiffany M. Field and Nathan A. Fox, eds., *Social Perception in Infants,* 1–30. Norwood, N.J.: Ablex.

———. 1988. Imitation, objects, tools, and the rudiments of language in human ontogeny. *Human Evolution* 3:45–64.

Meltzoff, Arthur N., and M. Keith Moore. 1977. Imitation of facial and manual gestures by human neonates. *Science* 198:75–78.

———. 1983. Newborn infants imitate adult facial gestures. *Child Development* 54:702–9.

Middleton, Russell, and Putney Snell. 1963. Political expression of adolescent rebellion. *American Journal of Sociology* 68:527–35.

Milgram, Stanley. 1970. The experience of living in cities. *Science* 167:1461–68.

———. 1974. *Obedience to Authority.* New York: Harper & Row.

Mill, John Stuart. [1861] 1979. *Utilitarianism.* Ed. George Sher. Indianapolis: Hackett.

Mischel, Walter, Yuichi Shoda, and Philip K. Peake. 1988. The nature of adolescent competencies predicted by preschool delay of gratification. *Journal of Personality and Social Psychology* 54:687–96.

Mischel, Walter, Yuichi Shoda, and Monica L. Rodriguez. 1989. Delay of gratification in children. *Science* 244:933–38.

Moffitt, Terrie E. 1990. Juvenile delinquency and attention deficit disorder: Boys' developmental trajectories from age 3 to age 15. *Child Development* 61:893–910.

Morgan, Lewis Henry. 1877. *Ancient Society.* New York: Henry Holt.

Morrison, J., and M. A. Stewart. 1973. The psychiatric status of the legal families of adopted hyperactive children. *Archives of General Psychiatry* 28:888–91.

Murdock, George P. 1965. *Culture and Society.* Pittsburgh, Pa.: University of Pittsburgh Press.

Murdock, George P., and D. R. White. 1969. Standard cross-cultural sample. *Ethnology* 8:329–69.

Myrdal, Gunnar. 1944. *An American Dilemma.* New York: Harper.

Naumburg, M. 1928. *The Child and the World.* San Diego, Calif.: Harcourt Brace Jovanovich.

Newman, Joseph, and Clark MacCauley. 1977. Eye contact with strangers in city, suburb, and small town. *Environment and Behavior* 9:547–58.

Nisbet, Robert A. 1953. *The Quest for Community.* New York: Oxford University Press.

References

Noble, Ernest P. 1991. Genetic studies in alcoholism: CNS functioning and molecular biology. *Psychiatric Annals* 21:215–29.

Noble, Ernest P., Kenneth Blum, Terry Ritchie, Anne Montgomery, and Peter J. Sheridan. 1991. Allelic association of the D_2 dopamine receptor gene with receptor-binding characteristics in alcoholism. *Archives of General Psychiatry* 48:648–54.

Noonan, John T. 1965. *Contraception.* Cambridge, Mass.: Harvard University Press.

Nussbaum, Martha Craven. 1978. *Aristotle's "De Motu Animalium."* Princeton, N.J.: Princeton University Press.

Oakeshott, Michael. 1962. *Rationalism in Politics.* New York: Basic Books.

Okin, Susan Moller. 1979. *Women in Western Political Thought.* Princeton, N.J.: Princeton University Press.

Okun, Arthur M. 1981. *Prices and Quantities.* Washington, D.C.: Brookings Institution.

Oliner, Samuel P., and Pearl M. Oliner. 1988. *The Altruistic Personality: Rescuers of Jews in Nazi Europe.* New York: Free Press.

Olmstead, A. L., and P. Rhode. 1985. Rationing without government: The West Coast gas famine of 1920. *American Economic Review* 74:1044–55.

Olweus, Dan. 1979. Stability of aggressive reaction patterns in males: A review. *Psychological Bulletin* 86:852–75.

———. 1984a. Development of stable aggressive reaction patterns in males. *Advances in the Study of Aggression* 1:103–37.

———. 1984b. Stability in aggressive and withdrawn, inhibited behavior patterns. In R. M. Kaplan, V. J. Konecni, and R. W. Novaco, eds., *Aggression in Children and Youth,* 104–37. The Hague: Martinus Nijhoff.

Olweus, Dan, Ake Mattsson, Daisy Schalling, and Hans Low. 1988. Circulating testosterone levels and aggression in adolescent males: A causal analysis. *Psychosomatic Medicine* 50:261–72.

Oxenstierna, G., et al. 1986. Concentrations of monoamine metabolites in the cerebrospinal fluid of twins and unrelated individuals: A genetic study. *Journal of Psychiatric Research* 20:19–29.

Ozment, Steven E. 1983. *When Fathers Ruled: Family Life in Reformation Europe.* Cambridge, Mass.: Harvard University Press.

Parsons, Talcott. 1951. *The Social System.* Glencoe, Ill.: Free Press.

Pateman, Carole. 1988. *The Sexual Contract.* Stanford, Calif.: Stanford University Press.

———. 1991. "God hath ordained to man a helper": Hobbes, patriarchy, and conjugal right. In Mary Lyndon Shanley and Carole Pateman, eds., *Feminist Interpretations and Political Theory,* 53–73. Cambridge: Polity Press.

Patterson, Gerald R. 1982. *Coercive Family Process.* Eugene, Ore.: Castalia.

References

Patterson, Orlando. 1982. *Slavery and Social Death.* Cambridge, Mass.: Harvard University Press.

————. 1991. *Freedom.* New York: Basic Books.

Pawelczynska, Anna. 1979. *Values and Violence in Auschwitz.* Trans. Catherine S. Leach. Berkeley and Los Angeles: University of California Press.

Phillips, Deborah, et al. 1987. Selective review of infant day care research: A cause for concern! *Zero to Three,* February 18–21.

Piaget, Jean. [1932] 1965. *The Moral Judgment of the Child.* Trans. Marjorie Gabain. Glencoe, Ill.: Free Press.

Pikas, Anatol. 1961. Children's attitudes toward rational versus inhibiting parental authority. *Journal of Abnormal and Social Psychology* 62:315–21.

Piliavin, Irving, J. Rodin, and Jane Piliavin. 1969. Good Samaritanism: An underground phenomenon? *Journal of Personality and Social Psychology* 13:289–99.

Piliavin, Jane A., and Hong-Wen Charng. 1990. Altruism: a review of recent theory and research. *Annual Review of Sociology* 16:27–65.

Piliavin, Jane A., John F. Dovidio, Samuel L. Gaertner, and Russell D. Clark, II. 1981. *Emergency Intervention.* New York: Academic Press.

Piliavin, Jane A., and Irving Piliavin. 1972. Effect of blood on reactions to a victim. *Journal of Personality and Social Psychology* 23:353–61.

Pinker, Steven. 1991. Rules of language. *Science* 253:530–35.

Pinker, Steven, and Paul Bloom. 1990. Natural language and natural selection. *Behavioral and Brain Sciences* 13:707–84.

Plomin, Robert, and Judy Dunn. 1986. *The Study of Temperament: Changes, Continuities, and Challenges.* Hillsdale, N.J.: Erlbaum.

Pollock, Frederick, and Frederic W. Maitland. 1959. *History of English Law Before the Time of Edward I.* 2d ed. Washington, D.C.: Lawyer's Literary Club.

Pollock, Linda A. 1983. *Forgotten Children: Parent-Child Relations from 1500 to 1900.* Cambridge: Cambridge University Press.

Popenoe, David. 1988. *Disturbing the Nest: Family Change and Decline in Modern Societies.* New York: De Gruyter.

Rachman, S. J. 1990. *Fear and Courage.* 2d ed. New York: Freeman.

Radke-Yarrow, Marian, Carolyn Zahn-Waxler, and Michael Chapman. 1983. Children's prosocial dispositions and behavior. *Handbook of Child Psychology* 4:469–545.

Raine, Adrian, Peter H. Venables, and Mark Williams. 1990. Relationships between central and autonomic measures of arousal at age 15 years and criminality at age 24 years. *Archives of General Psychiatry* 47:1003–7.

Rajecki, D. W., Michael E. Lamb, and Pauline Obmascher. 1978. Toward a general theory of infantile attachment: A comparative review of aspects of the social bond. *Behavioral and Brain Sciences* 3:417–64.

Rand, Alicia. 1987. Transitional life events and desistance from delinquency

References

and crime. In Marvin Wolfgang, et al., eds., *From Boy to Man, From Delinquency to Crime.* Chicago: University of Chicago Press.

Raphael, D. Daiches. 1947. *The Moral Sense.* London: Oxford University Press/Geoffrey Cumberledge.

Rapoport, J. L., M. S. Buchsbaum, H. Weingartner, et al. 1980. Dextroamphetamine: Its cognitive and behavioral effects in normal and hyperactive boys and normal men. *Archives of General Psychiatry* 37:933–43.

Rath, Louis, Merrill Harmin, and Sidney Simon. 1966. *Values and Teaching.* Columbus, Ohio: Charles E. Merrill.

Rawls, John. 1971. *A Theory of Justice.* Cambridge, Mass.: Harvard University Press.

Renken, Bruce, et al. 1989. Early childhood antecedents of aggression and passive-withdrawal in early elementary school. *Journal of Personality* 57:257–81.

Reuter, Peter. 1990. *Money from Crime: A Study of the Economics of Drug Dealing in Washington, D.C.* Santa Monica, Calif.: Rand.

Richards, Robert J. 1987. *Darwin and the Emergence of Evolutionary Theories of Mind and Behavior.* Chicago: University of Chicago Press.

Ridley, Mark. 1978. Paternal care. *Animal Behavior* 26:904–32.

Riesenfeld, Stefan A. 1962. Individual and family rights in land during the formative period of the common law. In Ralph A. Newman, ed., *Essays in Jurisprudence in Honor of Roscoe Pound,* 439–62. Indianapolis: Bobbs-Merrill.

Ritz, Mary C., R. L. Lamb, Steven R. Goldberg, and Michael J. Kuhar. 1987. Cocaine receptors on dopamine transporters are related to self-administration of cocaine. *Science* 237:1219–23.

Rorty, Richard. 1989. *Contingency, Irony, and Solidarity.* Cambridge: Cambridge University Press.

Rose, Richard J., Markkuu Koskenvuo, Jaaklo Kaprio, Seppo Sarna, and Heimo Langinvaino. 1988. Shared genes, shared experiences, and similarity of personality: Data from 14,288 Finnish adult co-twins. *Journal of Personality and Social Psychology* 54:161–71.

Rosenberg, Allison, and Jerome Kagan. 1987. Iris pigmentation and behavioral inhibition. *Developmental Psychobiology* 20:377–92.

———. 1990. Physical and physiological correlates of behavioral inhibition. *Developmental Psychobiology* 22:753–70.

Rosenhan, David. 1970. The natural socialization of altruistic autonomy. In J. Macaulay and L. Berkowitz, eds., *Altruism and Helping Behavior,* 251–68. New York: Academic Press.

Rossi, Alice S. 1977. A biosocial perspective on parenting. *Daedalus* 106:1–31.

———. 1981. On *The Reproduction of Mothering:* A methodological debate. *Journal of Women in Culture and Society* 6:492–500.

References

———. 1987. Parenthood in transition: from lineage to child to self-orientation. In Jane B. Lancaster, Jeanne Altmann, Alice S. Rossi, and Lonnie R. Sherrod, eds., *Parenting across the Life Span: Biosocial Dimensions*, 31–81. New York: De Gruyter.

Rothman, Stanley, and S. Robert Lichter. 1982. *Roots of Radicalism: Jews, Christians, and the New Left*. New York: Oxford University Press.

Rousseau, Jean-Jacques. [1758] 1913. *Discourse on the Origin and Foundation of the Inequality of Mankind*. In G. D. H. Cole, ed., *Rousseau: The Social Contract and Discourses*. London: Dent.

———. [1762] 1913. *The Social Contract*. In G. D. H. Cole, ed., *The Social Contract and Discourses*. London: Dent.

———. [1762] 1979. *Emile*. Trans. Allan Bloom. New York: Basic Books.

Roy, Alec, Byron Adinoff, Laurie Roehrich, et al. 1988. Pathological gambling. *Archives of General Psychiatry* 45:369–73.

Roy, Alec, Judith DeJong, and Markku Linnoila. 1989. Extraversion in pathological gamblers. *Archives of General Psychiatry* 46:679–81.

Royce, Joseph R., and Arnold Powell. 1983. *Theory of Personality and Individual Differences: Factors, Systems, and Processes*. Englewood Cliffs, N.J.: Prentice-Hall.

Rozin, Paul, and Jonathan Schull. 1988. The adaptive-evolutionary point of view in experimental psychology. In R. C. Atkinson, Richard J. Herrnstein, Gardner Lindzey, and R. Duncan Luce, eds., *Steven's Handbook of Experimental Psychology*, vol. 1, *Perception and Motivation*. New York: Wiley.

Rushton, J. Philippe. 1976. Socialization and the altruistic behavior of children. *Psychological Bulletin* 83:898–913.

———. 1980. *Altruism, Socialization, and Society*. Englewood Cliffs, N.J.: Prentice-Hall.

Rushton, J. Philippe, David W. Fulker, Michael C. Neale, David K. B. Nias, and Hans J. Eysenck. 1986. Altruism and aggression: The heritability of individual differences. *Journal of Personality and Social Psychology* 50: 1191–98.

Rutter, Michael. 1979. Maternal deprivation. *Child Development* 50:283–305.

Rutter, Michael, and Norman Garmezy. 1983. Developmental psychopathology. In E. Mavis Hetherington, ed., *Handbook of Child Psychology*, 4th ed., vol. 4, 775–91. New York: Wiley.

Rypma, Craig D. 1976. Biological bases of the paternal response. *Family Coordinator* 25:335–39.

Sagi, A., and M. L. Hoffman. 1976. Empathic distress in the newborn. *Developmental Psychology* 12:175–76.

Salkever, Stephen G. 1990. *Finding the Mean: Theory and Practice in Aristotelian Political Philosophy*. Princeton, N.J.: Princeton University Press.

References

Sanday, Peggy Reeves. 1981. *Female Power and Male Dominance.* Cambridge: Cambridge University Press.

Sartre, Jean-Paul. 1948. *Existentialism and Humanism.* Trans. Philip Mairet. London: Methuen.

Satterfield, J. H., C. M. Hoppe, and A. M. Schell. 1982. A prospective study of delinquency in 110 adolescent boys with attention deficit disorder and 88 normal adolescents. *American Journal of Psychiatry* 139:795–98.

Sawhill, Isabel. 1992. Young children and families. In Henry J. Aaron and Charles L. Schultze, eds., *Setting Domestic Priorities*, 147–84. Washington, D.C.: Brookings Institution.

Saxonhouse, Arlene W. 1985. *Women in the History of Western Political Thought.* New York: Praeger.

Schachter, Stanley. 1959. *The Psychology of Affiliation.* Stanford, Calif.: Stanford University Press.

Schalling, D. 1978. Psychopathy-related personality variables and the psychopathology of socialization. In Robert D. Hare and Daisy Schalling, eds., *Psychopathic Behavior*, 85–106. New York: Wiley.

Schalling, D., G. Edman, M. Asberg, and L. Oreland. 1988. Platelet MAO activity associated with impulsivity and aggression. *Personality and Individual Differences* 9:597–605.

Schanberg, Saul M., and Tiffany M. Field. 1987. Sensory deprivation stress and supplemental stimulation in rat pup and preterm humans. *Child Development* 58:1431–47.

Schelling, Thomas. 1980. The intimate contest for self-command. *Public Interest* 60:94–118.

Scheper-Hughes, Nancy. 1987. Culture, scarcity, and maternal thinking: Mother love and child death in northeast Brazil. In Nancy Scheper-Hughes, ed., *Child Survival.* Boston: D. Reidel/Kluwer.

Schmitt, D. R., and G. Maxwell. 1972. Withdrawal and reward allocation as responses to inequity. *Journal of Experimental Social Psychology* 8:207–21.

Scrimshaw, Susan C. M. 1984. Infanticide in human populations: Societal and individual concerns. In Glenn Hausfater and Sarah Blaffer Hrdy, eds., *Infanticide: Comparative and Evolutionary Perspectives*, 439–62. New York: De Gruyter.

Serpell, James. 1986. *In the Company of Animals.* Oxford: Basil Blackwell.

Segal, Nancy L. 1984. Cooperation, competition, and altruism within twin sets: A reappraisal. *Ethology and Sociobiology* 5:163–77.

Seligman, Martin E. P., and Joanne L. Hager, eds. 1972. *Biological Boundaries of Learning.* New York: Appleton-Century-Crofts.

Shedler, Jonathan, and Jack Block. 1990. Adolescent drug use and psychological health. *American Psychologist* 45:612–30.

Shepher, Joseph, 1983. *Incest: A Biosocial View.* New York: Academic Press.

References

Shils, Edward A., and Morris Janowitz, 1948. Cohesion and disintegration in the Wehrmacht in World War II. *Public Opinion Quarterly* 12:280–315.

Shorter, Edward. 1975. *The Making of the Modern Family.* New York: Basic Books.

Shostak, Marjorie. 1981. *Nisa: The Life and Words of a !Kung Woman.* Cambridge, Mass.: Harvard University Press.

Shweder, Richard A., Manamohan Mahapatra, and Joan G. Miller. 1987. Culture and moral development. In Jerome Kagan and Sharon Lamb, eds., *The Emergence of Morality in Young Children.* Chicago: University of Chicago Press.

Shweder, Richard A., Elliot Turiel, and N. C. Much. 1981. The moral intuitions of the child. In J. H. Flavell and L. Ross, eds., *Social Cognitive Development.* New York: Cambridge University Press.

Sidgwick, Henry. [1907] 1956. *The Methods of Ethics.* 7th ed. Reprint. Indianapolis: Hackett.

Singer, Peter. 1981. *The Expanding Circle.* New York: Farrar, Straus & Giroux.

Skinner, B. F. 1971. *Beyond Freedom and Dignity.* New York: Knopf.

Skinner, Quentin. 1978. *The Foundations of Modern Political Thought.* 2 vols. Cambridge: Cambridge University Press.

Smith, Adam. [1759] 1976. *The Theory of Moral Sentiments.* Ed. D. D. Raphael and A. L. Macfie. Oxford: Clarendon Press.

———. [1776] 1976. *An Inquiry into the Nature and Causes of the Wealth of Nations.* Ed. R. H. Campbell, A. S. Skinner, and W. B. Todd. Oxford: Clarendon Press.

Smith, Dorothy W., and Laurie Nels Sherwen. 1983. *Mothers and Their Adopted Children: The Bonding Process.* New York: Tiresias Press.

Smith, Robert J. 1983. *Japanese Society: Tradition, Self, and the Social Order.* Cambridge: Cambridge University Press.

Spiro, Melford E., with Audrey G. Spiro. 1975. *Children of the Kibbutz.* Rev. ed. Cambridge, Mass.: Harvard University Press.

———. 1979. *Gender and Culture: Kibbutz Women Revisited.* Durham, N.C.: Duke University Press.

Sroufe, L. Alan. 1983. Infant-caregiver attachment and patterns of adaptation in preschool: The roots of maladaptation and competence. *Minnesota Symposium in Child Psychology* 16:41–83.

———. 1985. Attachment classification from the perspective of infant-caregiver relationships and infant temperament. *Child Development* 56:1–14.

Sroufe, L. Alan, Byron Egeland, and Terri Kreutzer. 1990. The fate of early experience following developmental change: Longitudinal approaches to individual adaptation in childhood. *Child Development* 61:1363–73.

Staub, Ervin. 1978. *Positive Social Behavior and Morality*, vol. 1. New York: Academic Press.

Sternglanz, Sarah Hall, James L. Gray, and Melvin Murakami. 1977. Adult preferences for infantile facial features: An ethological approach. *Animal Behavior* 25:108–15.

Stockdale, James B. 1984. *A Vietnam Experience*. Stanford, Calif.: Hoover Institution.

Stockdale, James B., and Sybil Stockdale. 1990. *In Love and War*. Rev. ed. Annapolis, Md.: Naval Institute Press.

Stone, Lawrence. 1977. *The Family, Sex and Marriage in England, 1500–1800*. New York: Harper & Row.

———. 1982. Family history in the 1980s. In Theodore K. Rabb and Robert I. Rotberg, eds., *The New History: The 1980s and Beyond*, 51–87. Princeton, N.J.: Princeton University Press.

Stotland, Ezra. 1969. Exploratory studies in empathy. In Leonard Berkowitz, ed., *Advances in Experimental Social Psychology* 4: 271–314. New York: Academic Press.

Sumner, William Graham. [1906] 1959. *Folkways*. New York: Dover.

Super, Charles M. 1981. Behavioral development in infancy. In Ruth H. Munroe, Robert L. Munroe, and Beatrice B. Whiting, eds., *Handbook of Cross-Cultural Human Development*, 181–270. New York: Garland STPM Press.

Surgeon General's Scientific Advisory Committee on Television and Social Behavior. 1972. *Television and Growing Up: The Impact of Televised Violence*. Washington, D.C.: Government Printing Office.

Sussman, George D. 1977. The end of the wet-nursing business in France, 1874–1914. *Journal of Family History* 2:237–58.

Symons, Donald. 1979. *The Evolution of Human Sexuality*. New York: Oxford University Press.

Tafjel, Henri, M. G. Billig, R. P. Bundy, and Claude Plament. 1971. Categorization and intergroup behavior. *European Journal of Social Psychology* 1:149–78.

Taylor, Charles. 1989. *Sources of the Self: The Making of the Modern Identity*. Cambridge, Mass.: Harvard University Press.

Tec, Nechama. 1986. *When Light Pierced the Darkness: Christian Rescue of Jews in Nazi-Occupied Poland*. New York: Oxford University Press.

Thomas, Alexander, and Stella Chess. 1976. The evolution of behavior disorders into adolescence. *American Journal of Psychiatry* 133:539–42.

———. 1984. Genesis and evolution of behavioral disorders: From infancy to early adult life. *American Journal of Psychiatry* 141:1–9.

Thomas, Alexander, Stella Chess, and H. G. Birch. 1968. *Temperament and Behavior Disorders in Children*. New York: New York University Press.

References

Thomas, William I., and Florian Znaniecki. 1927. *The Polish Peasant in Europe and America.* New York: Knopf.

Thomson, Judith Jarvis. 1989. The no reason thesis. *Social Philosophy and Policy* 7:1–21.

Tiger, Lionel. 1970. *Men in Groups.* New York: Vintage Books.

Tiger, Lionel, and Robin Fox. 1971. *The Imperial Animal.* New York: Holt, Rinehart & Winston.

Tiger, Lionel, and Joseph Shepher. 1975. *Women in the Kibbutz.* New York: Harcourt Brace Jovanovich.

Tobin, Joseph J., David Y. H. Wu, and Dana H. Davidson. 1989. *Preschool in Three Cultures: Japan, China, and the United States.* New Haven, Conn.: Yale University Press.

Torgersen, Anne Marie. 1981. Genetic factors in temperamental individuality. *Journal of the American Academy of Child Psychiatry* 20:702–11.

Tracy, Paul E., Marvin E. Wolfgang, and Robert M. Figlio. 1990. *Delinquency Careers in Two Birth Cohorts.* New York: Plenum.

Trevethan, Wenda. 1987. *Human Birth: An Evolutionary Perspective.* New York: De Gruyter.

Triandis, Harry C. 1989. A strategy for cross cultural research in social psychology. In Joseph P. Forgas and J. Michael Innes, eds., *Recent Advances in Social Psychology,* 491–99. Amsterdam: Elsevier North-Holland.

Trilling, Lionel. 1965. *Beyond Culture.* New York: Harcourt Brace Jovanovich.

Triseliotis, John, and Malcolm Hill. 1990. Contrasting adoption, foster care, and residential rearing. In David M. Brodzinsky and Marshall D. Schecter, eds., *The Psychology of Adoption,* 107–20. New York: Oxford University Press.

Trivers, Robert. 1971. The evolution of reciprocal altruism. *Quarterly Review of Biology* 46:35–57.

———. 1972. Parental investment and sexual selection. In Bernard Campbell, ed., *Sexual Selection and the Descent of Man, 1871–1971,* 136–79. Chicago: Aldine.

———. 1983. The evolution of cooperation. In Diane L. Bridgeman, ed., *The Nature of Prosocial Development,* 43–60. New York: Academic Press.

———. 1985. *Social Evolution.* Menlo Park, Calif.: Benjamin/Cummings.

Trumbach, R. 1978. *The Rise of the Egalitarian Family: Aristocratic Kinship and Domestic Relations in Eighteenth-Century England.* New York: Academic Press.

Turiel, Elliot. 1983. *The Development of Social Knowledge.* Cambridge: Cambridge University Press.

Turiel, Elliot, Melanie Killen, and Charles C. Helwig. 1987. Morality: Its structure, functions and vagaries. In Jerome Kagan and Sharon Lamb, eds., *The Emergence of Morality in Young Children*. Chicago: University of Chicago Press.

Turnbull, Colin. 1972. *The Mountain People*. New York: Simon & Schuster.

Tyler, Tom R. 1990. *Why People Obey the Law*. New Haven, Conn.: Yale University Press.

Tyler, Tom R., Jay D. Casper, and B. Fisher. 1989. Maintaining allegiance toward political authorities: The role of prior attitudes and the use of fair procedures. *American Journal of Political Science* 33:629–52.

Underwood, Bill, and Bert Moore. 1982. Perspective-taking and altruism. *Psychological Bulletin* 91:143–73.

Urmson, J. O. 1973. Aristotle's doctrine of the mean. *American Philosophical Quarterly* 10:223–30.

Virkkunen, Matti, Judith De Jong, John Bartko, et al. 1989. Relationship of psychobiological variables to recidivism in violent offenders and impulsive fire setters. *Archives of General Psychiatry* 46:600–603.

Volkman, T. A. 1982. *The San in Transition*. Vol. 1, A Guide to N!ai, the Story of a !Kung Woman. Cambridge, Mass.: Cultural Survival.

Wagatsuma, Hiroshi, and George A. De Vos. 1984. *Heritage of Endurance: Family Patterns and Delinquency Formation in Urban Japan*. Berkeley and Los Angeles: University of California Press.

Walker, Lawrence J. 1984. Sex differences in the development of moral reasoning: A critical review. *Child Development* 55:677–91.

———. 1986. Sex differences in the development of moral reasoning: A rejoinder to Baumrind. *Child Development* 57:522–26.

Wallander, Jan L., and Nancy C. Hubert. 1985. Long-term prognosis for children with attention deficit disorder and hyperactivity. *Advances in Clinical Child Psychology* 8:113–47.

Walster, Elaine, G. William Walster, and Ellen Berschied. 1978. *Equity: Theory and Research*. Boston: Allyn & Bacon.

Watson, John B. 1928. *Psychological Care of Infant and Child*. New York: Norton.

Weiss, Gabrielle, and Lily Trokenberg Hechtman. 1986. *Hyperactive Children Grown Up*. New York: Guilford Press.

Weiss, Gabrielle, Lily Trokenberg Hechtman, et al. 1979. Hyperactives as young adults. *Archives of General Psychiatry* 36:675–81.

Weitzman, Lenore J. 1975. Sex-role socialization. In Jo Freeman, ed., *Women: A Feminist Perspective*. Palo Alto, Calif.: Mayfield.

Wemple, Suzanna Fonay. 1981. *Women in Frankish Society*. Philadelphia: University of Philadelphia Press.

Werner, Emmy E., and Ruth S. Smith. 1977. *Kauai's Children Come of Age*. Honolulu: University of Hawaii Press.

———. 1982. *Vulnerable But Invincible*. New York: McGraw-Hill.

References

West, Donald J., and David P. Farrington. 1973. *Who Becomes Delinquent?* London: Heinemann Educational Books.

———. 1977. *The Delinquent Way of Life.* London: Heinemann.

West, Mary Maxwell, and Melvin J. Konner. 1976. The role of the father: An anthropological perspective. In Michael E. Lamb, ed., *The Role of the Father in Child Development,* 185–217. New York: Wiley.

West, Max (Mrs.). 1914. *Infant Care.* Pub. no. 8 of the Children's Bureau, U.S. Department of Labor. Washington, D.C.: Government Printing Office.

Westermarck, Edward. [1906] 1971. *The Origin and Development of the Moral Ideas.* Freeport, N.Y.: Books for Libraries Press.

———. 1926. *A Short History of Marriage.* New York: Macmillan.

———. 1932. *Ethical Relativity.* New York: Harcourt, Brace.

White, Jennifer L., et al. 1992. Measuring impulsivity and examining its relationship to delinquency. Department of Psychology, University of Wisconsin at Madison. Manuscript.

Whitehead, Barbara Dafoe. 1992. *The Experts' Story of Marriage.* Council on Families in American Working Paper No. WP14. New York: Institute for American Values.

Whiting, Beatrice B., and John W. M. Whiting. 1975. *Children of Six Cultures: A Psycho-Cultural Analysis.* Cambridge, Mass.: Harvard University Press.

Wiessner, P. 1982. Risk, reciprocity, and social influence in !Kung San economics. In E. Leacock and R. B. Lee, eds., *Politics and History in Band Societies,* 61–84. Cambridge: Cambridge University Press.

Wilson, James Q. 1989. *Bureaucracy: What Government Agencies Do and Why They Do It.* New York: Basic Books.

———. 1991. *On Character.* Washington, D.C.: AEI Press.

Wilson, James Q., and Allan Abrahamse. 1993. Does crime pay? *Justice Quarterly* 9:359–78.

Wilson, James Q., and Richard J. Herrnstein. 1985. *Crime and Human Nature.* New York: Simon & Schuster.

Wilson, Margo, and Martin Daly. 1987. Risk of maltreatment of children living with stepparents. In Richard J. Gelles and Jane B. Lancaster, eds., *Child Abuse and Neglect: Biosocial Dimensions,* 215–32. New York: De Gruyter.

Wilson, Roberta, and James Q. Wilson. 1985. *Watching Fishes: Life and Behavior on Coral Reefs.* New York: Harper & Row.

Wolfgang, Marvin, Robert F. Figlio, and Thorsten Sellin. 1972. *Delinquency in a Birth Cohort.* Chicago: University of Chicago Press.

Wood, Gordon S. 1992. *The Radicalism of the American Revolution.* New York: Knopf.

References

Wrightson, Keith. 1982. *English Society, 1580–1680.* New Brunswick, N.J.: Rutgers University Press.

Zahn-Waxler, Carolyn, Marian Radke-Yarrow, and Robert A. King. 1979. Child rearing and children's prosocial initiations toward victims of distress. *Child Development* 50:319–30.

Zetterberg, Hans. 1979. Maturing of the Swedish welfare state. *Public Opinion,* October/November, 42–47.

Zinsmeister, Karl. 1990. Raising Hiroko. *American Enterprise,* 1:53–59.

Zuckerman, Marvin. 1978. Sensation seeking and psychopathy. In Robert D. Hare and Daisy Schalling, eds., *Psychopathic Behavior,* 166–85. New York: Wiley.

Index

Values, x, xi, 3
Values clarification, ix, xi, 6
van den Berghe, Pierre, 48
Veniens ad nos, 203
Victorian age, 172, 217
Vitoria, Francisco de, 209
Voltaire, 196, 219, 220, 221
Voting, 100, 115, 116, 248

Wages, 61–62, 63–64
Warrior societies, 173, 175
Watson, John B., 129
Werner, Emmy, 90
West, Donald, 11
West, Mary Maxwell, 171

Westermarck, Edward, 19, 185
Wet nursing, 19–20
Whiting, Beatrice & John, 47n.
Women, 71, 74, 201, 204; *see also*
  Gender
  dress and, 84
  evolution and, 70
  property and, 212, 213, 215
Wrightson, Keith, 20n.

Yąnomamö people, 166
You Just Don't Understand (Tannen), 187

Zinsmeister, Karl, 155